Nostradamus
The End of the Millennium

NOSTRADAMUS

THE END OF THE MILLENNIUM

PROPHECIES
1992-2001

V.J. Hewitt and Peter Lorie

BCA

LONDON · NEW YORK · SYDNEY · TORONTO

CN 4938

NOSTRADAMUS – THE END OF THE MILLENNIUM
was produced by Labyrinth Publishing S.A.

Art direction, illustrations and design by Malcolm Godwin

Typesetting by Dorchester Typesetting Group Ltd,
Dorchester, U.K.

Printed and bound by Mohndruck GmbH, Germany

C O N T E N T S

INTRODUCTION

SECTION ONE

SECTION TWO

SECTION THREE

SECTION FOUR

SECTION FIVE

INTRODUCTION

THE FIRE OF VULCAN

INTRODUCING AND UNDERSTANDING THE CODE

"*Maitre,* how do I begin to understand your prophecies?"

"First, you must destroy them."

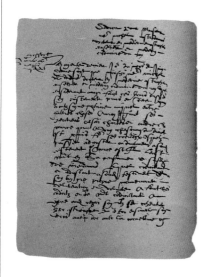

The handwriting of Michel Nostradamus.

WHEN THE MAN whom we know as Nostradamus was old, and knew that the great prophetic work that had occupied decades of his life was complete, he gathered together all his papers, notes, books and documents – records of a lifetime of secret prophecy – and burned them to ashes.

In the Preface to his prophecies, he writes that he offered them to Vulcan, the ancient Greek god who changed metals into weapons and tools. They burned with an extraordinary light, more brightly than might have been expected had they been ordinary documents, the flames illuminating his house as if it were a furnace.

Among the collection there were copies of centuries-old occult manuscripts and books, explaining ritualistic methods of calling up prophecy. These he also destroyed for fear of them falling into the wrong hands.

A few books and papers do not make the conflagration which Nostradamus describes. What else did he burn, or was it that he simply wanted us, his receiving descendants, to know that there was some great significance to this act of burning. Perhaps what we have today – those strange little verses known as "quatrains" – are not the real predictions at all. It may be that the papers he burned were the original and clear predictions which he had translated into the distorted form that we know today, in order that they might be disguised. Perhaps he recorded the act of burning simply to

draw attention to its significance. Nostradamus was not one to lightly discard an image. In fact, within the same Preface that he wrote, he tells us just this. He tells us that he condensed his original prophecies and wrote them in a twisted, obscure form to prevent the men of his time and future generations from knowing too much about how their world would change. The changes, he said, would be so great that these people would not comprehend his predictions until after they had happened. This prophecy is for sure correct!

Times have changed beyond all recognition between the period of Nostradamus' life and today. By contrast, a man from ancient Rome transported 1,200 years forward into the sixteenth century of Nostradamus would have found much that he could understand.

Latin and Greek were still spoken fluently by the educated. The Renaissance, based on the rediscovery of ancient Greek mathematics and astronomy, had just begun. Over a thousand years after Rome fell, animals and wheels were still the only source of transport.

But during the relatively short time – only 400 years – between Renaissance man and today, any visitor from the past would imagine that he had gone mad, or fallen into the clutches of demons! He would see people speeding about in cars, undertaking journeys of a few hours that in his time took weeks or months. He would see pictures, beamed into homes, of events taking place at that moment

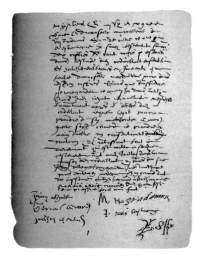

Above: A plaque commemorating the Prophet on the wall on the house in which he died on July 2nd 1566.

thousands of miles away. He would be told that within the space of sixty short years humanity had learned to fly and had landed on the moon, that people traveled to continents, unknown to him, in less than a day and that, while man was exploring other planets with machines, he was, at the same time, irreversibly damaging his own. And finally he would learn that the weapons man had developed were perfectly capable of annihilating the entire planet.

To realize that Nostradamus was this man – seeing all this extraordinary change from his home in old France – is to accept either that the whole idea is crazy, a fraud, or it is something that we need to give very serious thought to once more.

Yet, even in the twisted verses which are all he left to us, he gives the impression that he knew something of the changes occurring through the centuries to come. He describes situations that resemble, in part, historical events that have occurred since his day. Dramatic and vivid images scattered throughout his prophecies convey a feeling of changing society. Some of these images even call to mind the technology of the twentieth century – aerial combat, nuclear bombs, space travel. Yet every verse has a built-in distortion. There is no apparent continuity. It's a little like attempting to gauge the size and shape of objects in a room, looking through a deeply distorted mirror. At some point, and I think it was much earlier in his life than most other commentators believe, this prophetic genius set himself the monstrous task of drawing an entire planet into the light of a new day through the revelation of his power. Despite his gregariousness, there was a dark side to his

The signature of the Prophet.

character which betrayed the burden of a gift which he was unable to communicate fully to his own generation, but only to those living far distant in the future. We can fully understand such a problem. How could he have told his own people that in four hundred years' time human beings would be flying to the moon. They would simply have laughed!

We are the people to whom Nostradamus wanted to speak, the generation to whom he speaks clearly for the first time. We are the ones who will cross the invisible, but vital divide between one millennium and the next, between one age and another.

How could he do it? How could he prove to us, living four hundred years away from him, that the future could be accurately predicted?

First, he might have written his prophecies in a mixed-up fashion with just enough striking detail to keep generations fascinated by his words, until the time came when the key to them would be discovered again.

He knew that it *would* be rediscovered for he tells us so in a prophecy which we will examine in the last part of this book.

So what *did* Nostradamus destroy in his "Vulcan fire"? Surely it must have been the first prophecies that formed the basis for the twisted quatrains that we have today – the natural "ore" from which he crafted his fascinating and varied artifacts of prophecy. If they were destroyed, how can we ever know what they contained?

We must reverse the process by understanding what it was he intended, by "melting down" the verses we have until they reach

Strangely there are virtually no portraits of Nostradamus although his fame stretched across France during his lifetime. This painting on the opposite page is the only known likeness.

once again the state that he first wrote them in.

What is needed is a method that will break up the quatrains and leave us with the raw material containing new, clear predictions that arise out of the old confused ones.

During the pages of this book the reader will learn a revolutionary new code and its application – will learn exactly how to take Nostradamus' verses and turn them back into the original prophecies – and also see how they can be applied with the most astonishing accuracy. This book, then, is a book of mysteries and marvels, telling the story of a quest, offering delights and fears, as well as the solutions to one of the most exciting riddles that history has ever offered.

The coding system is intended to be usable by anyone, and a complete explanation and proof of the system exists in the back of the book. A brief explanation also follows hereafter.

On the other hand, if the reader is simply willing to take the system on, then the bulk of the book is made up of direct and dated predictions on all manner of world-wide subjects. Maps, charts, diagrams and map references are provided so that there can be no doubt as to the precision of many of these prophecies. Not all will be successful. The authors are still learning. But it is anticipated that a high proportion of the coming future stories will be fulfilled, as the authors have already experienced sound proof of the decoding mechanism and its power for accuracy when compiling the book. Predictions actually came true as they were being written!

Last then, in this introductory chapter, we take a brief look at the code itself. If further clarification or proof is needed, the reader should turn to the section entitled *The System Revealed in Full* at the back of the book.

S E C T I O N   O N E

BRIEF EXPLANATION OF
DECODING METHOD

ESSENTIALLY, THE SYSTEM IS QUITE SIMPLE. Nostradamus' original quatrains were written in old French, or Provence. Some of the letters that made up the lines of the verses were ancient in form, now no longer used, such as "f" instead of "s". In addition, the old spelling is often different to modern French. The first task of the decoder is to substitute the old letters for modern ones. But, and this is of fundamental importance, we do not discard the old letters (except in the case of the "f" to "s" which is merely a change of style). We simply raise it above the line – for example:

> *Le l**y**on **i**eune le vieux **f**urmontera,*
> *En champ bellique par **f**ingulier duelle,*
> *Dans cage d'or les yeux lu**y** crev**e**ra,*
> *Deux cla**ff**es **v**ne puis mourir mort cruelle.*

Apart from the obvious "f" versus "s" letters, which serve no purpose within the decoding system, we can see the old French/Provence spelling, for example, **ieune/young** is spelled nowadays as **jeune**. **Luy/him** is now lui.

The first task then, is to unlock the coded texts by modernizing the verse without losing the essential elements.

We change the medieval "f" to "s" and we correct some of the more outlandish spellings by putting the familiar letters in.

As we shall see in the coming pages of prediction, each verse retains the raised letters above the line as these "left-over" letters are going to show us how to date the prophecy.

And now begins the real fun! The next stage is to treat the prose story we find as a potential anagram. The words are literally placed in a melting pot of anagramatical change. Using various rules, as can be seen at the end of the book in the section entitled *The System Revealed in Full*, the prophecy transforms, not simply into **one** prediction, but into many different predictions, all arising out of the first and original verse. The result is an extraordinary series of events, all connected through space and time, and all resulting in precise and often awe-inspiring predictions. The prophecies are seen to move from the past, through the present into the future.

The letters above the lines are then isolated, together with the substituted letters within the lines and a numerical code is applied – each letter of the alphabet having an equivalent number – a=1, b=2, c=3 etc. etc. – giving us, in each case, the day, month and year of the prediction. This information can be found with each prediction under the heading "Time-Signal".

So to begin the book with some sense of order in time, and to provide some additional help with the system, we will move slowly, starting with the recent past – taking verses that have been proven true by events – and then, with the same verses we will also move subtly and surprisingly into the future.

The chains which, supposedly, held the Apostle Peter during his imprisonment in Rome. Serious doubts are now cast upon the authenticity of such holy relics as it has been proved, not only that Peter was never in Rome, but also, that the "Rock of the Church" may never have actually existed at all. Leaders of the early Christian sects were all called Peter. It would appear that Nostradamus knew that his prediction of the discovery of the tomb would open up all the troubles of a Pandora's box instead.

SECTION TWO

INTO THE EIGHTIES

USING THE SYSTEM

APPLYING THE RULES set for decoding the prophet, we can become prophets ourselves and make our own deliberations about any time in this coming decade, simply by working through the quatrains. In the coming pages we take a look through the eighties and into the early nineties, choosing a single quatrain that ranges across the most important issues of this last decade and into the next – issues that will continue to unfold through to the end of this millennium.

Nostradamus' quatrains contain the most extraordinary subtlety insofar as they seem to create a whole story in time and space which would appear quite impossible to see in such detail, even if we were present ourselves at the events, let alone years in their past. But in this section – *Into the Eighties* – we find yet another wonder. Once we start to melt down the verses and look behind the surface, they seem to glide, almost imperceptibly, from descriptions of our recent past into those of the future. It is as though Nostradamus was on a roller coaster of time, unable to resist the events that appeared beside the tracks as he sped by. We, the witnesses of his gift, watch the words and letters of a single prophecy somehow melt into a system and then emerge again and again in descriptions of exciting, earth-moving and often tragic events – events that we have watched unfold in recent years. We then see these same events develop through an ever-moving present into the near and more distant future. It is as though Nostradamus lived them all and simply invites us to do the same – as, of course, we shall.

To give an example of how this works, and to provide the source of this coming section of the book, we can examine a familiar single

Above: The recently discovered tomb was believed to have been that of St. Peter. When Constantine had founded the first Church in Rome it is thought that he removed the saint's bones from his original grave to protect them from deterioration and possible grave robbers. He then placed them in this secret hiding place.

quatrain taking it through the system explained at the back of the book to reveal some of the *many* predictions it contains. We start with the quatrain itself and the well-known modern interpretation of it – one which we already know something about – but by using the new system we can first bring fresh information to bear, keeping in mind what we learned in the first chapter, and then seeing how the same prophecy examines several separate events in different times once we begin to melt it down. We start with the papacy.

The basic verse or quatrain is number III.65, and this is where the story starts –

> *Quand le fepulchre du grand Romain trouné,*
> *Le iour apres fera efleu Pontife,*
> *Du Senat gueres il ne fera prouvé,*
> *Empoisonné, fon fang au facré fcyphe*

Using the decoding system we can firstly "modernize" the verse from its archaic form and also solve the distorted riddles in Line 2. As shown, we retain the archaic letters for dating –

> **n**
> *Quand le sepulchre du grand Romain trouvé,*
> **i**
> *Aprés le jour sera Pont suée fiel*
> **u**
> *Il ne sera prouvé, du Senat guères,*
> *Sacré scyphe empoisonné au son sang.*

And in modern English we find –

"When the tomb of the great Roman is found, after a day a Bridge will be sweating gall. It will hardly show. Not long of the Senate, the 'sacred chalice' is poisoned by his own blood."

The prophecy in its "normal" format is concerned with events which occurred between August and September of 1978. Albino Luciani was elected Pope John Paul I on 26th August 1978 following only one day's debate by the Conclave of Cardinals. By September 29th he was already dead. The official cause was a heart attack

John Paul only survived thirty days as Pope and yet in that all too brief time he endeared himself to the people as being a simple, compassionate and above all a true reformer.

but no death certificate was issued and no autopsy performed, leading to gossip that he was either murdered or committed suicide.

Nostradamus' description is precise – Pope John Paul I was killed by a condition in which his blood was poisoned by a rupture of the bile duct – "a sweating gall". The condition is also known as "uremia". ". . .the sacred chalice. . ." is ". . . poisoned by his own blood". However, this is not new to anyone who has examined Nostradamus' quatrains before. But if we take the quatrain through the complete meltdown process, something quite new begins to be revealed. Using the same letters of the modern French prophecy III.65, we place them into an anagramatical "pot", leaving out only those letters that we have selected to ask the question of the quatrain – i.e. if we want to know about the Pope, we withdraw the letters making up the word "Pope". Using the information gained from each of the separate lines of the verse to help us we produce a new prophecy from these remaining letters. The original raised letters remain in their original positions above the new letters.

The prose prophecy that results is made up of the letters in the original verse III.65, except for those new letters immediately below the raised letters that we added, and of course the letters that we used to ask the question. These new letters have been inserted into the text, using the information Nostradamus gave us in the hidden predictions for each separate line and keeping to one substitute letter per word. The system is therefore dependent essentially on anagram, with only one area of intuition – that of deciding what letters can be used as the substitute letters, those below the archaic letters that we have raised above the line. The choice of these substitute letters is made according to the sense of the prediction. This ability comes with practise. Having completed this anagram and letter substitution, we find the story begins to be revealed. For further and deeper explanation of this vital part of the decoding system, go to the last section of the book, where greater opportunity to practise the system is available.

>   q   u   n   o
> *Paul F coeur rasé d'arthrite, or Jean Paul I meurt*
>   n   s   n   g   u   s   r
> *d'uraemia, conduit de la bile cassé au temps de s'election.*
>   s   y   p   h
> *"Venise" ne sera prouvé guère sang empoisonné.*

Previous page: On August 25th 1978. Pope John Paul I, seated on his papal throne, carried by twelve attendants, is joyfully acclaimed by over 15,000 worshippers who attend his weekly audience.

Above: The previous, pious but strictly orthodox pope Paul had failed to win the hearts of many of his flock. John Paul, on the other hand, had captured their affection and it was with shocked disbelief that the news of his untimely death was discovered.

And in modern English we find –

"Paul VI's heart destroyed by arthritis, but John Paul I dies of uremia, the bile duct ruptured at the time of his election. "Venice" will hardly show poisoned blood."

John Paul II was shot in Rome by a terrorist, Mehmet Ali Agca, who promptly declared he was the reborn Christ. Many, including the pope, believe the plot had been encouraged by the U.S.S.R.

The letter "F" in the first line has a numerical value of 6. Paul VI died on 6th August of a heart attack during a severe bout of arthritis, but Nostradamus still insists that his successor died of uremia and that this condition was not apparent until it was too late. John Paul I is referred to as "Venice" because he was formerly Patriarch of Venice.

The body of the dead pontiff is
carried across St. Peter's square
towards the Basilica, only thirty days
after his triumphal consecration.

Using these same letters and the same prophecy we begin now
to notice how the prediction drifts forward in time as we use the
complete meltdown system once again, taking all the letters of the
prophecy and our knowledge gained from the line-by-line method
to help us. We find ourselves next in 1981:

>   **n**
> *En Roman – ou songe, dupe d'un Russie qui rouvre son haine sur*
>   **e**   **c**   **n**   **o**
> *URSS, US; Mehmet Ali Agca tire Karol, Jean Paul, des foules à la Place*
>   **n**   **n**   **g**   **y**
> *de St. Pierre. Le pape survie.*

In modern English –

*"In Roman – where he dreams – he is fooled by the Russian
who revives his hatred of the USSR and the US; Mehmet Ali Agca
shoots Karol, John Paul, from among the crowds in St. Peter's Square.
The Pope survives."*

On May 13th 1981, John Paul II, formerly Karol Wojtyla,
was shot by a terrorist, Mehmet Ali Agca in St. Peter's Square
who fired from among the crowds. The Pope always believed that there was a Russian influence behind the attempted
assassination.

Still on the same prophecy and once again, asking a different
question, continuing the meltdown process by producing another
anagram, we can now see how the bridge between past and future
is beginning to be made –

>   **s**   **uu**   **n**   **e**   **u**
> *Charles, Prince de Wales, épouse sa légère Diana Spencer au temple*
>   **u**   **o**   **s**   **s**   **s**
> *de St.Paul. Deviendra reine qui joint son roi songeur en rouvrir*
>   **y**   **p**
> *monarchie fugace.*

Diana Spencer and Charles, Prince of Wales. Not only has Lady Di enlivened a royal image which has become rather dull and tweedy, she has had an equally striking effect upon a rather serious and retiring husband.

In English –

"Charles, Prince of Wales, marries his frivolous Diana Spencer at the temple of St.Paul. She will become a queen who joins her pensive king in reviving a fleeting monarchy."

Diana has already shown an ability to "liven" up the monarchy in England with her natural public relations abilities, though Nostradamus tells us the sovereignty of Charles will be brief.

The "Time-Signal" tells us a lot –

	u		o s	s		s	y
Deviendra reine qui joint son roi songeur en rouvrir monarchie							
		p					
		fugace.					
	20	14	18	18	18	23	15
	4	1:9	1:9	1:9	1:9	3	3
	2	5	9	9	9	5	6
	4	19	19	19	19	3	3
	2	May	9 (2)	9	9	May	
	Apr	91	91	91	91	3	9

24 is 42: Nostradamus predicts here and elsewhere that Prince Charles will take the British throne in 1991 when he is still 42 – the date at the bottom left indicates that Charles will be crowned on 2nd May 1992. 4:4 x 2 = 8. Prince Charles was born in 1948. (Don't forget that for Nostradamus this was very much in the future!)

Important years for Charles will be 1995, 1999 (two events), 1993 and 1998.

Mikhail Gorbachev will be remembered for his "glasnost" policies which culminated in the demolition of over a hundred miles of walls and electric fences which divided East and West Berlin by a ring of death.

Our next extraction from this same quatrain involves us in the life and times of Mikhail Gorbachev, starting in March 1985 and sliding forward as far as 1994:

<pre>
        c   u   u
Mikhail Gorbachev devient chef de URSS. Il permet l'Europe de
                    n   n   u
    l'est de renoncer à le passé. Joint un groupe qu'est sans rangs, or
                    a   u
sans saper noyau – l'Europe.
</pre>

In English, this time, we find –

"Mikhail Gorbachev becomes leader of the USSR. He permits eastern Europe to renounce its past. It joins a group without ranks, but without undermining the nucleus – Europe."

The selection of remaining "upper" letters from our original quatrain, together with those below show us a time signal that indicates in 1992 there is a decision to allow the Eastern European countries into the European Community and that this will begin in 1994 after the 1st February.

Left: A Russian helicopter tests the levels of radioactivity.

Right: The official insignia for the Challenger mission. The tiny apple symbolizes the first teacher in space.

Moving slowly and inevitably forward in this Pandora's box of prophecy, all derived from one quatrain, we touch the future of nuclear power:

> **j   r   m   i**
> *Amerique: Navette spatiale Challenger explose à décoller.*
> **o   n s   n**
> *URSS: Chernobyl réponse avec feux dans un réacteur.*
> **g   s   r   s p**
> *Vous guident au point où su ne dure pas.*

And the English —

> *"America: the space shuttle Challenger explodes on take-off.*
> *USSR: Chernobyl replies with fires in a reactor.*
> *They guide you to a point where knowledge fails."*

On January 26th 1986 the space shuttle Challenger blew up less than two minutes after it was launched and still climbing. Seven astronauts were killed and the NASA shuttle program was grounded.

Three months later, on 30th April, the number 4 reactor at the Chernobyl nuclear power plant in Russia caught fire. Nostradamus tells us that there was more than one fire. The top of the reactor was blown off and meltdown of the core seemed inevitable at one point. The result of this catastrophe is still not fully certain.

The dating to this prediction (not shown here) gives a clear indication of the future. Between 1995–6, knowledge and technology surrounding space travel fails the human race as it appears to have reached an impasse based on contemporary knowledge. Between 1996-8, a new era of science begins; some major new discovery which again involves space travel. The 7th March 1999 is a vital date in this sequence, relating to a revolutionary kind of technology which comes about through theories about how black holes function in the universe (See Science and Technology predictions in third section).

Next we come to one of the early warnings of perhaps the single most significant prediction of an event due to occur in the USA during this last ten years of the current century.

>   **a**   **o**   **n**
> *En California séisme de San Andreas que previent un jour noir*
>   **s**   **a**   **c r s c**
> *Pour nations de l'Europe de l'est, le Mur est voie. Le vide attire*
>   **y**
>   *peuples.*
> **p**   **h**
> *Se gausse d'un guru.*

In English —
"In California an earthquake from San Andreas that warns of a
   black day.
For the East European nations, the Wall is on the way. The
   vacuum attracts the peoples.
A guru is derided."

Almost three hundred people were killed in an earthquake which occurred in the San Francisco area of California on 19th October 1989. Movement in the San Andreas fault was responsible. The "black day" is that of the huge earthquake which is expected by the Californian people some time in the future. The 1989 quake was seen as a warning. In the next section we can examine the coming quake of 1993.

Calculations indicate that May 1993 is the date for this major earthquake. Just one month after the 1989 quake the Berlin Wall was breached, an event that this generation hardly expected to witness. The breach caused a political "vacuum" with the collapse of the Communist regimes in Eastern Europe. There is also a suggestion within this prediction of a mass migration of peoples from east to west, something which we are now seeing come about at time of writing from Russia and other Eastern European countries into Central Europe.

But a major migration can also be expected between August 1993 and May 1995. The "derided guru" seems to refer to Nostradamus himself, to whom the authorities do not pay sufficient attention.

Above: Buckled streetcar tracks in San Francisco 1906. *Left:* Buckled houses after the 1989 earthquake show the awesome and wrenching power of such a natural catastrophe.

Some of the most horrendous prophecies center upon a Middle Eastern scenario. Nostradamus mirrors the biblical predictions of an apocalyptic confrontation and locates Armaggedon, the legendary site of the ultimate battle of good against evil, in the region. Yet it appears that the gulf war of 1991 is to be the last major battle fought by U.S. troops and the marine who looks out towards occupied Kuwait in the early part of 1991 will be too preoccupied on the home front to take part in the final apocalypse.

And now we arrive at what may be considered the trickiest and yet most significant point of this book – the present! Because of the constraints of book publishing – preparation of manuscript, pictures, printing and binding – which can take almost six months to complete, the present for the writer is the past for the reader. The text for this book was prepared, edited and adjusted around the end of 1990, during the Christmas period, and prior to the January 15th deadline set by the United Nations for Saddam Hussein to withdraw from Kuwait. Final changes and adjustments were made on the text proofs in February of 1991 and during that short time some of the most significant events occurred with regard to the troubles in the Middle East. None of the following predictions or those in the future section on the Middle East were changed, each one continuing to be fulfilled as time made its inevitable mark.

> j   c uu   o
> *Aprés Saddam Hussein envahie Kuwait, les Nations-Unis font*
> w   o   o   u
> *sanctions contre l'Iraq. Rat ronge péler. Leurre à promesse de guerre.*
> y   o
> *Fugue des peuples*

And the English version –

> *"After Saddam Hussein invades Kuwait, the United Nations make
> sanctions against Iraq. The rat gnaws to peel away. He deceives with
> a promise of war. The peoples run away."*

On the 2nd August 1990, Iraq invaded Kuwait and caused a global crisis. The world, through the United Nations, condemned Hussein and brought severe sanctions to bear on Iraq. Hussein threatened military retaliation on a huge scale and then positioned himself and his armies to fight a major war with the rest of the world – effectively this could be seen as a part of what Nostradamus might have enterpreted as the beginning of a Third World War. Seen from the distant past it would not be unrealistic to imagine that this planet has been permanently at war for the last two decades of the 20th century.

As on the previous page it is evident
that absolute rulers have a penchant
for creating edifices of themselves.
Saddam Hussein has a particularily
exhalted sense of his place in history.
Here he is seen meeting the great
6th century ruler of fabled Babylon,
Nebuchadnezzar. The mural on the
right from Iran tells quite another
story.

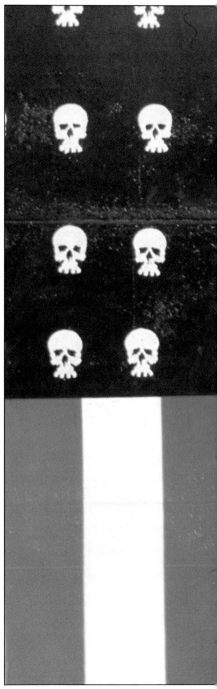

Nostradamus, in the above prediction, suggests that Hussein's
actions are a bluff throughout the political maneuvering before the
war began and indeed right up until the end of it, the desert rat
"gnawing" all the time at his "cage" to find a way to gain what he
wants – a small but rich part of Kuwait – and yet escape the power
of the United States and the United Nations. His techniques have
been those classically attributable to economic ambition in the hands
of a dictator – diplomatic maneuvers and unpredictable, intractable
behavior. Hundreds of thousands of foreign workers and their families have left Kuwait and Iraq, as Nostradamus predicted they
would. The story continues in the Middle East section of the book.
And in the meantime in Europe, we can take a look at the past/pre-
sent/future predictions surrounding Germany's reunification.

      p   v   i   p

Nulles, l'Allemagnes de l'ouest et l'est. Un pays que fera jour

      u   g

nouveau en l'Europe. Sera résine à cordes en air doux. Europe à

      s   h   c   p   h

rire non au sud. Gens sacrent.

"The Germanies of East and West are no more. One country which will make a new day in Europe. She will be the resin for the strings in a sweet tune. Europe will laugh, but not in the south. People curse."

As the economic power of the U.S.S.R. and its Eastern allies continues to disintigrate so hunger and homelessness become a nightmare. A unified and economically sound Germany increasingly finds herself as leader of the whole of Europe.

Nostradamus was quite adamant about the good that a unified Germany would bring – acting like "resin for the strings in a sweet tune" – very typical of his lyrical style with prophecy. Ultimately the whole of Europe will laugh, except for some cursing in the south. We may assume that this comes from the southern European countries such as Italy, which has recently spent much energy on pushing matters through with monetary policy – the Italian minister for Europe, Gianni de Michelis – who provoked Margaret Thatcher's crisis in late 1990. We may yet still see further problems from Spain, Italy and Greece. Predictions in the next section which relate to the later 1990s will show more detail to come.

The time-signal indicates that by 1995 Germany will have achieved her true role within Europe, the production of a "sweet tune" being the result. Between 1992-5 conditions in the south grow more troubled and by 1998 the European situation is not so happy, as we will see later in the book.

This one quatrain – III.65 – has revealed all that we have read so far in this section – taking us from the past through the ever-moving present into the future. But this is only a selection of what is available. Using this revolutionary new method of interpreting Nostradamus we can literally open new doors to the life that he prophesied - an almost unlimited picture. We have not included predictions that also arise from the system, directly within this one quatrain, related to the Iranian Revolution, the Iran-Iraq war, the IRA attempts to assassinate Margaret Thatcher, the Armenian earthquake, the recent changes in communism in Albania, the

Lockerbie air disaster in Britain. These can be drawn by any reader who cares to go deeper into the method provided, as can, of course, extensions of these past predictions and their "drift" forward into the future.

We can make a prediction through space – from one country into another – and through time – from one century into another. In this sense, provided we ask the right questions, the quatrains are like a written oracle. And what is perhaps most miraculous is the fact that we can achieve an almost unlimited number of interpretations from one single quatrain – once we know the date when it begins – and we can achieve the date by analyzing the letters above the line which Nostradamus left in the text to help us. (Further clarification of this method can be found at the back of the book)

As a final example for the end of this transition chapter, we can take one more interpretation close to the true starting point – the indicated date – of the quatrain number III.65 – July 1969 – giving us a startling piece of information that will guide us far into our own future –

    r   **n**   **u**   **u**   **v**   **p**
Dieu Apollo envoie Neil Armstrong a la lune. Utilise une
      o   **g**   **u**   **a**   **r**
technologie que se fanera. Série d'accidents serre NASA. Je prophétise
      s   **s**
un systeme plu, pur, dur

*"The god Apollo sends Neil Armstrong to the Moon. He uses
a technology which will fade. A series of accidents grips NASA. I
prophesy a more successful, purer and tougher system."*

During the next decade, space travel for the human race will be of major importance. According to Nostradamus, the method of traveling in space will be different from the one undertaken by NASA when Neil Armstrong commanded Apollo 11 to the moon in 1969. This prophecy directly predicts that there will be a reassuring change ("plus/plu" means "more/successful") which will enable mankind to travel more readily in space.

The time-signal indicates that the new technology will begin to emerge in 1992, bearing fruit for new space missions in 1998 and 1999. Once again it appears to be connected with a new form of physics created by fresh knowledge related to the theories surrounding black holes (see next section).

Using this method there should no longer be any problem with the previously rather "jerky" and vague interpretations made by various writers and interpreters of Nostradamus. The system provided here is natural, even sensuous in its fluid simplicity. Every quatrain possesses this capability – lacking the previous incoherence and fragmentation and containing an almost imperceptible "gliding forward" effect, from year to year and into the future, that we will now begin to sample in the next section.

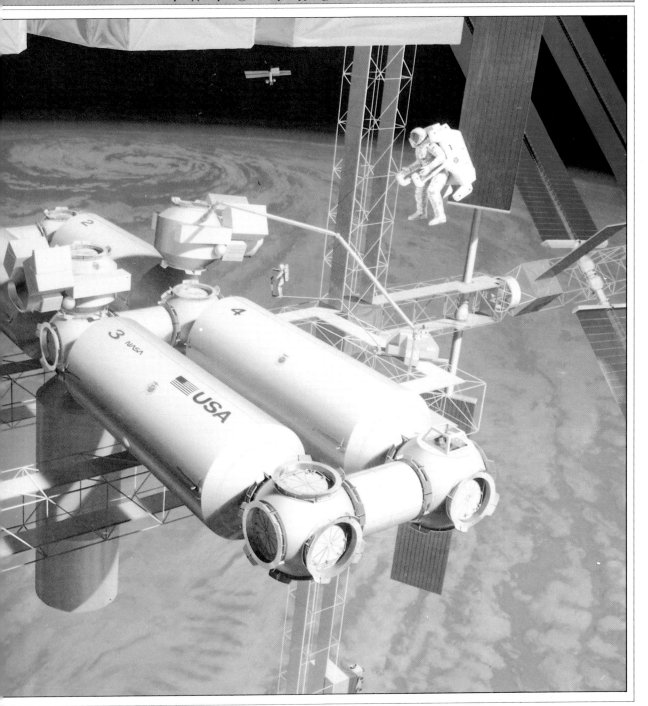

41

SECTION THREE

TOWARDS 2000

I N THE LAST SECTION we began the bizarre task of moving from the past, through the present and quite timidly into the future. The de-coding system set out in brief at the beginning of the book and complete at the end is the mathematics of the affair, but in section two we began to see how lyrical the device becomes when we put it to the test. It is as though we are using the art of a wizard – one who not only employs logic but also romance for his genius – the true craft of wizardry. Our predictions have invariably started in our past and moved forward into the future – like setting sail in a boat, we have found a suitable tide that runs our way and we have lifted our sails to a fresh breeze, ready to go, and yet we are still tied to the jetty with mooring ropes.

In order to slip those ropes and move out into the tide of the future, we must apply a simple additional method.

As the reader will have noticed, the dating system works largely, so far, on the basis that we know the dates that are being predicted. We can prove our system so long as we know where we are going. This may sound contradictory until we remember that the only purpose of working on the system up until now, has been to prove that it works – to build confidence in our ability to take the next step forward. Thus, in events that have not yet taken place, in the future, this system inevitably breaks down – or does it? Nostradamus, in fact, encoded a method of looking cleanly at the future, within the quatrains that he wrote and we shall see in this section how this works and how to apply it.

What arises out of the discoveries that we are about to make in this next section is that Nostradamus had a special place in his heart for the last ten years of the 20th century. As though there were some special significance to this era, almost all of the quatrains in the "Siécles" (Nostradamus' life work was entitled "Siécles" – in

As our present world seems to come to an end Nostradamus predicts that major institutions, like the Catholic Church, will lose support and credibility and will have become extinct by the end of the millennium. He sees the present pope as dying by 1995 and agrees with the 12th century prophet, Malachi, that there are only two popes left in the succession before the final fall of the Church of Rome.

English "The Centuries") seem to reveal material which effectively stops between the years 1991 and 2001! It is as though these years were the culmination of his most important message. All hitherto interpretations of the prophet's works have effectively been erroneous – the result of Nostradamus' determination to keep us all interested in his words until the right time arrived and the proper decoding system was discovered – that time has finally come and we can take full advantage of what he intended us to see.

Much is spoken about the end of the world coinciding with the last year of the 20th century. We seem to associate catastrophe with millennium ends – the last millennium end saw similar predictions and forecasts but, of course, nothing of the kind occurred. We seem to imagine that the forces of the universe that would be responsible for the end of a planet are interested in the dates that we have ascribed to our lives. What does existence care about the year 2000? It is only our own minds that make these assumptions. In any case, Nostradamus' predictions show a keen interest in a new religion that begins in the 21st century and takes mankind through a thousand years of peace and happiness. If we believe the prophet then we can look forward to a delightful future! The times of strife are now, not next century!

In a sense, though, our present world is coming to an end. Climatic factors are changing the physical world, social factors are altering our environment, technology is altering the scientific world, major institutions such as the Catholic Church will die in the next few years. One age is slipping away and another age coming into force – perhaps it is a new age, perhaps only another age that we can see as a repeat of a much older one that we thought had died.

In order to set sail out into the free breeze of the future, we have selected five prophecies. All the future predictions associated with the next ten years will be drawn from these five quatrains, worked in the manner that has been explained hitherto. We could have selected virtually any of the quatrains from "Siécle", there is no special magic about these five, except that they have been worked on by the authors and are therefore more familiar.

1.35 –

    y **i**

Le lion jeune le vieux surmontera,

    En champ bellique par singulier duelle,

        y **u**

Dans cage d'or les yeux lui crevera,

      v

    Deux classes une puis mourir mort cruelle.

1.42 –

      u

Le dix Calende d'Avril de faict Gotique,

    Resuscité encor par gens malins,

Le feu estainct, assemble diabolique,

    Cherchant les os du d'Amant et Pielin.

III.65

              n

Quand le sepulchre du grand Romain trouvé,

  i

    Le jour apres sera esleu Pontife,

                u

Du Senat gueres il ne sera prouvé,

    Empoisonné, son sang au sacré scyphe.

X.22

            u

Pour ne vouloir consentir au divorce,

    Qui puis apres sera cogneu indigné,

  y

Le Roi des Isles sera chassé par force

        y

    Mis à son lieu qui de Roi n'aura signe.

X.74

  u

An revolu du grand nombre septiesme,

          i

    Apparoistra au temps jeux d'Hecatombe,

Non esloigné du grand eage milliesme,

    Que les entrez sortiront de leur tombe.

Two of these verses – I.35 and III.65 appear in the first and last sections of this book. The other three are new treasure-troves for us to begin working on.

We are not going to interpret the three new verses at this point as our concern in the coming pages is for the future, and the future will arise out of the collection of letters that each verse holds. We can mention that verse I.42 has been previously identified with the introduction of the Gregorian Calendar in 1582 and verse X.22 with the abdication of Edward VIII in 1936. These are only the starting points in history of the two prophecies – the beginning of our treasure hunt – for once we know the mechanism that makes them move through time, i.e. that of asking the question of the quatrain by removing the relevant letters, then we can begin to take our steps forward along the most fascinating part of the journey.

The four verses then – I.42, X.22, I.35 and III.65 – will provide us with the basis for all the general predictions that we map out in the coming sections of the book about the future. All of them began at points in our past and can be moved forward through the coming years by the methods already explained.

However, the fifth verse – X.74 – is different. This verse begins its journey into the future from a starting point which is *still in* our future – the California Earthquake of 1993.

These five verses are capable of yielding up a massive amount of information on a great variety of subjects. We are only able to sample a very small selection in this book. We shall be seeing well-known names and places – people that we see regularly on our television screens, places that we read about in our newspapers. But these people and places will turn up in situations – under circumstances – that we have not yet experienced! The descriptions will be surrounding situations that have not yet occurred – the politics, economics, social developments and technological, scientific discoveries of the future – a time we do not know.

The precise starting point of the fifth verse we described above – X.74 – is just a little time before the California Earthquake in 1993. Its true starting point is the American and European celebrations that will take place in 1992 – the five-hundredth anniversary of the discovery of North America in 1492 by Christopher Columbus. And in the same way as Columbus set sail with a small fleet into the unknown, we are about to do the same – letting go the mooring ropes to sail out into the future.

S E C T I O N   F O U R

T H E   F U T U R E

EUROPE – GERMANY

"Germany in Europe" – 1991-1994

Drawn from verse III.65

    i n   **h**   **o**   **m**

L'Europe sera changé par l'Allemagne unifiée. / Trouvera que la

p   **o**   **s**   **o**   **s n**

sente d'or dure/à URSS. Fer à sud./Peuple songe à nouvel àge sur

y   **u**   **j**

en espace. Desirent science.

*"Europe will be changed by a united Germany. She will find that
the golden path stretches to the USSR: an iron one in the south.
People dream of a new and certain age in space. They want the
science."*

January 1991 Revellers celebrating the unification of the two Germanies.

NB – the / lines in the French verses indicate the breaks that correspond to the time-signal breaks. For a full explanation of the system and the following time-signals, please turn to the back of the book – "The System Revealed in Full".

Time-Signal

i	n	h	o	m	p	o	s	o	s	n	y	u	j
a	c	e	e	e	e	a	f	l	l	g	e	e	e
1:9	13	8	14	12	15	14	18	14	18	13	23	20	10
1	3	5	5	5	5	1	6	11	11	7	5	5	5
19	4	8	5	3	6	5	9	5	9	4	5	2	1
1	3	5	5	5	5	1	6	2	2	7	5	5	5
	194	8	May		9	95		95				92	
191	3		Oct	May	5	1 June							
						May		2 Feb		Dec 11			
						1	96						

EUROPE WILL CHANGE for the better between 3rd October 1991 and 8th May 1994 by the unification of Germany – Nostradamus indicates that this is beyond doubt. The change will inevitably create a "golden path" all the way to the borders of the Soviet Union, a shining future of peace, prosperity and scientific innovation in May 1995.

At the same time another path of "iron in the south" between 1st June 1995 and 1st May 1996 is being forged with troubles afflicting the Mediterranean, southern European countries of Italy and Greece. Other predictions verify this.

Between 11th December 1992 and 2nd February 1995 there will be "dreams" of a new space age. By "dreams" Nostradamus refers to revolutionary theories arising from "right-brain" intuition imposing themselves on the stale outmoded thinking of "left-brain", standard technological processes. (See Science and Technology predictions)

The ways of the more introverted "new age" thinking that will arise in the next years may well also contribute to this new science.

The Brandenburg gate has been the symbol of division of East and West ever since the wall was erected in 1961. Unarmed and relaxed East German soldiers line the wall as West Berliners mingle with the East for the first time in 30 years.

"Paris – Danger by Night" – 1991-1995

Drawn from verse X.22

>   i   i
> *Dans le cité de Paris, groupes des voyous errent / par*
>   i   i   o i   o a
> *les rues / commes loups, cognent ceux qui se hasardent / en*
>   i   y   r i n
> *soir, un force grisé que / nie la vie aux autres.*

"In the city of Paris, bands of young thugs roam the streets like wolves, beating up those who take risks in the evening, a drunken force which denies life to others."

Time-Signal

i	i	i	i	o	i	o	a	i	y	r	i	n
e	t	s	m	t	x	t	e	e	e	e	x	t
1:9	1:9	1:9	1:9	14	1:9	14	1	1:9	23	17	1:9	13
5	19	18	12	19	22	19	5	5	5	5	22	19
19	19	19	19	5	19	5	1	19	5	8	19	4
5	19	9	3	19	4	19	5	5	5	5	4	19
							Jan		5	Aug		194
195	1991	199	193	195	194	195	5	195	May	5	194	

D URING 1991–95 PARIS becomes a lawless city at night, terrorized by bands of youths who threaten the French capital's famed night life. 1992 is not included which may indicate a crackdown by the authorities which has no lasting effect. The year 199 (normally 1999) does not fit into the series and may refer to 19th September 1991 or 1993.

An incident involving drunken violence is highlighted on 5th January 1995.

Either actual loss of life occurs during the period from 5th May to 5th August 1994, or Nostradamus is referring to a curfew which results in Paris becoming a dead city at night. If so, this initial period may be extended to cover the whole of 1994.

"Britain in Europe." – 1992–1996

Drawn from verse III.65

>   **f**   **g**
> *Le Royaume-Uni se trouvé partie d'une grande alliance*
>   **n**   **j**   **s**
> *de l'Europe: / souverainetés / des nations perdu. /*
> **e**   **u**   **a**   **g**
> *An l'espace atmosphérique / personnes choir sur US.*

"The United Kingdom finds itself part of a great European alliance;
the sovereignty of each nation lost.
In a year of outer space, people will fall on the USA."

Time-Signal

f t	g e	n e	j t	s d	e a	u i	a e	g i
6	7	13	10	18	5	20	1	7
19	5	5	19	4	1	1:9	5	1:9
6	7	4	10	9	5	2	1	7
19	5	5	19	4	1	19	5	19
196	7	Apr	91:10		5	192	1	197
	May	5	2001	94	Jan		May	

T HE UNITED KINGDOM, which did not exist in Nostradamus'
lifetime, is, at present, being swept along in the irresistible
tide of events unfolding in Europe. This process will surely accelerate. It will have reached a crucial stage during the period
between 7th April and 5th May 1996, indicating that European
monetary and economic union will be achieved by that stage.

During the years 1991–2001 the sovereignty of all nations will
be lost in the formation of this great European alliance, including,
perhaps, some, if not all republics from the Soviet Union. Europe

The "Iron Lady", Margaret Thatcher, in characteristic battle mood. This latter-day Queen Boudicea has fought to retain British sovereignty and currency in a Europe which seeks to have more common aims. Nostradamus clearly indicates that national pride and interests will be swept aside by the wider considerations of a Super-Europe.

Thatcher, from her first year to her resignation as Prime Minister of the U.K. has always assumed almost heroic status. The British Sunday Times wryly captures this Joan of Arc-like quality in both her first year of glory and her final martyrdom in 1990.

will have seen nothing like it since the fall of the Roman Empire 1,600 years ago.

The year when this great decision will be made is 1994, already the target year for closer monetary union and a prominent factor in the causes leading up to Mrs. Thatcher's resignation in November 1990. (In another prediction, Nostradamus indicates that she will be re-elected leader of the Conservatives in 1995, but in opposition. Possibly this is a last-ditch, but futile, attempt to fight Britain's inevitable inclusion in the new super-Europe.) See WORLD FIGURES.

There are great achievements in space exploration during the year from 5th January 1992.

Turning to the space accident dated 1st May 1997, the non-sexual use of *personnes* may indicate that one or more astronauts are women.

A clue to the nationality of the spacecraft is located in the anagramatic
$$g$$
phrase: *choir sur US*

$$g \quad u$$
which becomes *Russie choir* – "Russia will fall".

The spacecraft is Russian. 1st May is a day of national celebration in the Soviet Union as it is throughout Europe. The space mission may be timed to coincide with this date, but goes horribly wrong. (See AMERICA predictions.)

"Fraud Destroys Swiss Financial System."
— 1995

Drawn from verse X.22

    i   **r**   **c**   **i**

Pour quoi prouve La Suisse sa voracité / — non par direct

     n   **s**   **i**   **d**

cours du change, mais / en session illégale de fourberie que

    o   **i**   **y**

ruine / sa reputation, système d'argent?

"For what does Switzerland show her hunger — not through a direct rate of exchange, but in an illegal session of cheating that destroys her reputation and money system?"

Time-Signal

i	r	c	i	n	s	i	d	o	i	y
e	t	a	t	d	m	e	b	t	t	t
1:9	17	3	1:9	13	18	1:9	4	14	1:9	23
5	19	1	19	4	12	5	2	19	19	19
19	8	3	19	4	9	19	4	5	19	5
5	19	1	19	4	3	5	2	19	19	19
	198	Mar		Apr			Apr	195		195
195		1	1991	4	93	195	2		1991	

Increasingly Switzerland finds herself out in the economic cold surrounded by the increasingly stable currencies of the European partners. The once solid and certain stability of her own Swiss Franc had begun to appear vulnerable by the beginning of the last decade of the 20th century.

THE COMPLETE PREDICTION is phrased as a question, illustrating Nostradamus' opinion of the futility of this illegal activity, involving huge deception connected with the rate of exchange between Swiss francs and other currencies.

The deception is gradually uncovered between 1995-1998, but operates secretly between 1st March 1991 – 4th April 1993.

An important date in the detection process may be 2nd April 1995.

During 1995 Switzerland's financial reputation and consequently her wealth are destroyed, with the revelation of this secret fraud operating from 1991.

"Michael Returns to Roumania" — 1992

Drawn from verse III.65

           u   **o**
La Roumanie, séparé des pays autres de la Revolution, se leurre.
     s   **n**   **u**   **c**
Les joindra / quand Michael revient. Fusionne, / éponge rage de son
  s   **c**   **p**   **h**
pays / en guerir un peur sur.

"Roumania, separated from the other countries of the Revolution, deceives herself. She will join them when Michael returns. He merges and absorbs the rage of his country in the healing of a sour fear."

Time-Signal

u	o	s	n	u	c	s	c	p	h
a	e	r	l	i	d	y	i	e	r
20	14	18	13	20	3	18	3	15	8
1	5	17	11	1:9	4	23	1:9	5	17
2	5	9	4	2	3	9	3	6	8
1	5	8	2	19	4	5	19	5	8
2	95		4		93		193		14
	June								
Feb	98								
6									
					4	May			Aug
			Feb	192	Mar			June	16
					4	95		195	

x-King Michael en route in the
lane between Geneva and Bucharest.
However, he was turned back from
is own country.

Ex-King Michael and his family attempt to re-enter Roumania in 1990 but are turned away at the border. Nostradamus predicted that it will take another year before the monarch can return to his stricken and turbulent country.

I N THE EAST EUROPEAN REVOLUTIONS that we have seen during 1989 and 1990, Roumania's uprising was markedly different from the other countries. She had been ruled by a family dicta-torship masquerading as a communist government. Her revolution was violent and bloody in order to eliminate the autocratic force of Ceausescu on Christmas Day 1989. Nostradamus states clearly what we have begun to see during the course of 1990 – that the story is not yet over – the country "deceives" itself. True democracy arises only between 2nd June 1995 to the 6th February 1998, several years after ex-king Michael of Roumania, forced into abdication by the Communists in 1947, has returned on the 4th February 1992 to help cope with a highly turbulent and angry period between 4th May 1993 and 4th March 1995. The healing of his bitter and fearful country takes place between 14th August 1993 and 16th June 1995.

Nostradamus does not refer to Michael as King, which may indicate that he will not adopt a formal political or constitutional role.

"Turkey Wars with Greece – Saddam Hussein in the Middle East." – 1991 – 1998

Drawn from III.65

> **s**   **n**   **l**   **p**
> *La Turquie, Grèce rouvrent la guerre, tandis qu'au sud*
>
>   **p**   **s**   **i**
> *la Chypre fêle. / S Hussein pousse notre pouvoir / fané à*
>
> **s**   **o**   **j**   **p**
> *l'écart. / Noue damier méditerranéen. Son, sang.*

"Turkey and Greece reopen the war, while to the south Cyprus shatters. S.Hussein thrusts our fading power aside. He knots up the Mediterranean draughtboard. Noise, blood."

Time-Signal

s r	n t	l r	p q	p t	s i	i f	s l	o t	j i	p a
18	13	11	15	15	18	1:9	18	14	10	15
17	19	17	16	19	1:9	6	11	19	1:9	1
9	4	2	6	6	9	19	9	5	1	6
7	19	8	7	19	19	6	2	19	19	1
	194		8	196	199		9	195	191	6
97			July			196	2			Jan
		Aug								
		198	7							

It is difficult, at the time of writing, in early 1991, to see Saddam Hussein remaining in power and yet Nostradamus sees him as an ultimate survivor in some form or another. Even if he is personally eliminated his legend could well be used as a rallying focus for Arab and Palestinian unrest. Martyrs are often more useful to revolutionaries than leaders who are alive. Lenin must surely be a perfect example.

TURKEY AND GREECE go to war over the island of Cyprus, long a source of dispute, and at present partitioned between these two countries. The delicate balance of rule is shattered and Cyprus suffers severe damage, economic and material, from the outbreak of conflict. The relevant dates are 8th July 1994, 1997 and 7th August 1998.

As the first draft of this book was being completed, the world was locked in confrontation with Iraq over its invasion of Kuwait.

This prediction indicates that Saddam Hussein, the President of Iraq, survives the Gulf War, both physically and politically. The information given here should be linked with the "Israel Defeated" prediction (See MIDDLE EAST), which states that in a war with Iraq, Syria and Egypt, Israel will be defeated and overrun.

"S.Hussein thrusts our fading power aside ..."

As the descendant of Jews, although his family had converted to Roman Catholicism, Nostradamus identifies personally with the downfall of Israel, expressing a tacit sorrow. This personal identification also occurs in the MIDDLE EAST prediction referred to above. It is not stated that this is the end of the experiment which began with the recreation of the state of Israel almost 2000 years after it fell to the Roman sword, but it does look very much like it.

Saddam Hussein pursues his path to power in the Middle East between 1996–9. Israel's resistance begins to weaken after the period 9th February 1995 and 2nd September 1996.

The final part of the prediction might have been thought to have been a consequence of Hussein's growing victory over Israel, but the date tells us differently.

As the first draft of this text was completed it seemed, according to the primary dates in the time-signal, that Hussein might complicate the power structure in the Mediterranean on 6th January 1991. The UN had then just passed a resolution authorizing the use of force if Iraq had not withdrawn voluntarily from Kuwait by 15th January 1991.

The primary time-signal suggests that conflict would break out on or near the 6th January between Iraq and the powers ranged up against her over the invasion of Kuwait and then spill over into the Mediterranean. The last two words of the prediction convey better than most the impact of war.

Left: Turkey's President Ozal attempts to court the European Community and the U.S.A. while, at the same time, having to live with his Islamic neighbors. Turkey's long-standing emnity with Christian Greece, founded on grievances as long past as the Ottoman Empire, is always likely to erupt in non-rational ways. *Right:* Greek and Turkish Summit Conference held in June 1988. The two symbols of Cross and Crescent eloquently attest to the religious undertow of any relationship between the nations.

In the event, the Gulf War began on 16th January at a few minutes to midnight, British time, when Allied aircraft took off on the first of continuous bombing raids over Iraq.

And here is a perfect example for us to see the use of the Supplementary Dates, as, if we include them, the Dating System reveals this information –
Time Signal – Final Section

15	15th
1 }	
6 }	16th
1	January
191	1991

The phrase "he knots up the Mediterranean draughtboard" has also become more clear. A few days before the conflict began, tourists were told to leave holiday resorts, including Cyprus, at the eastern end of the Mediterranean. During the conflict, Iraq launched missiles at Israel inflicting damage on Tel Aviv and Haifa on the Mediterranean coast. American forces were also moved into Turkey as a precaution against Iraqi attack.

THE MIDDLE EAST

"Israel Defeated by her Arab Neighbors." 1995–1998

Drawn from verse III.65

>   u   o   m   o   o   r
> *Sans guet Amerique chaude Israel fait la guerre / contre les*
>   o   e   c   n   j   u s   s   u
> *Palestiniens. Un rond / de l'Egypte, Syrie, Irak est plus / fort pour*
>   p   h   s
> *nous. / Vannent à perte de / vue.*

"Without the sentry – 'hot' America – Israel makes war against the Palestinians. A circle of Egypt, Syria and Iraq is too strong for us. They winnow a wasteland as far as I can see."

Time-Signal

| u | o | m | o | o | r | o | e | c | n | j* | u | s | s | u | p | h | s |
t	e	i	e	t	s	i	r	t	y		t	l	f	o	t	t	u
20	14	12	14	14	17	14	5	3	13	10	20	18	18	20	15	8	18
19	5	1:9	5	19	18	1:9	17	19	23		19	11	6	14	19	19	20
2	5	3	5	5	8	5	5	3	4	10	2	9	9	2	6	8	9
19	5	19	5	19	9	19	8	19	5	1	19	2	6	5	19	19	2
192	5	193	5	195	98	195	5	193	4		192	9			196	198	92
		May		May			Aug		May				Feb				
Feb	5	Mar	5										96 5				
195		195															

* There is no letter "K" in the French alphabet so that in our coding system it possesses no value, numerically.

THE INSERTION OF MANY SUBSTITUTE letters in the meltdown process of Nostradamus' verses seems invariably to indicate a sensitive subject. As we have seen before, Nostradamus has a personal identification with the Jewish peoples of Israel and brings himself into the prediction directly.

ddam Hussein   Yasser Arafat   King Hussein   Hosni Mubarak   Hafez Assad

America, if we look again at the panoramic future history of the world, is very much occupied with her problems of agricultural depletion after the terrible droughts and the massive earthquake of 1993. According to the time-signal the loss of interest in her foreign policy, at least with regard to Israel, begins in the run-up to the earthquake – 5th May 1992 – 5th May 1993 and continues crucially between 5th February and 5th March 1995. This attitude also continues further into the decade.

Israel apparently takes this opportunity to attack her Palestinian Arab neighbors. According to the prophecy Israel's war continues between 1995 and 1998 and is not only concerned with the Arabs living in the West Bank, since she already occupies this territory, but with the Palestinian camps based in Syria and Iraq under such leaders as Yasser Arafat. In this case Syria and her neighbors would certainly enter such a war.

The prophecy states that the result of this decision is catastrophic for Israel as Egypt, Syria and Iraq form a circle around the country, probably cutting off her Mediterranean access.

The Arab alliance has been formed prior to the attack between 9th February 1992 and 4th May 1993. It holds until 5th February 1996 when Israel begins to lose the war – for, as Nostradamus states, her enemies are too strong. Between 1996 and 1998 Israel is devastated and presumably overrun by Arab armies. The last date – 1992 – seen at the right-hand end of the time-signal, is a final warning both to Israel and America that this grim prospect is "seen" by Nostradamus and perhaps could be avoided if noted by the authorities involved.

America's involvement with Saddam Hussein in Iraq and Kuwait must have a major bearing on the predicted war brought about by Israel. According to the predictions we have already seen and others that are yet to be included here, Hussein is still around in his leadership position into the mid-90s which suggests that his quest was not thwarted successfully during 1991.

This rather doomy prediction seems to suggest the end of the modern nation of Israel almost 1,900 years after the devastation it suffered at the hands of Rome.

A Palestinian girl runs past Israeli troops in Old Jerusalem, a gay butterfly of hope caught amongst drab military khakhi in 1990. By the time the next major conflict erupts in the region this girl, herself, could be a mother. What hope for any of the children of the region?

N O R T H   A M E R I C A
The California Earthquake
Predictions

W E Begin this very significant part of the book with a rather strange prophecy – one that does not reveal itself so readily as others so far. The following pages, though, will tell a remarkable story, one that alters the course of history if all or even some of these predictions are fulfilled – bringing the biggest single earthquake to hit the United States in its civilized history.

Unlike other verses in the book, before we get into the interpretation of this one we will take a brief look at the original verse itself, and then the method by which we decode this strange piece of prophecy.

Verse X.74

u

An revolu du grand nombre septiesme,

i

Apparoistra au temps jeux d'Hecatombe,
Non esloigné du grand eage milliesme,
Que les entrez sortiront de leur tombe.

"*A completed year of the great number seven*
It will appear during the Games of the Hecatombe
Not far from the great age-year
As you enter them they will come out of their tomb."

The subject does not immediately show itself, but the solemn tones of this prophecy sound a chilling note. What are the clues trailed by Nostradamus that lead to the revelation of its secrets?

Firstly the anagrams and word-games. The French word *revolu* means "completed", but is also a precise anagram for *louver* – meaning "claw up", a powerful, almost "revelatory" description for earth movements.

The French word *septiesme* has been distorted to indicate that it contains another word – in this case *seisme* – earthquake.

These first hints indicate the likely subject of the verse, and the tone of the prophecy indicates a major event. What, then, were the *"Games of the Hecatombe"? Hecatombe* is usually translated as "slaughter", but the term comes from the Roman festival in honor of Hecate, goddess of night and the underworld, or the realm of the dead. These Games were held in much the same way as our modern Olympic Games but with animal sacrifices to the goddess. Nostradamus' analogy, taking all the senses of the verse into consideration, is that this event is going to occur at the time of the next Olympic Games – "Not far from the great age-year" – the end of the millennium.

Spain, the host of the 1992 Games, is synonymous with bullfighting, the slaughter of animals, and no place in Spain more so than Barcelona, where the Games will be held.

So the "completed year of the great number seven" could begin in 1992 and end in 1993 – *seven* years away from AD 2000 – "the great-age year."

If we then commence the melt-down process, taking the second line anagramatically, we find further information –

     s   i

Roi apparait au temps jeux d'Hecatombe
"A King appears at the time of the Games of Slaughter."

Line two then becomes a reference to the Coronation of Charles III, the present Prince of Wales, in 1992.

The prophecy describes a period beginning in 1992 with the Coronation of Charles III and the Olympic Games in Spain and ending in 1993 with a great earthquake seven years away from the new millennium.

And then the last line –

"As you enter them, they will come out of their tomb."

Littered throughout Nostradamus' prophecies are statements in the "you" form – direct instructions to any interpreter who manages to understand them as such. This instruction says, "the more you enter into the codes and understand them, the more lives will be saved."

This brief beginning gives us enough of a starting point to delve deeper into the verse with some confidence. But now, what about the dating of the predicted event?

DATING THE QUAKE
In Lines One and Three are hidden codes.
Line One

u
An revolu du grand nombre septiesme

This is the complete line. To locate the date of the earthquake, remove the following phrase from the line

u
An revolu du grand séisme
louver
"A complete year clawed by a great earthquake".

The letters below are what remain of the line.

n	o	m	b	r	e / p	t	e
13	14	12	2	17	5 / 15	19	5
4	5	3	2	8	5 / 6	19	5
	9	3	2	8	5 / 6 + 1 = 7	9 + 5 = 14 = 5	

Look carefully at these final numbers – they hold the key to the dating of the earthquake.
93 2   8 May (5th month)   7   5

The date and time that clearly emerges is –
8th May 1993 at 7:05

The earthquake is prophesied to happen on 8 May 1993 at 7:05.
The number "2" indicates the scope of the whole prediction - the complete year would therefore be 2nd May 1992 – 8th May 1993.
The letters "p", "t" and "e" come from the distorted *septiesme/seven*. It seemed natural to follow the sequence until 7 emerged. This is the *hour* of the earthquake. The sequence then

In this outline map of California and Western Nevada the shaded yellow area, which extends from Pahute Mesa in the north to Cabot Colonet in the south, shows the region of greatest seismic disturbance. The line stretching from the Juan De Fuca plate in British Columbia to the Peru-Chilean Trench in the south shows the front line where the Pacific Plates meet the land masses of North and South America. This uneasy region, which includes the San Andreas fault, is a zone of intense volcanic activity, having over 30 potentially active volcanoes along its leading edge. It is this clash of giants which creates the devastating quakes, eruptions and slides which have dogged the area for the last century.

Opposite: As the Pacific plate (shown as grey in the diagram) moves under the lighter American plate, huge explosive forces release energies greater than a thousand bombs of Hiroshima. Seismic waves from each cataclysmic scenario will rock the land and coastal seas with quakes well in excess of eight magnitudes.

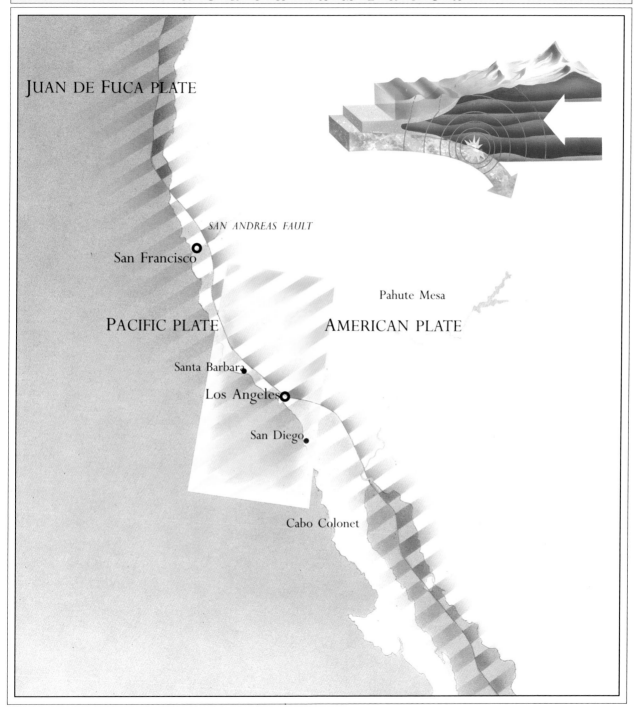

JUAN DE FUCA PLATE

SAN ANDREAS FAULT

San Francisco

PACIFIC PLATE

Pahute Mesa

AMERICAN PLATE

Santa Barbara

Los Angeles

San Diego

Cabo Colonet

produces 5 – the actual minute when the earthquake begins. This time is confirmed several times in the following predictions.

California is in the Pacific Time Zone – we can assume that Nostradamus is using Pacific time, not European time. The word "zone", appearing in the predictions, is a device indicating map co-ordinates, but he may also have employed it to confirm the local-time factor.

Whether it is 7:05 in the morning or evening, cannot clearly be deduced, but the reference to Hecate, goddess of night, death and the underworld might suggest that it is 7:05 p.m.

As the earthquake hits the seaboard cities the pent-up emotions of many underprivileged groups could well explode. The heavily policed and partitioned societies living in the cities are likely to be the center of crumbling law and order. One prediction tells of killings and looting which follow the earthquake which "hurls Santa Barbara like dice…Soon groups kill to survive". This moment of truth between the "haves" and the "have nots" is settled amidst the tragedy of a nation divided and torn apart.

If the earthquake were to happen in the evening, casualties would be multiplied many times. Millions of people would already be indoors, the rush-hour traffic having cleared. Rescue efforts would be severely hampered by poor light and the true devastation would not be visible until next morning.

Line Three   *Non esloigné du grand eage milliesme*

The solution to this very strange and distorted riddle is located by extraction and anagram.

Non loin du grand age millèsime —
"Not far from the great age-year"

The letters that remain provide the answer.

e	s	g	e	e
5	18	7	5	5
5	9	7	5	5

5 + 9 = 14   (5) + 7 = 21 (3) + 5 = 26 (8) + 5 = 31 (4)

The bracketted numbers, (5), (3), (8) and (4) make 20 = 2000

The answer to the riddle "not far from the great age-year" is AD 2000.

Finally, the prophecy number again confirms the date, using the standard decoding device of X = 11.

X.74 = 11 74   7 + 1 = 8   4 + 1 = 5
                        8th   May

        Year - 1 1 7 4
                7 + 4 + 9   4 + 7 + 1 + 1 = 13
                    9   1   3
            =   193   =   1993

All the following predictions extracted from Prophecy X.74 confirm California as the location of the earthquake.

They make grim reading, but it should be obvious that their ultimate aim is not to frighten, but to ALERT and WARN.

"As you enter them, they will come out of their tomb."

A NOTE ON THE DATING

Since the day, month, year, even the hour, of the quake have already been detected, the dating system automatically reflects that change of emphasis, although the techniques employed are the same.

Sections in the time signals may begin or end with 93, or, in many cases, with 5, meaning May. Some sections contain sequences of days – and, where this is vital, "clocks" giving the actual hours and minutes.

Where a series of days appears, the base date, or starting point, will be 8th May, the predicted date of the earthquake.

The Supplementary Dates Section is retained.

Almost ninety years ago in the great earthquake of 1906 troops were called in to stop looting. Law and order are usually the first casualties in countries which have such wide disparities of wealth as there are in the cities of California.

"California clawed up."
7:05 – 8th May 1993

Drawn from verse X.74 Decoded

L'Amerique: aprés Roi Charles et Jeux Olympiques, / un
(b   p   o)

grand séisme de San Andreas en California / louve Etat.
(g   g   m)

Mort tombe en tentes. / Pudeur, danger boiter de zone.
(u   e   m l)

"America: after King Charles and the Olympic Games, a great earthquake from San Andreas in California claws up the State. Death falls among the tents. Decency and danger will limp away from the zone."

Time-Signal

b q	p c	o y	g a	g f	m e	u n	e a	m r	l e
2	15	14	7	7	12	20	5	12	11
16	3	23	1	6	5	13	1	17	5
2	6	5	7	7	3	2	5	3	2
8	3	5	1	6	5	4	1	8	5
2	9	May 8	8	13	8	6	18 19	13 8	10 May
2:8	=	10	1	+	92	=	93		

BEGINNING IN 1992 and ending in 1993, The coronation of King Charles and the Olympic Games will be followed by a great earthquake, triggered off by a shifting in the San Andreas fault. The earthquake is predicted for 8th May 1993, wreaking huge damage throughout California. Continual tremors and aftershocks will occur after 8th May for at least 13 days.

As a technological and agricultural economy, California outranks most countries in the world. Its leading aerospace and computer industries are situated near the west coast. And, of course, there is Hollywood, the powerhouse of the American film industry which reaps billions of dollars every year from world-wide movie, TV and video sales.

All this is in jeopardy.

The prediction suggests that, following the earthquake, huge camps are set up to accommodate the survivors, but death appears among them during the first six days from 8th May. Possible causes are rioting and disease. Between 8th – 19th May there will be a slow trek, by the more law-abiding citizens, northwards away from the danger zone, including groups of less seriously injured able to walk. Significant dates are 10th, 13th, 18th and 19th.

Still melting down the same verse – X.74 – we can find further information –

"Mass Evacuation." – 1992–1993

p   **l**   **p**   **m**

Evacuation en masse débute des cités et villes avant

p   **j**   **n**   **g**

séisme / Rugir le trafic. / Gouverneur de l'Etat organise

m   **m**   **q**   **n**   **u**   **m**

l'exode au bord / ou reste dehors / rond, ombre, zone.

"A mass evacuation begins from cities and towns before the earthquake. The traffic will roar. The State Governor organizes the exodus to the border where it stays outside the ring, the shadow, the zone."

Time-Signal

p	l	p	m	p	j	n	g	m	m	q	n	u	m
c	c	v	v	f	v	t	e	o	s	s	d	r	e
15	11	15	12	15	10	13	7	12	14	16	13	20	12
3	3	21	21	6	21	19	5	14	18	18	4	17	5
6	2	6	3	6	1	4	7	3	5	7	4	2	3
3	3	3	4	6	3	19	5	5	9	9	4	8	5
	92	6	Mar	12			5	July	5	July		8	May
	93	3	Apr		193		May	8	Sept	9		8	May

There is a surrealist atmosphere surrounding this family which calmly dines out complete with tablecloth on salvaged furniture amidst a shattered city in 1906. However, such scenes of peace are unlikely to be common in the next great quake as the incidence of crime has increased beyond all imagination since the turn of this century and Nostradamus clearly sees looting and rioting commonplace as many survivors seek refuge in the North and East.

BEAR PHOTO
S.F. 234.

ETWEEN 6TH MARCH 1992 AND 3 APRIL 1993 there is mass evacuation from Californian towns and cities to other states – apparently a voluntary exercise, with little or no help from the authorities. The sound of traffic driving away will be heard for twelve months, day and night, according to the time-signal dating.

After the earthquake, the State Governor organizes a further exodus of survivors from the state to the border (with Nevada) where they stay. After 5th July this operation ceases, either because there are no more survivors or because those left prefer to try and live where they are.

Between 5th July and 9th September, refugees remain in the camps before, presumably, either traveling back into California or settling elsewhere.

The "ring, shadow, zone" phrase contains the date 8th May twice, which may indicate that there are two major earthquakes as well as a number of severe aftershocks stretching over a period of time.

Damage to houses in the 1989 earthquake which Nostradamus foresaw as only a warning of the catastrophy to come.

THE AREA OF THE EARTHQUAKE

The words "ring, shadow, zone" contain map co-ordinates demonstrating that the area of the "ring" is where the greatest seismic disturbance occurs. The "shadow" on the western and northern parameters of the "ring" receive a lesser impact, while the "zone" is that region *outside which* all those hoping to avoid injury or death should remain.

N
ROND

			13
17	14	13	4
			4
8	5	4	4
			25
	13	17	21

$$17 + 21 = 38$$
$$5 - 2 = 3 \quad 2 - 1 = 1$$

The map co-ordinates are 117–121 degrees longitude by 31–38 degrees latitude.

Note that the calculation includes the date of the earthquake – 8-5 – 8th May.

We can see from the map that the area of greatest seismic disturbance is huge, lying south of the San Andreas fault, extending to the coast, west of Santa Maria and passing directly through the area of San Diego. One the following prediction states that San Diego will disappear beneath the Pacific Ocean. The area stretches southward to points in the Pacific east of Baja California, the peninsula which forms one side of the Gulf of California. A further prediction states that half this territory will be flooded. Enormous geographical changes will occur in this region.

U
OMBRE

		20			
14	13	17	5		
		2			
5	4	8	5		
		24		17 + 22 = 39	4 – 2 = 2
	9	17	22		7 – 1 = 6

The map co-ordinates of the "shadow" area are 117-122 degrees longitude and 26-39 degrees latitude.

This area overlies the "ring" co-ordinates, showing a rim of territory, including San Francisco, where the geographical impact is not so great. Predictions tell of refugees arriving in many thousands in the city.

M
ZONE

			12		
24	14	13	5		
			3		
6	5	4	5		
			23	15 + 20 = 35	3 – 2 = 1
	11	15	20		2 – 0 = 2

The map co-ordinates here are 115-120 degrees longitude and 12-35 degrees latitude.

The "zone" area drawn by Nostradamus is huge, describing the area outside which people should withdraw if they wish to escape injury and death.

The "safety zone" co-ordinates overlap the others given. Therefore, the area of safety *outside which* people should withdraw to the east is 115-117 degrees longitude and 12-35 degrees latitude. The line marking the border of the "safe region" passes close to Las Vegas. Another prediction states that the gambling city becomes a refugee camp after the earthquake.

The safety zone applies to the west coast of the South American continent as far south as 12 degrees latitude which cuts across Nicaragua. Apart from seismic disturbance, this indicates the impact of giant tidal waves originating in the earthquake region. The following predictions support this conclusion.

Nothing comparable to the predicted earthquake in 1993 has yet been experienced in America. Even the worst quake in 1906, shown on the left, is likely to be viewed as a minor event in comparison.

LOGISTIC PROBLEMS

Not only do you have the immediate physical problems of the earthquake, geographical changes, aftershocks, the recovery of the dead and dying, the danger of buildings collapsing, subsidence, flooding – all of which are detailed in following predictions – but these predictions represent a huge social catastrophe. How is it possible to feed hundreds of thousands of people suddenly left without means of support? How is aid got to them if roads and airports are destroyed?

It is clear from these predictions that most of those in the area of the earthquake at the time will have to struggle through to safety themselves if they are to survive.

Therefore, the regions to the north-west, north and east of the earthquake area itself are going to be inundated with refugees.

Continuing the meltdown we move on –

"San Diego Disappears Beneath the Sea."

p

San Diego: dur rond. Batiments tomber. Le peuple

g

rotir. L'agonie agrandir. Une masse brune au-dessous la

m   z   o   d

mer que se jette sur le cit_ piteux / comme une avalanche.

"San Diego: a harsh ring. Buildings fall down. The people will roast. The agony will increase. A brown mass beneath the sea which rushes upon the pitiful city like an avalanche."

Time-Signal

p a	g a	m s	z u	o c	o u	d c
15	7	12	24	14	14	4
1	1	18	20	3	20	3
6	7	3	6	5	5	4
1	1	9	2	3	2	3
	7	93	8	May	5	
7				12	9	7

THE 8TH MAY APPEARS in the center of the time-chart. Left, 7, shows the hour at which the earthquake is predicted to begin. The exact time is 7:05, but the section shows 7:07.

This may indicate that in the first two minutes, buildings fall to the ground and people burn to death, either from fire or electrical accidents.

The city's agony grows. Between 9 and 12 minutes past 7, the Pacific Ocean towers and rushes upon San Diego like an avalanche. Afterwards the city is a brown mass beneath the waters. The geography of this part of the United States will be permanently changed as a result of the earthquake and huge flooding.

The word *Rond* disguises map co-ordinates (see map).

Right: Projected new coastline based upon areas most likely to be flooded. The depth of the saline tidal waters will probably be quite shallow but will render the once fertile land completely useless.

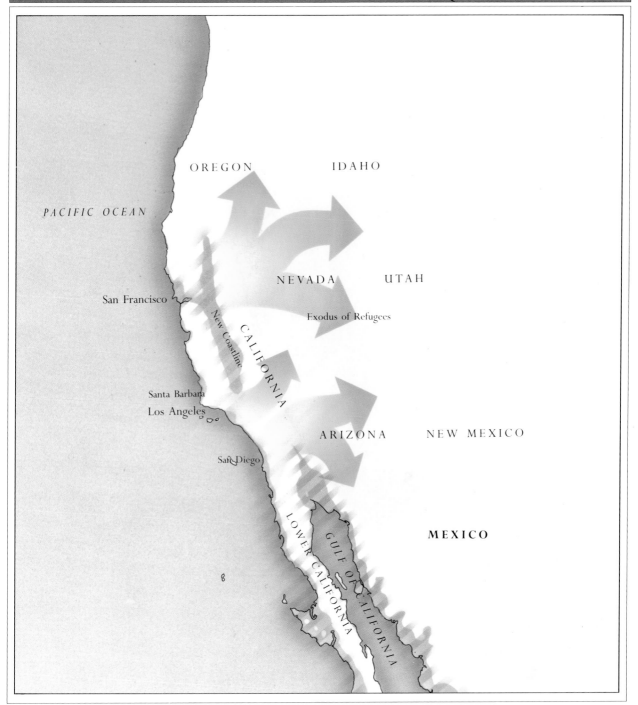

"Giant Waves Hit Mexico."

p   p   p

En demi Baja déluge grand tombe et tonne. Enormes

h   d   m   l   z r

vagues / du Golfe de Californie brisent tot sur les rives du

r   me

Mexique. Avancent aussi loin que Sonora trempé.

"In half Baja (California) a great deluge falls and thunders. Soon, enormous waves from the Gulf of California break upon the shores of Mexico. They reach as far as steeped Sonora."

Time-Signal

p a	p n	p s	h v	d f	m f	l i	z v	r d	r c	m n	e q
15	15	15	8	4	12	11	24	17	17	12	5
1	13	18	21	6	6	1:9	21	4	3	13	16
6	6	6	8	4	3	2	6	8	8	3	5
1	4	9	3	6	6	19	3	4	3	4	7
				1 (0)							
	12	6	8th		7		8	8	8	11	May
May		9	93	1 +	6 (7)				193	18	14

Any sudden disturbance of the ocean bed can generate tidal waves which can travel at 400 miles per hour and can reach the shore as a series of waves up to 200 feet high.

ONCE AGAIN WE HAVE it confirmed that the earthquake occurs on 8th May 1993. At midnight on the 8th/9th May, five hours after the earthquake has begun, half of Baja California, the tongue of land forming one side of the Gulf of California, is battered by a huge flood from the Pacific, which falls and thunders like cannon fire on the land. Half the land lies under water, perhaps permanently. The fact that the "9th" date is used here, interlinked with 12 o'clock indicates that, as we have already suggested, the earthquake happens at 7:05 p.m. on 8th May, with the flood occurring at midnight. This continues until six.

During the first twelve hours, from seven to seven, "tsunami",

or giant tidal waves, sweep across the Gulf of California towards Mexico's mainland.

The number 8 occurs three times, not only confirming the date, but perhaps also indicating the number of hours before the first wave hits Mexico - 24 - but the worst do not arrive until 11th May (the bigger the wave, the slower it travels).

The waves reach inland as far as the region of Sonora, leaving it steeped or soaked, like marshland. The flood's greatest impact is felt between 11th, 14th and 18th May.

"Los Angeles Undermined."

>   t   p
> *Dure ombre. Los Angeles gémir: miné, le cité gronde,*
>   j   a   a
> *ondule. / Paix. On happe revue dangereuse. / Les morts*
> a   d   a m   u   z   m
> *bloquent rue. Constructions / en grandins, nombre ne tient.*

"*A harsh shadow. Los Angeles will groan. Undermined, the city rumbles and undulates. Peace. A dangerous inspection is snatched. The dead block up the street. Buildings in tiers, a number do not hold.*"

Time-Signal

t c	p n	j n	a e	a r	a o	d c	a n	m g	u n	z n	m n
19	15	10	1	1	1	4	1	12	20	24	12
3	13	13	5	17	14	3	13	7	13	13	13
19	6	1	1	1	1	4	1	3	2	6	3
3	4	4	5	8	5	3	4	7	4	4	4
		7	10	9	May		5	10	6	10	7
193	8	4	May	8		8		26			

ONCE AGAIN WE SEE that the quake is timed to begin at 7:05. Between 7:04 and 7:08, the city of Los Angeles will actually groan with the stress being put upon its foundations by seismic activity, waves rippling through the ground, which will rumble and undulate.

The word *paix/peace* is a time word.

```
15    1   1:9    22
 6    1   19      4
 6 + 1 = 7    4 + 1 = 5    9 (9 minutes or 9:00)
```

The time, 7:05, is once again evident. The figure "9" indicates either nine minutes after the quake begins, or 9:00 – almost two hours after. This probably defines the length of the quake – nine minutes or 115 minutes. Let us hope that it is the former.

In the great earthquake of 1906 San Francisco suffered a 40 second shockwave followed ten seconds later by another of similar duration. By the time the fires were extinguished three days later the city lay twisted, broken and scorched by fire. Now it is believed that the death toll was over 3000; over 500 city blocks were destroyed and 300,000 people were made homeless. The shock waves prophesied by Nostradamus may last

an hour and a half so the destruction and number of deaths could be far more terrible than that of 1906.

Above: Fighting fires in the San Francisco earthquake of 1989.

The 9th and 10th May see a dangerous inspection after the quake, probably to search for victims and survivors, and from the onset of the disaster, the streets and buildings will be blocked by the dead.

Buildings are sheered away, their floors resembling the tiers of theaters. Many, of course, fall to the ground. The number "26" seems significant. This may be either the full length of time it takes to destroy Los Angeles, or a record of the number of major buildings destroyed during the quake's effect on the city.

Dure ombre/harsh shadow is a geographical reference to the extent of the quake (See map)

"Hollywood Film Studios Collapse."

buu   m   j   v   d   x

Hollywood goguenard anerie tragique. Sera / à la traine les

u g   m   m   z   d

autres en préparations pour / le séisme. Le sol tombe. Les / studios

e   t m   b

s'écroulent, pas un seul indemné.

"Mocking Hollywood — a tragic stupidity. It will lag behind the others in preparations for the earthquake. The ground subsides. The studios collapse, not one undamaged."

Time-Signal

b	m	j	v	d	x	u	g	m	m	z	d	e	t	m	b
y	u	a	s	a	l	s	u	s	l	l	s	o	s	u	l
2	12	10	21	4	22	20	7	12	12	24	4	5	19	12	2
23	20	1	18	1	11	18	20	18	11	11	18	14	18	20	11
2	3	1	3	4	4	2	7	3	3	6	4	5	19	3	2
5	2	1	9	1	2	9	2	9	2	2	9	5	9	2	2
Feb	4		93	Aug		9		93	May	8	33	May		193	2
5th	Mar			1	Feb		92				29	20	15	6	4

WITH YEARS OF EXPERIENCE at making fantasy disaster movies – including the finest details and realistic setting – Hollywood pays little or no attention when the real thing is about to arrive!

Between the 4th February and 5th March 1993, Hollywood ridicules the notion of the predicted earthquake, perhaps fearing but not believing the predicted destruction of the film industry, the biggest reason for the town's existence.

From 9th August 1992, it lags behind other towns and cities in making preparations.

Again, for the umpteenth time, we see 8th May as the date of the commencement of the quake. Within 33 minutes of the quake beginning, all the buildings and studio lots collapse.

"San Francisco – Refugees Flee Devastation"

　　　　　u　x　　　　　d　　b　　d
Je nomme Saint Francois que retentira de bruit éloigné
　　　　　g　　m　　　　　　　m　　e
du sol paralléle séisme. / Puits, pompes gondolent. Après
　　　z　　o　　　d　　u　　b
un veille, refugiés arrivent tot à marcher.

"I name 'Saint Francis' which reverberates with distant sound from the ground parallel to the earthquake. Shafts, pumps buckle. After a night watch, refugees soon arrive on foot."

Time-Signal

u	x	d	b	d	g	m	m	e	z	o	d	u	b
a	f	i	i	i	r	s	l	p	l	f	v	t	c
20	22	4	2	4	7	12	12	5	24	14	4	20	2
1	6	1:9	1:9	1:9	17	18	11	15	11	6	21	19	3
2	4	4	2	4	7	3	3	5	6	5	4	2	2
1	6	19	19	19	8	9	2	6	2	6	3	19	3
16	14	10	6	4	7	93	14*	11		May 8			
17	23	42	8	20	8	28	16*	22	24	30	33	19	3

9 May 11 hours after 7:05 6:00 a.m.　　24 May 11 hours after 7:00 p.m.
14　"　　"　　"　　9:00　　　　　　10 May 30　"　　"　1:00 a.m.
16　"　　"　　"　　11:00　　　　　　　　33　"　　"　4:00 a.m.
22　"　　"　　"　　5:00 p.m.

　*The numbers 14 and 16 can be reduced to 5 and 7, or 7:05, the time of the earthquake, an added confirmation to the date in this section.

　This prediction contains an amazing amount of information, including a prime device which confirms, once and for all, the rule of the "Substitute Letter" (one substitute letter per word).

　The name "San Francisco" has been changed to the French equivalent – *Saint Francois*. Nostradamus confirms this in the most extraordinary way – he states that he himself NAMES the city in this prediction, lest anyone should think this is an arbitrary decision on the part of the interpreter!

The financial district of San Fransisco. The disruption of the entire banking and finance system of the west coast has far reaching consequences for the entire federation and especially for an economy already in recession. The United States will lick its economic wounds long after the turn of the century and its status as a super power could crumble in much the same manner as that of the U.S.S.R. in 1990.

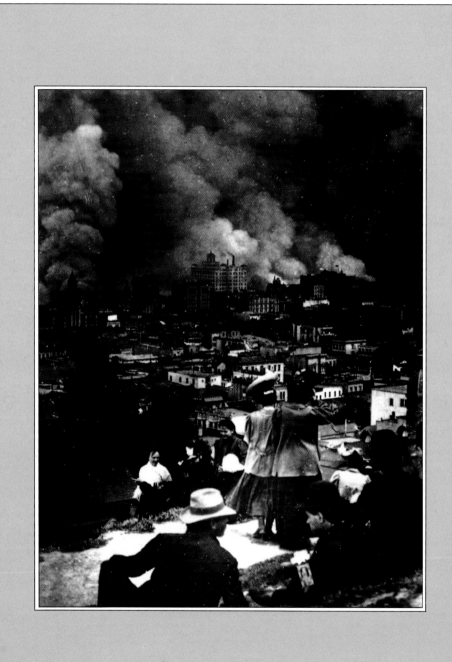

The left-hand part of the time-signal counts the number of minutes during which people in San Francisco hear the terrible sound of the earthquake reverberating through the ground beneath their feet. It begins one minute before the earthquake, at 7:04 and continues until at least 8:28 – a period of one hour and twenty-four minutes. Most earthquakes last only a few minutes, excluding aftershocks.

The period 7:42 – 8:20 is produced from the number 19 on three occasions, suggesting that the loudest reverberations occur then. Sound waves take longer to travel through rock than through air and the sound during this period would be coming from the southern part of the State where the destruction is worst.

In San Francisco itself, "shafts and pumps buckle", referring to mineshafts and other underground shafts, water and sewage systems, wells, gas stations and any other facility which uses pumping equipment.

The right time-signal again seems to confirm that the earthquake occurs at 7:05 p.m. on the evening of 8th May 1993.

Nostradamus says that it is after a "night watch" that refugees from the earthquake region begin to arrive. This makes sense. If the earthquake occurred at 7:05 a.m. people fleeing from the area would not take eleven hours of sunlight to begin arriving. They would appear within an hour or two. But amidst such devastation and at night, they would have to stay put until daybreak.

However, by 10th May they are arriving at night with perhaps a lighting system set up to guide them (San Francisco could have lost its electricity supply at first), together with, perhaps, the first rescue attempts to bring groups of refugees out.

Refugees arrive on foot – no roads are passable for vehicles within the earthquake region itself to the northwest of the state.

"California after the Earthquake."
1993-1995

Drawn from verse III.65

The Golden Gate bridge is predicted to be severely damaged on May 8th 1993 and is either totally rebuilt or extensively repaired. The work of reconstruction begins in 1994 but is not completed until 1999.

> l   p   e j
> *Amerique, non sagesse,/recouvre du séisme – prédit,/su, vu en o*
> o   s   n   a   uu   d
> *California; San Francisco /pont rasé / reconstruit; Hollywood haut/*
> a   g   a
> *repeuplé. Guerre en Europe*

"*America unwisely recovers from the predicted, known and seen earthquake in California; the destroyed San Francisco bridge rebuilt; the heights of Hollywood repopulated. War in Europe.*"

Time-Signal

l	p	e	j	o	s	n	s	a	n	d	a	g	a
i	r	i	u	f	c	t	a	c	o	t	e	r	o
11	15	5	10	14	18	13	18	1	13	4	1	7	1
1:9	17	1:9	20	6	3	19	1	3	14	19	5	17	14
2	6	5	1	5	9	4	9	1	4	4	1	7	1
19	8	19	2	6	3	19	1	3	5	19	5	8	5
	6	195	1	95			94	Jan	4	194			9
192	Aug			Aug		19	Jan	3	May		May	8	5
			Mar		93								
			6										

NB – uu is only a split form of w and does not form a true substitute or have any numerical value.

NOSTRADAMUS, IN OTHER PREDICTIONS indicates that the California earthquake of 1993 will surpass all others hitherto experienced in magnitude. In ferocity it will exceed Krakatoa (1888). In his verse X.74 he states that the prospect is not all darkness, however, and that lives will be saved because the prediction of the quake is known before it happens and a mass evacuation of the region will take place.

In the prediction on the previous page, the prophet insists once again that a sequence of events, not at all characteristic of this cynical age, will help the situation – prediction followed by belief in prediction, followed by action based on this belief and finally the quake itself. Normally, our response in the past has simply been disbelief followed by inaction followed by the event, by which time everyone has forgotten that there was a prediction in the first place and those that have not put it down to coincidence!

The problem is that the human mind is so conditioned to disbelieve in the process of prediction, or anything else unexplained, that it has an automatic "cut-out" process which denies the truth. Even as these words are being read, many people will simply shrug their shoulders and cast the ideas contained herein aside as crankish nonsense. It may be, however, that in 1993 the California earthquake will help re-establish the powers of prediction again. California is, after all, one of the most forward-looking areas of the world when it comes to esoteric concepts.

Geographical references for this massive quake are clearly defined – America, California, San Francisco, Hollywood, Europe. Nostradamus wishes us to be in no doubt about the point he is making. The *whole* of America will recover from the quake, not simply one state. America is *looking back* on the quake, predicted for 8th May 1993. All of California awaits this disturbance of the earth.

The time-signal indicates, in the left-hand column, that in 1992 "America unwisely recovers....", this being *before* the quake has occurred in terms of chronology! But Nostradamus often played this game with his prophecies. If we can visualize the bizarre nature of his verses, spread across time as though it were a tapestry, past, present and future all laid out before him. We, as characters stitched into this tapestry, are now observing the situation in *his* future, but with the event still in *our* future! The predicted event, however, discusses the quake as though it were in the past! The whole thing becomes very hard to be sensible about! The line in this case is split into time frames – the first three words in 1992, but referring to an event in 1993 about which America unwisely acted, perhaps because not sufficient concern was given to the prophet's warning before the quake, which then resulted in worse losses of life – a consideration of regret *after the quake*. Perhaps we can see by this stream of time and space just how extraordinarily difficult it must have been to construct the verses in the first place – let alone the complexity of the codes to hide the truth from the intermediate generations.

Looking again at the time-signal – by 6th August 1995 America is already recovering from the quake. During the time span between 6th March 1993 and 1st August 1995 there is intense public interest in the earthquake in San Francisco. The quake happens on May 8th 1993 and the Golden Gate Bridge is severely damaged so that perhaps the remaining parts still standing are pulled down and rebuilding commences after 19th January 1994.

Between 4th January and 3rd May 1994 the "heights of Hollywood" begin to be repopulated – a casual statement which suggests that the area must have been severely affected by the quake. The suggestion is clear and creates a strange picture of the most famous fantasy factory in the world being empty and like a ghost town for a considerable period of time.

The verse suggests indirectly that the worst part of the quake damage is suffered in the east and south of the area, not in the north.

The last line switches dramatically to Europe and if we examine the time-signal once again we see that there is war there two years after the quake has taken place.

Bridges are often the earliest casualties in earthquakes so are built stronger in regions of seismic disturbance. In the 1989 earthquake a section was damaged on the Oakland Bay bridge but was repaired in a relatively short time.

NORTH AMERICA – AFTER THE QUAKE

"America Burns" - 1993 - 1996

Drawn from verse III.65

    o   **p**   **j**   **p**

Aprés le séisme, les Etats-Unis/fusant dans un rayon qu'étend de t rive à

        t   **p**   **p**   **n**   **g**

rive./ On rougir. Sous chaud soleil,/ la récolte en feu, troupeaux

    s   **c**   **h**

meurent./ Grain rare.

"After the earthquake, the United States is crackling within a radius which stretches from coast to coast. Everything will redden. Under a hot sun, crops are on fire, flocks and herds die. Grain is scarce."

Time-Signal

ɔ	p	j	p	t	p	p	n	g	s	c	h
!	t	t	t	r	i	t	f	x	t	i	a
14	15	10	15	19	15	15	13	7	18	3	8
11	19	19	19	17	1:9	19	6	22	19	1:9	1
5	6	1	6	19	6	6	4	7	9	3	8
2	19	19	19	8	19	19	6	4	19	19	1
5	196	191	196	198	196	196	4	7	199	193	8
Feb						June		Apr		Jan	
										Mar	8	191

Even in the late 1980's a drought threatened Californian farmlands. This will intensify during the next five years until the once rich and fertile region becomes hardly more than desert.

AFTER THE CALIFORNIA EARTHQUAKE of 1993 detailed in the last pages, the statement that United States "is crackling" indicates that a major burning of the earth, presumably crop failure and drought, continues over a period. "Everything is reddened" — land and people are flushed with the heat, probably suffering from the effects of too much heat and the exhaustion of dehydration. Nostradamus is viewing an America as if it were a time/space map with "redness" as the general picture he wished to convey.

The devastation of American agriculture by climatic change develops out of global warming over a period of years, but there is particular emphasis on the 5th February 1996. Uncontrollable brush and forest fires will begin again in 1991, as they have already done so in 1990 with the California and Arkansas fires. Over the years to 1996, this problem increases until almost every state experiences it. Between 1996-8 almost everywhere reddens in the heat, indicating widespread problems with many deaths.

Grain is scarce over the period from 8th March 1991 to 8th January 1993, perhaps because of vital supplies being stored in order to overcome fears of future scarcity. We may even see similar scenes as are presently being experienced in Moscow, with queues for food in the streets, or rationing of food. This would be a first for America.

Forest fires like the one opposite at Yellowstone, devastated one and a half million acres in the Western states in 1988 after a long drought. *Above:* An army helicopter flies towards the fire for a water drop. When pitted against raging fires such as these even the most sophisticated technology seems pitiful.

"Spacecraft crashes on America" – 1997

Drawn from verse III.65

    g   **o**   **o**   **n**   **j**

Un vaisseau / spatial Russien choir sur l'Amerique. / Deux personnes morts.

       s   **p**   **o**   **a**

Le Chef Yeltsin ne fera guére entendre / l'acrimonie. Dupe prouvé au sang

 s

perdu.

"A Russian spacecraft will crash on America. Two people killed. The leader Yeltsin will hardly listen to the acrimony. A fool shown up by bloodshed."

Time-Signal

g i	o i	o i	n r	j x	s z	p f	o t	a m	s e
7	14	14	13	10	18	15	14	1	18
1:9	1:9	1:9	17	22	24	6	19	12	5
7	4	4	4	1	9	6	5	1	9
19	19	19	8	4	6	6	19	3	5
			4	Jan		6	195	Jan	
197	194	194	Aug	4	96	June		3	95

I N THIS PREDICTION we see the first part of the time-signal dating the most important aspect of the story – 1997. This is the year, as we will see in the "Science and Technology" predictions, when physics opens up new areas of scientific discovery that will influence space travel. Everything else that comes, time-wise, thereafter in this prediction is in reference to that discovery.

The prediction also links up with another which we will find later in the book (Britain in Europe) in which a crashing spacecraft is mentioned. The craft in the prediction on this page appears to crash on 4th August 1994. If Boris Yeltsin is still President of Russia then, this indicates that the Republic of Russia is running its own space

It would seem from this prediction that Boris Yeltsin (above) has managed to oust President Gorbachev (inset) from power. It may, however, suggest that the Republic of Russia is running a space program independently from the Federation of Soviet states.

program independent of whatever remains of the Soviet Union. The fact that he does not listen to objections indicates that the space program will continue to be pursued but will run into other difficulties between 6th June 1995 and 4th January 1996.

On 3rd January 1995 there is to be a bitter argument between the US and Russia. Nostradamus seems not to be impressed by the leader's response.

WORLD FIGURES

"Margaret Thatcher – Conservative Leader Again." – 1996

        n   **s**   **u**   **u**   **n**

Quand le pont / plonger, sionisme sévir. Aurore lueur prés feux. / Paul –

          p   **d**   **o**   **j s**   **p**

gué à Dieu. Margaret Thatcher /remonte à devenir chef des / Conservateurs

    y

– sans loins.

"When the bridge will submerge, zionism will rage. Dawn, a glimmer beside the fires. Paul – a ford to God. Margaret Thatcher remounts to become leader of the Conservatives – without the reins."

Time-Signal

n	s	u	u	n	p	d	o	j	s	p	y
t	r	m	r	x	t	h	t	f	d	v	i
13	18	20	20	13	15	4	14	10	18	15	23
19	17	12	17	22	19	8	19	6	4	21	1:9
4	9	2	2	4	6	4	5	1	9	6	5
19	8	3	8	4	19	8	19	6	4	3	19
194		92	2	Apr	196	4	195	1	Sept	6	195
						Aug		Oct		Mar	
	98	3	Dec					196	4		

Thatcher as seen by the British newspaper, the Evening Standard. The image of the ex-prime minister of the U.K. in the role of Marlene Dietrich in "Blue Angel" is particularly effective as Margaret Thatcher has never hidden her distrust of Germany. Her general anti-European stance was just one of the issues which cost her the leadership of the country in 1990.

AMERICA WILL BE MUCH INVOLVED in the problems of the after effects of her own home tragedy, the California earthquake – the Golden Gate Bridge, for example will have been so seriously damaged that the remnants of it will be pulled down and the whole thing rebuilt. As we have seen in earlier quake predictions, places like Hollywood will literally no longer exist. There

will be little space for serious foreign affairs interest so that her relationship with Israel will be neglected. During the years between 2nd April 1992 and 3rd December 1998 the zionist movement will dominate the political scene creating great turmoil and conflict. Pope John Paul II will pass away.

"Dawn, a glimmer beside the fires" – fires presumably raging across the United States, ruining crops, animals and causing human and economic devastation. This "dawn" – rising in the east – may also have some relevance to Middle Eastern conflict with Israel (see Middle East predictions).

"Paul – a ford to God..." This is a reference to John Paul II's prophetic and historical significance. His election to office in 1978 was the catalyst for the first political movement in the Polish ship-yards at Gdansk which led to the rise of the *Solidarity* movement. His reign has thus seen the fall of communism in Europe and its gradual retreat in the Soviet Union. It has been the "ford" by which the nations of Europe will cross to unity, and at his passing, he will go to God with this aspect of the world's changes best remembered. It is, moreover, the divine reason why his tragic predecessor, John Paul I, died so early.

Karol Wojtyla, John Paul II, had been destined from birth to oversee these momentous events in Europe, which will alter the course of the world for centuries to come. The destiny was shown in other predictions long before its occurrence and this may be seen, in the light of Nostradamus' predictions, as the reason for the quick change in papal office.

This remarkable prediction emerged during the summer of 1990, months before the political earthquake which led to Margaret Thatcher's resignation on 22nd November 1990. According to Nostradamus, the story of Margaret Thatcher as a political phenomenon is not yet over.

She rises to prominence once more on 4th August 1996. Between 1st September 1995 and 4th October 1996, she appears to be climbing back to power as leader of the Conservatives, perhaps even becoming Prime Minister of Great Britain again. The date 6th March 1995 may be the time of her re-election to leadership of the party. However, there is the hint that she may only become leader of the opposition, as perhaps the Conservatives are no longer in power.

A tearful and not so "Iron Lady" leaves No. 10 Downing Street for what appeared to be the last time.

"Mitterrand Government Accused."
1994–1998

Drawn from verse I.42

<pre>
    e   x   d   d
France: Scandale politique. Michel Noir cite /
           a   e   i   d
    le feu gouvernement du Mitterrand concernant / largesses,
    d   t   i
corruptions. Blessé a l'assaillant / Hébraique.
</pre>

"France: political scandal. Michel Noir cites the late government of Mitterrand concerning gifts and corruptions. Wounded by a Hebrew assailant."

Above: Michel Noir, right wing mayor of Lyon.

Time-Signal

e a	x n	d o	d t	a r	e r	i n	d r	d o	t n	i r
5	22	4	4	1	5	1:9	4	4	19	1:9
1	13	14	19	17	17	13	17	14	13	17
5	4	4	4	1	5	19	4	4	19	19
1	4	5	19	8	8	4	8	5	4	8
May 8			194	1 May			4 Apr			
	5 May			Aug 8		194	Aug 5		194	198

I N DECEMBER 1990 MICHEL NOIR, mayor of Lyon and a leading member of the French right-wing party RPR, resigned from both the party and his parliamentary seat, an action viewed as a long-term step towards his standing in the next French presidential election in 1995.

During the period 5th to 8th May 1994 Noir accuses the Mitterrand government of corruption. The scandal arises from 1st May (when he possibly makes his decision to speak out) to 8th August.

He may obtain evidence of such corruption during 4th April and 5th August.

Although the number 198 would normally mean 1998, here it is possibly 19th August, the date of the attempted assassination mentioned in the prediction.

It does not say whether he recovers, or whether he goes on to become President of France in 1995.

Above: Francois Mitterand at a press conference during the Gulf crisis.

"George Bush re-elected" – 1992

Drawn from verse III.65

    u   **u**   **u**   **e j**

Le président / américain George Bush, non Quayle, vouer encore à L'Union.

   s   **u**   **p**   **s**   **a**   **u**   **s**   **p**

Aprés sera séisme prédit. / L'avenir guide à reconstruire le pont / de

        h

San Francisco.

"*The American president George Bush, but not Quayle, vows again to the Union. The predicted earthquake will happen after. The future directs the reconstruction of the San Francisco bridge.*"

Time-Signal

u	u	u	e	j	s	u	p	s	a	u	s	p	h
i	c	b	r	n	r	r	i	i	i	i	t	e	c
20	20	20	5	10	18	20	15	18	1	20	18	15	8
1:9	3	2	17	13	17	17	1:9	1:9	1:9	1:9	1:9	5	3
2	2	2	5	1	9	2	6	9	1	2	9	6	8
19	3	2	8	4	8	8	19	19	19	19	19	5	3
				Jan		92	196	199	191	192	199	6	Aug
192	93			14	Aug	8						May	3

George Bush's firm overseas policy makes him the most popular president in 50 years. But will that popularity remain when he has to deal with the ordeal of America's internal problems and the forthcoming disasters on the West Coast?

ALTHOUGH GEORGE BUSH is re-elected President in 1992, his running mate this time is not Vice-President Dan Quayle. The earthquake predicted for California occurs after the Inauguration on 14th January 1993 (May 8th). Bush's presidency lasts until 1996. The date 8th August 1992 is significant in this prediction for Bush and his second term of office. Finally, it appears that the San Francisco Golden Gate Bridge will be completed again some time between 3rd May and 6th August 1999.

"President Nelson Mandela." – 1994

Drawn from verse 1.35

    j   **y**   **x**

L'Afrique du sud – Le President Nelson Mandela lui-même, un moribond,

        y   x   v   **y**   **u**   **u   r**

gère le role / des voix noires/ pullullants. Séche chaleur / croft. Un virus

    u

      caserné cueille page.

"South Africa: President Nelson Mandela himself, a dying man, manages the register of multiplying black voices. The dry heat grows. A quartered virus plucks a page of history."

Time-Signal

j	y	x	y	x	v	y	u	u	r	u
f	n	d	d	o	o	s	h	t	n	n
10	23	22	23	22	21	23	20	20	17	20
6	13	4	4	14	14	18	8	19	13	13
1	5	4	5	4	3	5	2	2	8	2
6	4	4	4	5	5	9	8	19	4	4
July		9		9	3	5	2	192		10
	4	4	Apr	10		9	Aug		Aug.	

Above: Nelson Mandela and his wife Winnie, who during 1991, appeared in court charged with kidnapping and assault. By 1994 both seem to have survived a case which may have proved too embarrassing for a government to press, engaged as it was in a policy of reconciliation with a black community headed by Mandela himself.

I N SOUTH AFRICA, Nelson Mandela is President on 4th July 1994. Though a dying man, he has overseen the huge task of vote registration and electoral reform for the black South Africans (10th April 1993). The country is, like others, severely affected by climatic change. A hot drought is spreading (2nd August 1995). Meanwhile, a virus, possibly AIDS, has been quartered in the country since 10th August 1992. Its arrival marks the end of a page of history.

"Fonda and Turner before the Senate."
– 19th April 1993

Drawn from verse III.65

>   h   g   l
> *Mai, un pis-aller. Jane Fonda, Ted Turner vus prédiction publié du seisme*
>   n   g   a   p   h
> *roule / pont cassé, / voyageront au Senat que les ouir, / or se leurre sans*
>   e
> *un respect.*

"May, a last resort. Jane Fonda, Ted Turner having seen the prediction of the rolling earthquake, the broken bridge, will travel to the Senate, which will hear them, but deceives itself without reason."

Time-Signal

Mai is a time word – 12 1 1:9 = 3   1 19
                                = 19 4
                                = 19th April 1993.

h	g	l	n	g	a	p	h	e
l	b	i	t	t	t	i	l	t
8	7	11	13	7	1	15	8	5
11	2	19	19	19	19	1:9	11	19
8	7	2	4	7	2	6	8	5
2	2	19	19	19	19	19	2	19
Aug	7	192	194	197	192	196	8	195
2	Feb						Feb	

The time word *Mai* gives the date of this last desperate appeal by two famous names as 19th April 1993. The earthquake is predicted for 8th May and it is clear that this prediction describes events immediately before it occurs.

Previous page and right: Jane Fonda and Ted Turner. It is likely that the actress-activist might well voice a strong belief in the prophecies of Nostradamus. It would also be logical that Ted Turner, as chairman of cable News Network might give backing to any renewed interest in the prophet.

Jane Fonda and Ted Turner, at time of writing, are due to be married. Some while before the earthquake is due to occur they will become convinced of the validity of the predictions and will travel to the Senate in Washington to appear and make an appeal for evacuation of the area and special aid for the damage expected. Although the Senate will listen to their appeal it will be too much to expect formal government to take a serious interest in something so apparently "vague" as a four-hundred year old prophecy in this scientific age. They will not give this as their reason for non-action, however.

The time-signal dates indicate that Fonda and Turner will become increasingly concerned between 2nd February and either 7th August 1992 or 1993 (this is not entirely clear). The Golden Gate Bridge also appears once again here but the information is not quite clear either, insofar as this interpretation indicates that the bridge remains collapsed after the quake until 1994 whereas other verses indicate that it will be pulled down for rebuilding.

In 1992 and 1996/7, Fonda and Turner will become further involved in the quake's results – debates and discussions with the political legislature – and from 8th February 1995 it will be made clear that the Senate will refuse to take action based on the approaches of these two well-known personalities.

"Tom Cruise – A New Role." – 1992

Drawn from verse X.22

    n   **u**   **y** **c**   **u**

Aprés séisme Tom Cruise enhardir les gens qui ont peur pour ses vies. / Sera

     d   **i**   **o**   **y**   **i**   **n**   **u**   **a**   **i**

vouloir rester en California. / Pacifiera l'ordre social / que soigne gens / durs.

"After the earthquake Tom Cruise will give courage to those people who are in fear for their lives. He will determine to stay in California. He will calm the social order that cares for a hardened people."

Time-Signal

n	u	y	c	u	d	i	o	y	i	n	u	a	i
m	e	i	t	s	t	r	f	r	l	e	e	s	r
13	20	23	3	20	4	1:9	14	23	1:9	13	20	1	1:9
12	5	1:9	19	18	19	17	6	17	11	5	5	18	17
4	2	5	3	2	4	19	5	5	19	4	2	1	19
3	5	19	19	9	19	8	6	8	2	5	5	9	8
Apr 2		195	193	92	194		5 May			6	2	91	
3 May						198	June	8	192	May			198
										June			
										5	95		

TOM CRUISE is evidently due to find himself in a new part! His new role will be concerned with very real issues, backed by his determination to remain in California during the earthquake, thus helping others who will fear the coming disaster. This brave decision will be incepted in 1992 as the predictions surrounding the coming quake will have reached a large audience around the world. His decision will be particularly significant during the period from 2nd April – 3rd May 1995 during the run-up to the second anniversary to the quake when there will be some warnings regarding yet another quake. Cruise will remain in California during the period 1994 – 1998.

There will be much unrest concerning the coming quake during the period from 5th May – 8th June 1992 which Cruise will help to pacify.

SCIENCE AND TECHNOLOGY

"*Siécles* * Alters the Human Brain." – 1999

Drawn from verse I.42

g t   **f**   **b**

La fiche prophétique Siécles alignera les cerveaux / humains des gens qui

l   **t**   **e**   **t**   **t**   **i**

désirent le science de Nostradamus. / Ont du bol, à cause / d'amas dans

i

linceuls.

"The prophetic timetable Siécles will align the human brains of people who want the science of Nostradamus. They are fortunate, because of the mass of ideas within the shrouds."

Time-Signal

g a	t s	f h	b g	l n	t s	e u	t u	t s	i s	i s
7	19	6	2	11	19	5	19	19	1:9	1:9
1	18	8	7	13	18	20	20	18	18	18
7	19	6	2	2	19	5	19	19	19	19
1	9	8	7	4	9	2	2	9	9	9
1999	-	8	Feb	1999		May	92	1999	1999	1999
1	July		August	11		2nd				

Siécles is the French title of Nostradamus' work of prediction - The Centuries.

NOSTRADAMUS STATES CLEARLY in this prediction that the continued use of predictive devices such as the study of his own verses, can eventually result in a personal power to predict on the part of the student. The "shrouds" describe the distorted quatrains of the Siecles.

By the 1st July 1999, just before the end of the millennium, the power of prophecy has become an established ability acceptable to mankind. This appears to begin its process from 2nd February 1992, perhaps as a result of this book.

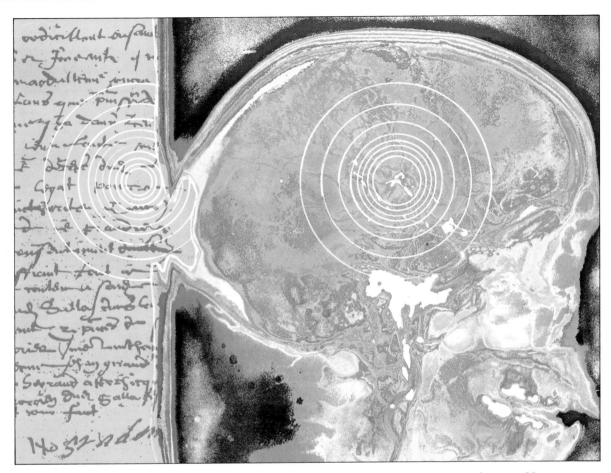

It is recognised that our perceptions are largely formed by what we expect to perceive. Nostradamus cuts through our habitual view of the material world and the idea that the future is not really accessible to us. The prophet clearly shows that it can be seen by those attuned to it.

It is important to note the emphasis on a change of brain usage, or brain pattern – a change that is needed to accept and use prediction as a real force in life. One of the major reasons why this has not been possible during this century until now is the presence of "rational" science and its determination, also backed by the established Church, not to accept anything that does not emanate from the thinking or reasonable capacities of the brain. This is becoming so patently absurd as a dictum that the human brain is opening up to the unreasonable at last, and finding it continuously fascinating. The presence of the "unreasonable" chaos theories illustrates this. If chaos can be converted from unreasonable to reasonable simply by understanding, so also can prediction.

"Computers Calculate Chaos." – 1996

Drawn from verse I.35

       y   **p**   **y**

Dix ordinateurs jumellent, liquide a gueule, morcellent/ calculer sans lier les

    y   **a**

les unités. Révéle du chaos, un rêve nouveau, simple. Gère loix mûrir les

      x

cubes purs.

"*Ten computers are paired off, liquid to the mouth. They break into pieces to calculate without binding the units. Revealed by chaos, a new and simple dream. It manages laws to mature pure cubes.*"

Time-Signal

y l	p t	y s	y t	a s	x e
23	15	23	23	1	22
11	19	18	19	18	5
5	6	5	5	1	4
2	19	9	19	9	5
5	196	5	195	91	9
Feb		Sept			=2000

THE FOCUS OF THIS PREDICTION IS CHAOS, referring to the theory which first rose to prominence in the 1970s. Scientists have chosen the subject as their most recent and popular fashion, making chaos the center of widespread theoretical experimentation.

Readers will not perhaps readily appreciate the nature of chaos as its modern application has developed. To give a simple example – scientists involved in chaos theory use the half-serious example of the flapping of a butterfly's wings. This might seem a totally random affair with little or no likely effect on the surroundings – so to speak, a random and ineffective movement. But modern science has actually linked what it calls "sensitive dependence on initial

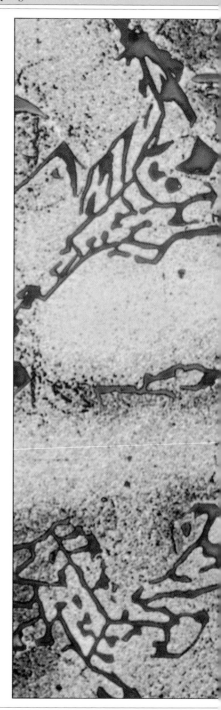

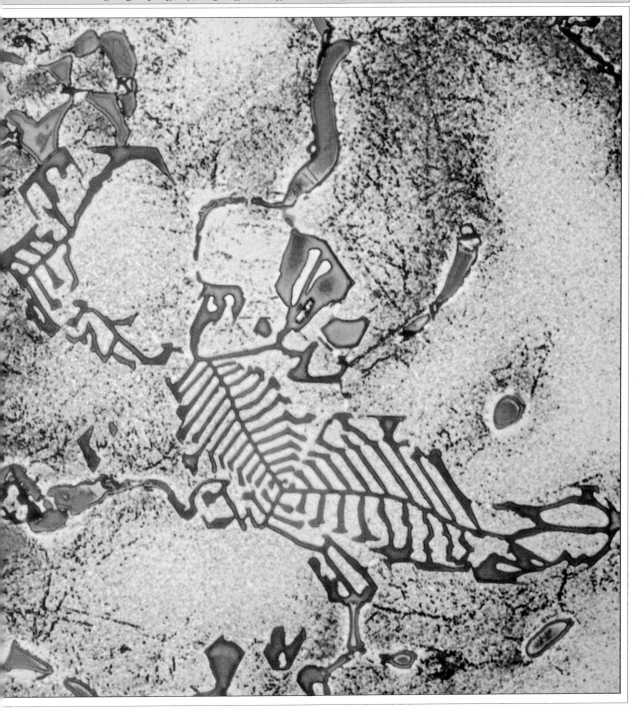

conditions" to traceable results - the movement of butterfly wings, say in the Pacific Ocean, to the upsurge of a hurricane! The concept, actually exemplified, indicates that even the tiniest movement or change of physical activity anywhere on the planet touches the rest of the planet – even though the change that occurs may be of infinitesimal value – it still theoretically has an effect.

Chaos theory therefore explains that in a sense chaos is only something which we don't necessarily understand. Chaos in this context is therefore irrelevant and anything which we consider chaotic may in fact be perfectly sensible.

Chaos theory is now a highly developed factor of mathematics and is being applied to all manner of hitherto unfathomable aspects of science and matter. The ecosystem of this planet is, of course, a prime target for chaos theory.

The prediction on this page might easily seem a perfect example of chaos theory. The arrangement of the melted-down words was one of the most difficult to figure out and this factor has two effects – firstly that it indicates the nature of the prediction, but secondly it also gives way to other possible interpretations. The problem is that much of the scientific theory involved, although it may have been clear to the prophet Nostradamus, is not apparent to us. It has not happened yet and we do not have much to go on!

Essentially we are being told about a computer system that has not been developed but appears to have something to do with five pairs of computers working together. "Liquid to the mouth" suggests that one of the pairs feeds the other with information – perhaps some kind of random system to illustrate the senses of chaos in any given situation. These streams of information may change their form or nature when transmitted to one another.

The computers start their work on 5th February 1996 following a simple new theory proposed on 5th September 1995. The use of the word "dream" indicates a right brain source. Nostradamus uses this analogy frequently.

Very large computer capacity is required to prove the theory which proposes the new laws of chaos and the final date is 2000 when mathematical models involving pure cubes will be produced. Using such models perhaps we will be able to predict ecosystems and other complex systems enabling mankind to reverse the ecological damage that has occurred.

Previous page: "Chinese Script" is an apt name for the complex dendrites of various trace metals found in this aluminium-silicon alloy. Existence creates such seemingly chaotic patterns which the human mind promptly seeks to give some sense of order. Perhaps chaos is merely a concept which reflects that particular obsession.

Right: The Cray machine, at the US National Supercomputing Center at the University of Illinois, uses "parallel processing" which allows information to be processed in a way analogous to that which occurs within the human brain. Such computers can be seen as the parents of the forthcoming generations of super machines which promises to be radically more intelligent than their ancestors.

"Mission to Mars." — 2000

Drawn from verse X.22

      i   i   i r   r

Mars connu. Voyage à la planéte / près le Grand Age. Puissance nouvelle

  i   i   i   r   s   i   r

que / croît / au lieu de diminuer. Un succés / foudroyant. Possession

     s   i

hors de roquette.

"Mars known. A journey to the planet near to the great age. A new power which grows instead of lessens. A staggering success. Possession outside the rocket."

Time-Signal

i	i	i	r	r	i	i	i	r	s	i	r	s	i
a	t	e	u	l	e	t	l	m	u	t	n	d	t
1:9	1:9	1:9	17	17	1:9	1:9	1:9	17	18	1:9	17	18	1:9
1	19	5	20	11	5	19	11	12	20	19	13	4	19
19	19	19	8	8	19	19	19	8	9	19	8	9	19
1	19	5	2	2	5	19	2	3	2	19	4	4	19
191		198		Aug		2000		198		2000	Aug	Sep	2000
2000		May	2	2	195		Feb	3	92		4	4	

19/19 refers to the year 2000. 19+19 = 38 = 11 = 2 = 2000

MARS, OUR CLOSEST PLANETARY NEIGHBOR after the Moon, is visited for the first time by humans during a space voyage which ends in a landing on the red planet in 2000, perhaps a breathtaking piece of millennium – ending drama. The planning for this begins in 1991.

A new technology is mentioned in the verse, heralded by the statement that it "grows instead of lessens." The new method of travel will not make use of the massively heavy and quickly expended fuels that An entirely new form of energy transforms the old rocket-style spaceships into strange and alien shapes. This starship flies high above the gigantic Olympus Mons situated in the Amazonia Planitia region of Mars. The ancient volcano rises 15 miles above the surrounding plains and is the tallest mountain in the solar system.

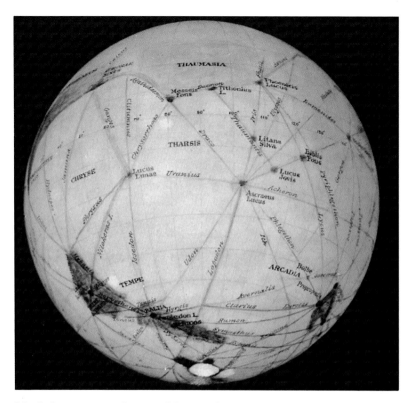

lifted the moon rockets so laboriously out of the earth's atmosphere. The new form of propulsion will create the possibility of much longer and more economical space travel. "Near to the great age a new power" may indicate that test runs will be undertaken before the trip to Mars, perhaps once again using our old friend the moon as the testing ground. The new power system will become increasingly successful between the period of 2nd August 1995 and 2nd May 1998. By 2000 the new technology will be extensively in use.

Research development begins on 3rd February 1992 and continues until 3rd February 1998 with ever increasing reward.

The dates 4th August to 4th September 2000 may designate the stay on Mars. Nostradamus indicates that the new process continues to use rockets but that the technology may require much smaller ones – the entire craft then being able to land on the planet. No claim is made for any one country – perhaps because it is a joint global operation.

At the beginning of the century the astronomer, Percival Lowell, produced detailed maps of Mars showing what he supposed to be a great artificial system of canals. These, of course, turned out to be a hopeful optical illusion but his idea of life on Mars could turn out to be less of a fantasy.

"Aliens Televized." – August 1998

Drawn from verse 1.42

    d   **d**   **d**   **c**

Personne télévise à chemin étrangers / intelligents du ciel du semblant

              h   **d**   **d**   **l**

cassé, boiteux. Les fera fuire. Rapatrie quoiqu'ils / remanient ca la croyance.

"On a road someone televizes intelligent aliens from the sky with a broken, limping appearance. He (or she) will put them to flight. He sends them home, although here they alter belief."

Time-Signal

d	d	d	c	h	d	d	l
r	n	n	e	r	r	r	y
4	4	4	3	8	4	4	11
17	13	13	5	17	17	17	23
4	4	4	3	8	4	4	2
8	4	4	5	8	8	8	5
	20		9	8	8		
						6	
	20	19	9	8	Aug	Aug	5

Many so called abductees agree the head of the alien shown above represents a recognizable portrait of space visitors who supposedly regularly visit earth. Many of those who claim to have seen such creatures often remember under hypnosis, experiments, abductions and meetings with these remarkable aliens. Will the TV image be anything like this reconstruction made under the direction of Whitley Strieber in his book Communion?

T HIS UNIQUE AND PERHAPS TRAUMATIC EVENT seems to be reflected in the rather unusual time-signal chart. The date given for the encounter is August 1998 and the number "20" may refer to the number of aliens caught on film. There is some doubt about the day-date but this may be taken to be 5th August, while the first showing of the film is likely to be 6th August 1998.

Despite the fact that this sounds like something out of a science-fiction movie, the prediction follows all the rules we have established and can therefore be taken as seriously as any other prediction.

Someone, perhaps an amateur camera-person, happens across a group of creatures which evidently appear to be aliens "from the sky" while on a road on Earth. Nostradamus goes so far as to describe the beings as having a "broken, limping" movement which we may take either to be associated with alien biology or an injury. The aliens flee and return to their home world but the capturing of the images on film alters public opinion in regard to the existence of alien or extra-terrestrial life which has hitherto been a bone of considerable contention all over the world with many reports and conflicting information from sometimes very convincing sources.

Nostradamus gives us no information about the location of this encounter, except that it is on a road somewhere. The French word "casse" can also mean "cracked voice" so that we may also hear sounds of the aliens on the film.

Two images which evoke the popular idea of alien space craft. On the right artist Tim White perfectly captures the flying saucer myth. *Above:* A vast mothership hovers over Devil's Tower, Wyoming, in Spielberg's film, Close Encounters of the Third Kind.

RELIGION & MYSTICISM

"A New World Religion" – April 1993

Drawn from verse I.42

        d   **v**

Le lendemain millièsme le Christianisme fait face à l'étrange doctrine /
b   **b**   **t**   **o**   **a**

qu'encercle science et religion, deux hauts associés du Dieu / qui pat de
l

sape.

*"In the next millennium, Christianity faces a strange doctrine which
encircles science and religion, two high associates of a God who suffers
from undermining."*

Time-Signal

d m	v i		b e	b c	t t		o o	a e	l e
4	21		2	2	19		14	1	11
12	1:9		5	3	1:9		1:9	5	5
4	3		2	2	19		5	1	2
3	19		5	3	19		19	5	5
4	193		2	Feb				1	Feb
Mar			May	3	2000		Aug		
								195	5

*Above:*Muslim girls praying in an Indonesian village. Islam is rapidly overtaking Christianity as the largest religious order in the world. But both remain "Religions of the Book", sharing with Judaism beliefs which were written as long as four millennia ago. They all rely on the sanctity of age as hallmarks of their authenticity. Any new religion will be one born in an age of information and science and is not likely to rely on the accuracy of scribes. *Far right:* A Voodoo priest of Haiti.

BEGINNING 4TH MARCH 1993, Nostradamus sees the rise of a new world religion to be at its peak during the coming millennium. The last major world religion to appear came 1,500 years ago – the beliefs of Islam. Because the dating mechanism in this volume only covers the years up to 2001, the period of the next millennium cannot be dated but described verbally only. (Nostradamus evidently divided his coding process according to centuries and millennia. For further details see last section)

The new religious doctrine will challenge Christianity by combining science and religion as part of one creed and from this meltdown

we can gather that the period between 2nd February and 3rd May 2000 is a significant time for the new growth of belief.

Christianity has been seriously undermined in the last centuries by the uneasy association of religion and a science which seems to reveal a mechanistic universe without a spiritual dimension. The presence in Christianity of a distant God has also brought dissatisfaction to a growing intelligence among the young and old alike who look for a more personal creed that brings God into the presence of humanity rather than one that punishes in life and promises only bliss after death.

In this respect Christianity will be seriously threatened as a religious and spiritual force between 1st February and 5th August 1995. Other predictions, such as the falling of the Christian Rome given earlier in this book, also add force to the predicted changes in religion.

"Osho Rajneesh." 1994 – 1995

Drawn from verse III.65

Osho Rajneesh, un guru raréfie, empoisonné, rapproche deux pays. Peu à
           r   **l**

           g   **r**   **d** **n**
peu, son mouvement luit / avec plus éclat en l'Inde et Amerique.

           r
Son sang sera dessus.

"Osho Rajneesh, a thin, poisoned guru brings together two countries.
Little by little, his movement shines more brightly in India and America.
His blood will be upon it."

Time-Signal

r	l	g	r	d	n	r
h	x	m	p	t	m	e
17	11	7	17	4	13	17
8	ї 22	12	15	19	12	5
8	2	7	8	4	4	8
8	4	3	6	19	3	5
98			8	194	Dec	
8	Apr		June		193	5
Aug	4	93				

O SHO RAJNEESH was the leader of a spiritual movement which created two experimental communities in Oregon, America, and Poona in India. His teachings against organized religion were regarded as highly controversial. Prior to his deportation in 1985, he was imprisoned and subsequently claimed that he had been poisoned by American government agents during this period.

"Thin" describes his emaciated appearance during his last years in India and Nostradamus appears to confirm he was indeed poisoned, although by what or whom is not clear.

During the period between 4th August 1993 and 8th April 1998 India and America are drawn closer together by the followers which he left, known as sannyasins. This period begins soon after the predicted earthquake in America and may herald a change of heart in the American authorities towards Eastern mystical teaching. America is destined to undergo great spiritual change during the next decade.

This revitalized relationship between the peoples of Osho and the American authorities will come about as a result of events during the period between 8th June 1993 and 5th December 1994. "His blood will be upon it" suggests that it is admitted that Rajneesh was deliberately given a slow-acting poison as a result of pressure on the authorities by the fundamentalist Christians who objected to his teachings.

Previous page: Osho Rajneesh helped by one of his disciples during a convalescence after his imprisonment in the U.S.A. *Above:* His body is carried to the funeral pyre in Poona, India, 1990. Substantial evidence has been gathered which shows he was poisoned with a slow acting radioactive substance while being held in custody in America.

"Women Priests in the Church of England."
1992-1998

Drawn from verse X.22

         o   **o** **i**
Archevêque de Canterbury consacre les femmes, prêtres. L'Eglise
    o   **s**   **r**   **s** **i**   **u**   **i** **y**
Anglicane / si auréolé. Voire, / quasi sourire poli du pape / donne signe
    r   **a** **i**
du soin / que se nuit.

"The Archbishop of Canterbury consecrates women priests. The Church of England greatly glorified. Indeed, a polite half-smile from the Pope shows a sign of concern that harms him."

Time-Signal

o b	o m	i t	o e	s l	r e	s e	i l	u e	i e	y e	r q	a e	i t
14	14	1:9	14	18	17	18	1:9	20	1:9	23	17	1	1:9
2	12	19	5	11	5	5	1	5	5	5	16	5	19
5	5	19	5	9	8	9	19	2	19	5	8	1	19
2	3	19	5	2	5	5	11	5	5	5	7	5	19
5 May			195		98	Sept		192		195	8 Jan*		
2 Mar			195	Feb	5	12			May	5	July	5	1991
					Aug								
				92	5								

* Here, 8th January most likely refers to 1992.

DECISION WILL SOON BE TAKEN within the Church of England establishment to admit women priests. The first two groups will be ordained by the Archbishop of Canterbury himself on 2nd March and 5th May 1995 to demonstrate the authority of the Church behind its decision.

Between 5th August 1992 and 5th February 1998 the Church of England is exalted by the prospect of this influx into the priesthood, possibly drawing larger congregations and numbers of women applicants for holy orders.

Between 12th September 1992 and 5th May 1995 the papacy becomes secretly alarmed, perhaps by the thought that women worshipers will be more drawn to a Church which has many women priests than to one which has none. It tries to disguise its apprehension with a polite, somewhat patronizing, attitude.

This policy is not successful, because Pope John Paul II has already made his position clear, perhaps with statements of opposition issued during the period 5th July 1991 and 8th January 1992.

Barbara Harris is consecrated in Boston as the first woman bishop in the United States. While such a progressive lead is given by America the clergy of the Church of England are known to be as conservative and reactionary as the Papacy. If this bastion of male supremacy falls to women then the Pope may well feel his own power slipping.

"AIDS in the Catholic Priesthood." 1992

Drawn from verse I,35

    y   **u**   **u**   **y**
La maladie AIDS en la prêtrise catholique. / Les homesexuels corromptent
          y u   **x u**
les juvéniles. / L'urne prétend que, vu leur vie à Croix, c'est mal.
      i u
/ Le clergé ruiné, bagnard.

"The disease AIDS in the Catholic priesthood. Homosexuals corrupt juveniles. The urn/ballot box asserts that, considering their life dedicated to the Cross, it is evil. The clergy destroyed, convict."

Time-Signal

y	u	u	y	y	u	u	x	u	i	u
a	t	h	t	t	q	o	t	a	e	a
23	20	20	23	23	20	20	22	20	1:9	20
1	19	8	19	19	16	14	19	1	5	1
4	2	2	5	5	2	2	4	2	19	2
1	19	8	19	19	7	5	19	1	5	1
4	192	2	195	195			4	194	2	Feb
Jan		Aug				Dec		Jan	195	1
				Sept						
				197		5				

AFTER 4TH JANUARY 1992 the Roman Catholic Church will no longer be able to disguise the numbers of their priests who are both HIV positive and already developing the AIDS disease.

By 2nd August 1995 many juveniles (both male and female?) will have been sexually infected by a priesthood, one of whose primary vows is that of celibacy.

Because *l'urne* has two meanings, Nostradamus is possibly referring to two social developments. Firstly, the deaths of many young

people will persuade society that their corruption by priests is not only immoral, but evil. Secondly, an electoral process will introduce legislation with severe penalties against knowingly infecting another person. Dates indicated are 2nd January 1994 and between 4th December 1995 and 5th September 1997.

As a result, from 1st February 1995 many priests are not only socially ruined, but imprisoned.

HEALTH, DISEASE AND SOCIETY

"Sound Waves Kill Cancer." – 1992 – 1998

Drawn from verse III.65

>   h   j   u
> *Aprés repartition donne la fréquence single pour agir sur malades, vagues de*
>   **u   u   a   y   h eu**
> *son tuent/les cancers. Deviennent mous./ Leurs poisons partent / de corps.*

"After assessment gives the unique frequency to operate on the patients, waves of sound kill the cancers. They become lifeless. Their poisons leave the body."

Time-Signal

| h | j | u | u | u | a | y | h | e | u |
t	n	n	t	s	t	i	t	d	c
8	10	20	20	20	1	23	8	5	20
19	13	13	19	18	19	1:9	19	4	3
8	1	2	2	2	1	5	8	5	2
19	4	4	19	9	19	19	19	4	3
			(=10)						
									Feb
2 Jan 1992				92	191	195	198		93
4 Oct 1994									
1 Feb 1998									

THE CLINICAL RENDITION of this meltdown befits both the description of the medical treatment described and the profession of the prophet, who was himself a physician during his lifetime. New methods of cancer treatment will develop over the six years between 1992 – 1998. Important dates are 2nd January 1992, 4th October 1994 and 1st February 1998. First experiments indicate that sound waves leave cancer growths lifeless. These take place between 1991-2. The treatment becomes more and more successful during 1995-98, with the residues of cancer leaving patients completely cured. February 1993 may prove to be a turning point.

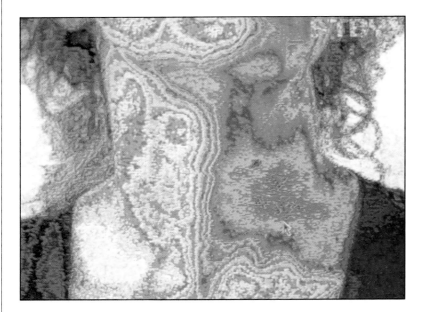

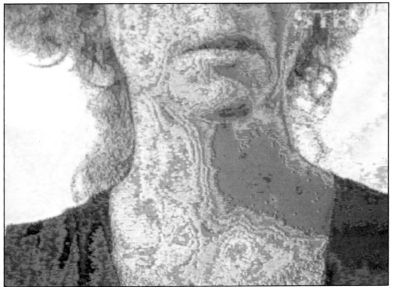

There are many hi-tech, alternative, diagnostic techniques available at present. The images here, for instance, show a patient before and after electro-crystal therapy, one of the many treatments which utilize color as a therapeutic tool. The top computer generated image shows the patient before treatment. According to the therapist the red "kundalini" energy is misplaced in the throat chakra. This can cause health problems. After color therapy the area around the throat is predominantly a blue and beneficial energy and correct for that region of the body. Similar treatment with sound could open up an entirely new therapy technique.

Medical experiments and diagnostic tests will fix the precise and unique sound frequency at which individual cancers may be killed. This may well include a kind of tissue typing, both of the cancer and the individual patient.

"Medicine Reverses the Ageing Process." – 1991-1998

Drawn from verse I.35

     c **y**
La médicine nouvelle traite la maladie d'âge; les vieux, jeunes crûs avec
r   **y**   **l** **r**   **i**   **r** **u**
peau lisse. Les séniles/perdent confusion./ Luxe robotique. Un/ rythme pur
    l   **l**
   rue grumeaux.

"New medical treatments for the disease of ageing; the old, grown young with smooth skin. The senile lose their confusion. Robotic luxury. A pure rhythm kicks at lumps."

CHILDHOOD

Time-Signal

c	y	r	y	l	r	i	r	u	l	l
e	a	a	s	t	f	t	n	t	e	e
3	23	17	23	11	17	1:9	17	20	11	11
5	1	1	18	19	6	1:9	13	19	5	5
3	5	8	5	2	8	19	8	2	2	2
5	1	1	9	19	6	19	4	19	5	5
Mar	13		95	Feb	8		198			
May	1		91		196		194	195 9th Feb 7th April, 5th June or 195 + 5 = 2000 4th Feb 2nd April		

MATURITY

OLD AGE

ONE OF THE SOCIAL PROBLEMS of the nineties will be the older population of Western countries. Much emphasis will be placed on finding new treatments to reverse or halt the ageing process. According to Nostradamus, this research will prove successful. Successful tests allowing physical rejuvenation will come first between 1st May 1991 – 13th March 1995.

These fibroplasts, growing out of living tissue placed in a culture medium, demonstrate the diminishing ability of cells to replace and reproduce themselves with age.

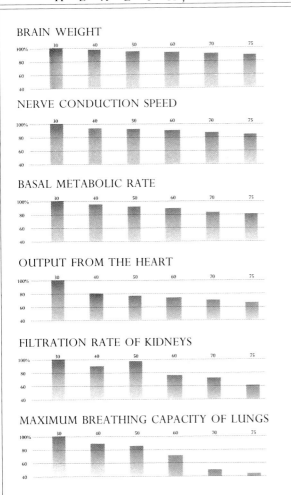

BRAIN WEIGHT

NERVE CONDUCTION SPEED

BASAL METABOLIC RATE

OUTPUT FROM THE HEART

FILTRATION RATE OF KIDNEYS

MAXIMUM BREATHING CAPACITY OF LUNGS

The six graphs show the decreasing efficiency of different organs in the human body as they age. These are plotted from 30 to 75 years of age and show a fall of range of between 9% for brainweight to 57% efficiency of the lungs.

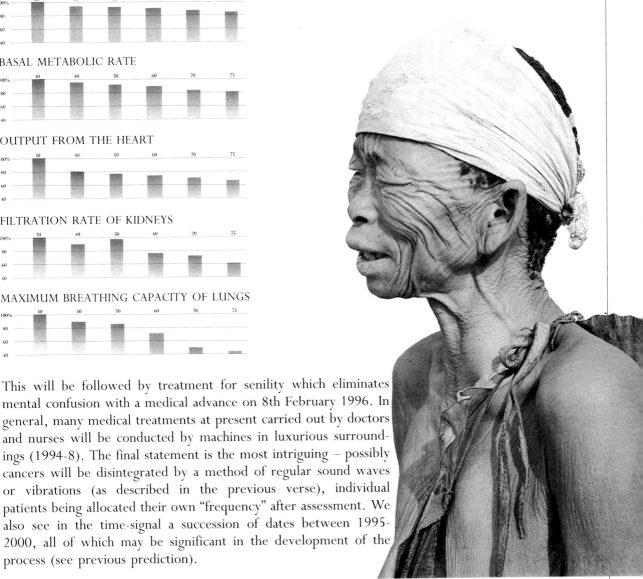

This will be followed by treatment for senility which eliminates mental confusion with a medical advance on 8th February 1996. In general, many medical treatments at present carried out by doctors and nurses will be conducted by machines in luxurious surround-ings (1994-8). The final statement is the most intriguing – possibly cancers will be disintegrated by a method of regular sound waves or vibrations (as described in the previous verse), individual patients being allocated their own "frequency" after assessment. We also see in the time-signal a succession of dates between 1995-2000, all of which may be significant in the development of the process (see previous prediction).

"The Power of Genetics." – 1995

Drawn from verse X.22

                                                           o
La génétique donne pouvoir sur le corps humain par dresser une carte. /
                    i   i   y   a
Indique coeur d'une cellule. / Rase virus isolé. / A cas soi, signe soigné
        i
    par foyer sis.

*"Genetics gives power over the human body by making a map. It
indicates the heart of a cell. It destroys the isolated virus. On the case
itself, the symptom treated through the located center of infection."*

Time-Signal

o t	i e	i l	y e	a e	i e
14 19	1:9 5	1:9 2	23 5	1 5	1:9 5
5 19	19 5	19 2	5 5	1 5	19 5
195	195	192	May 5	Jan 5	195

THE HUGE TASK OF CHARTING a blueprint of the genetic structure of the human body has already begun. It has been estimated that it will take ten years, but Nostradamus states that this extra knowledge will help to heal many medical conditions by 1995. In that year the internal structure – "the heart" of each cell will be defined. From 5th May 1992 to January 1995 new treatments using genetic techniques will have begun to isolate and destroy viruses within the living cell. At present many medical conditions can only be treated by suppressing the symptoms with drugs. By 1995 the true cause of symptoms will be located and corrected within the genetic structure itself.

Diagram of the Human cell. At the center is the nucleus containing 23 pairs of chromosomes made up of thousands of genes, each coding an individual protein. The labyrinthine structure which surrounds it is a vital pathway for enzymes and hormones moving within the cell, while the small bean-like shapes are the mitochondria.

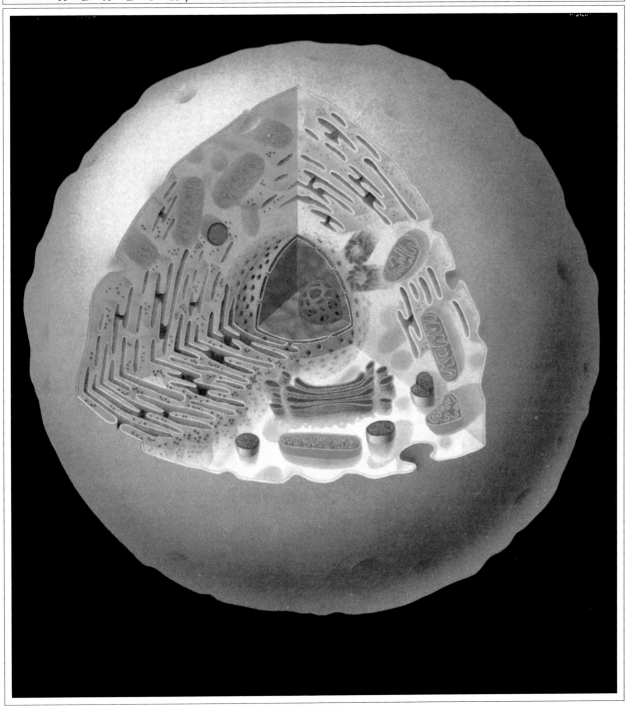

"Education." – 1994 – 1996

Drawn from verse I.42

   d   s   b   i   h

Chaque enfant recoit l'education single. / Moniteurs ne gêner pas

a   s   dd   i   e

cerveau. S'apprend loix / tellement beaucoup plus facilement / qu'il

i   i

distance adultes.

"Each child receives a unique education. The instructors will not constrict the brain. It teaches itself laws so much more easily that it outstrips adults."

Time-Signal

d u	s o	b u	i e	h t	a p	s n	d p	d p	i n	e u	i n
4	18	2	1:9	8	1	18	4	4	1:9	5	1:9
20	14	20	5	19	15	13	15	15	13	20	13
4	9	4	19	8	1	9	4	4	19	5	19
2	4	2	5	19	6	4	6	6	4	2	4
Apr		Apr		198	1					May	
2	94	2	195		June	94	1	1	194	2	194
				Aug 1				(95 twice)			
				196							

I N ALL THE SOCIAL CHANGES which Nostradamus describes and certainly with respect to education, the dates given, although significant in themselves, also mark a point when we will witness a new development and its continuing impact on society.

Children will receive individual attention in schools in such a way as to encourage a unique education, designed to draw out latent talents and creativity. Between 2nd April 1994 and 2nd April 1995 an educational pilot scheme may be introduced. Its results are then favorably assessed and the experiment becomes much more widespread between 1 August 1996 – 1 June 1998.

Back in the 1950's children had active and creative means of expression. Even poor children, as shown in the photograph, managed to devise complex games with only a piece of chalk. By the late 1970's and early 1980's over exposure to packaged concepts offered by television coupled with its almost hypnotic radiant light source has seriously impaired a whole generation's ability to construct abstract ideas. By the 1990's government authorities admit that the education system has all but collapsed and that 80% of children in the U.S. today are under- educated and unlikely to meet even the most modest requirements of industry.

The "instructors" in this scheme do not constrict the growing brain's learning abilities as may have been the case in previous educational systems. It is as though the chemical and electrical make-up of a child's brain receiving this new teaching is found to be physically different from that of a child receiving a conventional education. Nostradamus indicates that it learns "laws" rather than facts which it can then apply to a wide field of study.

As early as the initial scheme of 1994-5, it becomes clear that the new teaching methods enable children to learn at a rapid rate. On 2nd May 1994, only a month after the beginning of the scheme, children evidently compete with and even begin to outstrip adults.

It may be that the "instructors" are computers equipped with specially created learning programs based on individual assessments. Each child will have its own "school" entirely devoted to developing his or her abilities. New methods of fast learning now being pioneered in the States may also be involved.

T H E   F A R   E A S T

"Hong Kong and China" – 1995-6

Drawn from verse III.65

            n   **d**

Aprés Russie se rend dur empire, en sequelles les Chinois se radoucent

u   **a**   **j**   **c**   **s**   **o**   **p**   **y**

gouverner sur leur/tenants. Hongkong/pourra fié. Pape aux Anglais./

              e

Hume va à foi.

"*After Russia gives up her harsh empire, in the aftermath the Chinese soften the government of their tenants. Hong Kong will be trusted. A pope among the English. Hume goes with faith to the foe.*"

Time-Signal

n r	d h	u g	a e	j s	c k	s f	o a	p x	y i	e i
13	4	20	1	10	3	8	14	15	23	5
17	8	7	5	18		6	1	22	1:9	1:9
4	4	2	1	1	3	9	5	6	5	5
8	8	7	5	9		6	1	4	19	19
Apr	4		6	91 Mar				6	195	195
8	Aug	9			193			Apr		
							May			
						96	1			

RUSSIA HAS GIVEN UP her "harsh empire". Possibly a loose confederation of new nation-states has been formed.

Following the Russian example, China relaxes her hostility towards Hong Kong, which is free to continue as a capitalist economy. Dating indicates that China's government mellows considerably from its former orthodox communism between 4th April – 8th August 1995-6.

Previous page: Hong Kong in 1990
compared with the colony in 1967
(opposite) shows the massive
expansion area with the threat of the
Chinese takeover.

Hong Kong is "a tenant" – Nostradamus is aware that the official handover of the colony by Britain does not occur until 1997. ("K" is omitted because it is not an element of the numerical alphabet. "3" refers to the three countries of the United Kingdom which form the British Crown governing Hong Kong prior to the handover to China).

Between March 1991 – 1993 Hong Kong will begin to be trusted by her future Chinese masters. Her economic future becomes much more secure.

It becomes clear that before long a new pope will have come on the scene. Possibly John Paul II is ailing at this time.

Britain's Cardinal Hume, Archbishop of Westminster, will become the next pope in 1995. (See Religion predictions). The period here is 6th April 1995 to 1st May 1996, although other predictions suggest January or October 1995. The numbers 6 and 4 in the set above add up to 10 or 1, possibly also referring to either October or January. Therefore October is more likely because it falls within this period.

"Hume goes with faith to the foe" ("a" in French means both "with" and "to") may describe a peace mission undertaken by the new pope to southern Europe in 1995 (see EUROPE predictions). If 195 also refers to October this means he would depart on or by the 5th of the month (19 = 1:9 = 10 = October 5 = 5th).

"China Survives Alone." – 1991 – 1995

Drawn from verse III.65

>   **u**   **q**   **y**   **r**
> *La Chine dure seule, ourlée a démocraties. / On ménage rapports.*
>   **s**   **u**   **u**   **f**
> *Juin/ Pont cassé nuire à son voisin le Japon. Le pire/ des vagues*
>   **d**   **r**   **h**
> *énormes fera tuer nageurs.*

"China survives alone, hemmed in by democracies. Relationships are handled with care.

   June – the 'broken bridge' will harm her neighbor Japan. The worst of huge waves will kill swimmers."

Time-Signal

| u | q | y | r | s | u | u | f | d | r | r | h |
a	e	i	s	j	o	e	i	m	f	t	r
20	16	23	17	18	20	20	6	4	17	17	8
1	5	1:9	18	10	14	5	1:9	12	6	19	17
2	7	5	8	9	2	2	6	4	8	8	8
1	5	19	9	1	5	5	19	3	6	19	8
9		195	98		Feb 2		196	12		198	8
1	May			91	5	May			Sept		
											Aug

BETWEEN MAY 1991 AND 1995 China sees her former communist allies becoming democracies in the new world order. She survives for the time being as the last communist state, but handles these new relationships with sensitivity between 1991 and 1998, indicating a significant event at the beginning of this period.

Student flags in Peking, China. This demonstration in 1990 was put down by the authorities as ruthlessly as ever, with many of the leaders being given harsh sentences, apparently to dissuade others who might revolt.

The China Wall. Many commentators wonder how long China can resist the ideological and economic pressures of the democracies which surround her borders. As the last great outpost of communist power how long can China maintain her sense of splendid isolation?

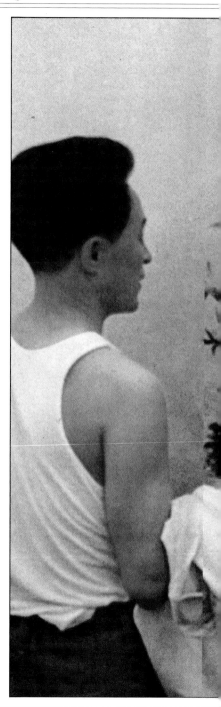

Between 5th February and 5th May 1996 China's neighbor Japan bears an increasingly heavy burden. From other predictions we know that this arises from huge investment in an America which becomes economically unstable in the first half of the decade.

An earthquake in California is predicted elsewhere, as we have seen, for 8th May 1993. The reference to "the broken bridge" is the San Francisco bridge which will be destroyed. Hollywood will be devastated. The Japanese have recently begun buying up leading Hollywood film companies.

This could be regarded as a localized disaster, if it were not for the fact that in the years following the earthquake the base of American power, her agriculture, is ruined by climatic change. Between 8th August and 12th September 1998 Japan's economy becomes fragile and many suffer as a result.

This seems to be an economic warning rather than a literal one, because of the precise information given in the next prediction, "Japan's Economy Hurt". But it is possible that, following the earthquake, the "Ring of Fire" – volcanoes and earthquake regions surrounding the Pacific Ocean – will be highly disturbed, sending out huge tsunami or giant waves over a vast region in which Japan is included.

"Japan's Economy Hurts." – 1993 - 1996

Drawn from verse III.65

     o   **d**   **s**   **o**   **s**
L'économie du Japon sera mal affecté / par le séisme grand / en
    u   **n**   **o**   **v**   **p**   **o**
l'Amerique. / Le pire su n'est passé. / Agriculture – vue en ruine. / Yen
  h   **u**   **p h**
fragile dure sac. Nus se noyer.

*"Japan's economy will be badly affected by the great earthquake in
America. This is not the worst knowledge. Agriculture (America's) – a
ruined sight. The fragile yen endures pillage. Those unprotected will
drown themselves."*

Time-Signal

o	d	s	o	s	u	n	o	v	p	o	h	u	p	h
i	f	l	m	e	m	e	a	l	e	i	f	c	e	y
14	4	18	14	18	20	13	14	21	15	14	8	20	15	8
1:9	6	11	12	5	12	5	1	11	5	1:9	6	3	5	23
5	4	9	5	9	2	4	5	3	6	5	5	2	6	8
19	6	2	3	5	3	5	1	2	5	1:9	1:9	3	5	5
May 4														
	196													
195	4		95		92			Mar 6		195	195		8	Aug
	June	Feb	3	May	3	95	Jan	2	May			193	5	May
		May		Feb										
		92	3	95	3									

THIS PROPHECY READS like an economic report – about the
future. America's current deficit in the early nineties is massive. Uncontrollable circumstances add to this burden until
America's economy is broken. From the California earthquake, due
on 8th May 1993, Japan can no longer play "angel", because the
demands on her economy become such that even this technological
giant of the post-war world cannot sustain the demands – 4th June
1995 - 4th May 1996. The economic damage sustained by the earthquake takes place earlier, between 3rd February 1992 and February

1995. These dates are repeated twice in the chart indicating that they affect America and Japan equally. Note that the damage begins to occur a year *before* the predicted earthquake, probably as investors "play safe" and begin to switch their holdings elsewhere.

Worse is to come after January 1995. Nostradamus predicts that America's agriculture is visibly ruined between 6th March and 2nd May 1995. The yen will be most vulnerable to financial attack between 5th May 1993 - 8th August 1995.

Tokyo Stock Exchange. The Japanese Yen remains the most stable and sought after currency even into the 1990's. But, linked as it is with the economy of the United States, this could become vulnerable if anything happened to its major market outlet.

AFRICA

"AIDS from Africa." — 1993

Drawn from verse III.65

            n

AIDS pullule en Mediterranee d'Afrique. Sang sera navigué, volé. La peste
      n   **u**   **s**   **n**   **g**

rase Roma. Pontife/prie. Scythe rouvre Europe au sud — / pan. Nord;
j   **h**

soucis sur océan.

"*AIDS swarms in the Mediterranean from Africa; blood will be navigated and flown. The plague brings down Rome. The Pope prays. A scythe reopens a section in the south of Europe. In the north, concerns over the ocean.*"

Time-Signal

n	n	u	s	n	g	j	h
v	i	t	r	a	d	i	a
13	13	20	18	13	7	10	8
21	1:9	21	17	1	4	1:9	1
4	3	2	9	4	7	1	8
3	19	3	8	1	4	19	1
4	193	Feb	98	Apr	7	191 + 9 = 2000	
Mar		3		1	Apr		

LITTLE PUBLICITY HAS BEEN GIVEN in the West to the devastating effects of AIDS in Africa which resembles a plague in the Middle Ages. By 4th March 1993, AIDS will be "swarming" in the Mediterranean. Nostradamus compares it with the gathering of millions of locusts to convey the magnitude of the problem. He knows the virus is carried in blood and other bodily fluids. Europe is unable to repel a disease silently arriving on every ship and aircraft. Rome is racked by this epidemic. So what is left? Only prayer. But the Pope, too, is destroyed.

Throughout these predictions Nostradamus makes constant references to war in southern Europe and the Middle East. (See EUROPE and MIDDLE EAST predictions). The scythe, a death symbol, points to Europe being attacked (3rd February 1998). Pan also identifies the oldest Greek god; Greece becomes vulnerable to an attack from a "scythe", possibly a disguised reference to Turkey.

$$\text{pan / section / Greece?}\quad\frac{\mathbf{n}\qquad\qquad 13}{1}$$

This is a map reference. Reverse 13 to 31 and extend 1 to 10, add these together, we achieve the number 41.

41 degrees latitude crosses the map very near Istanbul, the capital of Turkey, traversing the Aegean Sea into northern Greece. This may mean that the attack comes from Turkey (1st – 7th April 1991).

Deep concerns arise over a section of a northern ocean – the Arctic – which may show higher levels of pollution, or rising sea-levels

Prostitutes in Bangui laughingly show an 'AIDS Monster' poster. But the problem in Africa is anything but a joke and governments who simply cannot afford the costs of routine HIV tests are tardy in educating the population. Although condoms help prevent the spread of the syndrome many are Catholic communities and the Pope has banned their use. Caught between poverty and dogma the people of Africa will suffer terribly in the last decade of this millennium.

as the ice melts under the greenhouse effect, even a new hole in the ozone layer. One exists already over Antarctica.

$$\mathbf{g}$$
Nord   13   14   17   4

With geographical directions, all numbers should be included.

$$\begin{array}{ccccc}
 & & & & 7 \\
13 & & 14 & 17 & 4 \\
 & & 27 & 44 & \\
71 & & & & \\
71 & + & 74 & = & 145
\end{array}$$

145 degrees longtitude by 71-74 degrees latitude fixes the location of the rising concern as the Arctic ocean.

Deep concern remains until the year 2000.

"Refugee Millions Die in Sudan." — 1998

Drawn from verse X.22

     c   **n**   **r**   **r** **i**

Afrique – millions des gens refugiés voraces voyagent / au Soudan. Puis

    i   **s**   **i**   **i**   **d**   **r**

/ mises au / lieux où meurent, / corps à soir, sinon ceux-là qu' /

     o   **i**   **r**

échappent rôder à / l' / Egypte.

"Africa – millions of voracious refugees travel to the Sudan. Then they are put in places where they die, corpses by the evening, except those who escape to wander about Egypt."

Time-Signal

c e	n g	r f	r t	i a	s m	i x	i m	i p	d x	r u	o t	i l	r t
3 5	13 7	17 6	17 19	1:9 1	1:9 12	18 22	1:9 12	1:9 15	4 22	17 20	14 19	1:9 11	17 19
3 5	4 7	8 6	8 19	19 1	19 3	9 4	19 3	19 6	4 4	8 2	5 19	19 2	8 19
Mar 12 12 June 198				191	193	94	193	194 196	4 Feb	8	195	192198	

T HE DATING SYSTEM in this prediction alters the whole sense of the message. Between 12th March and 12th June 1998 in Africa, millions of starving refugees are on the move. The build-up to this situation begins in 1991 in Sudan where attempts will be made to marshal the refugees and place them in camps (1993-4). From 8th February 1994 to 4th February 1996 a huge number die in less than a day (which suggests, among other causes, an uncontrollable epidemic). A number escape over the border with Egypt in 1995. Between 1992-8 Egypt is severely affected by the refugee problem in Sudan on her southern frontier.

Already in 1990 this situation began to build up. Millions face death from famine in Sudan and Ethiopia because the rains have failed in the Horn of Africa.

Refugees in Ethiopia 1990. Few Western nations have any concept of the sheer numbers involved in the African tragedy. It is not a matter of thousands dying of hunger, disease and AIDS but of tens of thousands. By the end of this decade Nostradamus predicts that these numbers will dramatically rise to hundreds of thousands and even millions.

A U S T R A L A S I A

"A Fight for Rights." – 2000

Drawn from verse III.65

 p c r r s o
L'Australie / sent durer ouragans, du furieux peuple / aborigéne,
 s h s s s c
pendant / qu'en Nouvelle-Zélande / le / gouvernement / pose honneurs
 y j
aux Maoris pacifiques.

"Australia will experience lasting political storms from a furious aboriginal people, while in New Zealand the government treats the pacific Maoris honorably."

Time-Signal

| p | c | r | r | s | o | s | h | s | s | s | c | y | j |
l	i	u	x	u	b	e	q	z	l	t	n	x	s
15	3	17	17	18	14	18	8	18	18	18	3	23	10
11	1:9	20	22	20	2	5	16	24	11	19	13	22	18
6	3	8	8	9	5	9	8	9	9	9	3	5	1
2	19	2	4	2	2	5	7	6	2	19	4	4	9
6	193	8	Aug	92	May		Aug		92	199	Mar	5	9:1 = 10
Feb			Feb	4	2	95	7	96			4	Apr	

* The combination 9:1 = 10 refers to the year 2000 (90 + 10 = 100), rather than 1991, although time may prove differently. This conclusion is reinforced by the appearance of 1999 just before this section.

Map Reference:
 y j
aux Maoris pacifiques
 23 10 = 1
 22 18

Previous page: Demonstration for Aboriginal rights in Sydney, Australia. *Right:* Maori women singing during the Royal Jubilee Tour at Gisbourne, New Zealand.

With the treaty possibly taking effect in the year 2000, the final thought is that these numbers could also be map references.

23 + 22 = 45   18 − 1 = 17 = 170

45 degrees latitude cuts across the southern end of New Zealand's South Island, while 170 degrees longitude divides the island roughly in two.

COULD NOSTRADAMUS BE ATTEMPTING to offer a location for newly acquired territorial lands for the Maori nation under a treaty with the New Zealand government?

The problems could be about land rights of indigenous peoples, the aborigines in Australia and the Maoris in New Zealand.

The Australian government (6th February 1993, possibly the date of a general election) is "harsh" towards its aborigines' claims for which they are campaigning. This refusal to deal unleashes political storms, perhaps even violent resistance from 4th February to 8th August 1992. This comes to a head on 2nd May 1995.

In New Zealand the government treats the Maoris honorably – perhaps offering a treaty which recognizes the Maoris as a sovereign nation with territorial rights – 7th August 1996. This was the solution adopted by the American government to end the Indian wars of the last century. Possibly land approximating to 45 degrees latitude, 170 degrees longitude will be ceded in perpetuity to the Maoris. The process of recognizing the sovereignty of the Maori nation continues from 1992-9, with the process being completed during the year 2000 between 5th March and 4th April.

Nostradamus describes the Maoris as *pacifiques* – members of the great sweep of Polynesian peoples which migrated through the Pacific ocean and settled on its numerous islands. But *pacifiques* also means "calm" – Maori leaders do not adopt the violent tactics of the aborigines, whose history is one of suffering and decimation at the hands of white settlers.

S C I E N C E & E C O L O G Y

"A Poisoned Earth." – 1995

Drawn from verse III.65

n   **p**

Roi Charles, l'homme fié éprouvé de grand travail / sentinelle

n y   **o j**   **p**

pour terre empoisonnée au scie, quand USA casse, fuse. Guerres –

au

danger en Europe, sud en sus.

"King Charles, the steadfast man tested by a great task – sentinel for an earth poisoned by the saw – when the USA cracks and crackles. War – danger in Europe, as well as to the south."

Time-Signal

n	p	n	y	o	j	p	a	u
m	e	e	i	e	f	r	d	e
13	15	13	23	14	10	15	1	20
12	5	5	1:9	5	6	17	4	5
4	6	4	5	5	1	6	1	2
3	5	5	19	5	6	8	4	5
Dec	4	195		5	Jan		9	
3	Oct			Nov	12		5	

Charles, the present Prince of Wales and heir to the British throne, is an ardent campaigner on behalf of the environment. He is unique amongst recent royalty in that he has both strong views on the ecology of the planet and the courage to voice them in public.

CHARLES III WILL RULE BRITAIN in this decade, but there is an even greater destiny unfolding for him - leader of the battle to save an earth "poisoned by the saw".

In this one phrase Nostradamus encapsulates all that is wrong with our planet. We have sawn down the trees, the lungs of the earth, which could have absorbed much of the pollution we have been putting out for decades.

The device *n/m* which appears in *l'homme fie* proves the lineage and therefore the identity of "King Charles".

3 = 2 = 5
1 = 1 = 2

In 1952, Queen Elizabeth II inherited the monarchy after the death of her father George VI. "2" in the device refers to Queen

Elizabeth the Second (II) and "3" to her eldest son, who will be Charles III. The device appears in the time-signal above.

Between 3rd October and 4th December 1995 Charles III takes on a leading role in the worldwide campaign to save the environment.

"When the USA cracks and crackles … " *Casse* means "to crack like a nut" and must describe initially the great earthquake in 1993 (see AMERICA). One of the "cracks" may be the San Andreas fault, but California is criss-crossed with a multitude of such lines. "Cracking" may also refer to the fragmentation of American society under increased stress.

The center of conflict also refers to Europe as she finds herself threatened from within, as well as from the south.

Part of the danger may come from Sudan, according to certain letters in the phrases:

   a u

*sud, en sus _*can be linked to the name "Sudan". (see Africa).

America is burning. Europe faces conflict. The crisis period is 5th January – 12th November 1995.

"A New Hole in the Ozone Layer." – 1993-1997

Drawn from verse III.65

                      s   g   s   p
Le grand Trou dure en niveau d'ozone sur l'Antarctique. / Ocean
   s   s   p   l   a   p   p s
d'Arctique – encore un ouvre. / Il ménace à ruiner le monde / que ne
g   h   j
pare pas scythe, fosses fusés.

"*The Great Hole continues in the ozone layer over Antarctica. The Arctic ocean – another one opens up. It threatens to ruin the world, which cannot by itself avoid the crackling scythe, the crackling pits.*"

Time-Signal

| s | g | s | p | s | s | p | l | a | p | p | s | g | h | j |
z	s	t	c	q	c	e	c	e	d	q	n	a	t	f
18	7	18	15	18	18	15	11	1	15	15	18	7	8	10
24	18	19	3	16	3	5	3	5	4	16	13	1	19	6
9	7	9	6	9	9	6	2	1	6	6	9	7	8	10 or 1
6	9	19	3	7	3	5	3	5	4	7	4	1	19	6
			June		June		2 July			June		7 198		10 or 1
96	97	199	3	97	93	5	3	9		7	94	Jan		June

THIS PREDICTION warns that the entire world will be touched by the problems of the ozone hole in the atmosphere over Antarctica which will continue to cause concern from 1996 to 1999. But then we will see a new hole over the Arctic Ocean emerging and developing between 5th June 1993 and 3rd June 1997. This second hole will confirm to the world's scientists and ecologists just what is happening.

The reference to a "scythe" is an indication of the "cutting" power of heat over crops when the sun shines through a broken atmosphere.

The world cannot "by itself" avoid the consequences (from "ne" including "s", making the verb reflexive as well as negative). Perhaps Nostradamus offers us his help by predicting the new hole, giving humanity a chance to prepare. The problem begins on 7th June 1994 and continues to between 7th January and 10th June 1998. The device "J10" at the end of the time chart may indicate that the problem will continue for 10 years further into the year 2008.

The use of the word "fosses" may refer to the pits that are used to bury farm animals, thus pointing to large-scale slaughter or natural death of animals such as cattle, sheep and pigs who expire from heat and exhaustion or thirst and starvation or disease.

The use of the word "crackling" is likely to refer to widespread drought or global warming or perhaps even land-fires brought about by the excessive heat.

The overall message is that there is to be a greater threat to mankind from his own gradual corruption of the environment than from any potential war between nations. Ultimately, the predicted disasters could bring mankind together enough to make him forget his perpetual differences!

The greatest message that has come back from all the space missions is that the planet is an undivided whole. Whatever happens on one side of the globe can have far reaching consequences for the rest.

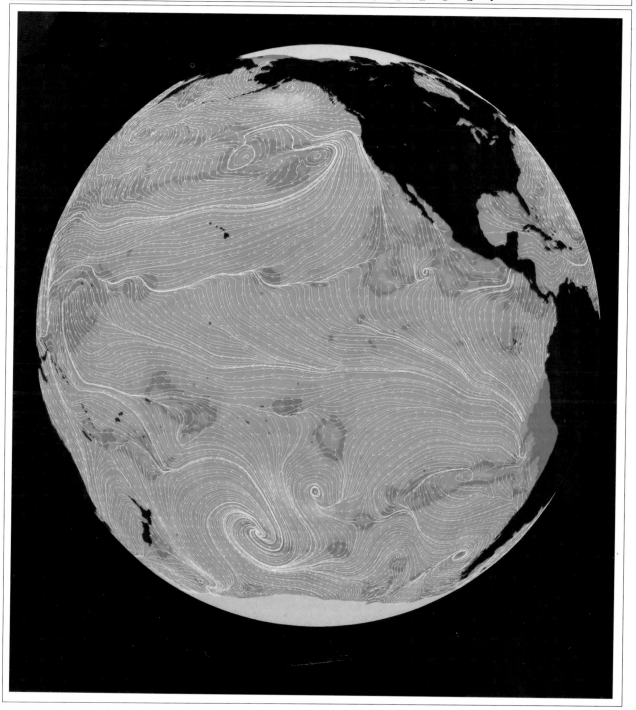

"The Black Hole Explained." – June 1995

Drawn from verse III.65

e

La physique nouvelle décrire trou noir. Après Juin, ère autre commence.

e

Elle a / porte./

e   p   s   h

Soudan, sas d'Afrique, va. En Nations-Unis peur des / groupes sanguins.

"The new physics will describe a black hole. After June, another era begins. It has a gateway.
Sudan, the sieve of Africa, goes. Among the United Nations there is fear of blood groups."

Time-Signal

e	g	e	p	s	h
i	t	q	i	e	i
5	7	5	15	18	8
1:9	19	16	1:9	5	1:9
5	7	5	6	9	8
19	19	7	19	5	19
		5	196		198
195	197		July	95	

Right: Our present understanding of a black hole suggests that a star which collapses upon itself reaches a critical density which is greater than can be sustained in our universe. It then drops out altogether, leaving an empty black hole in space. Some scientists believe that these mysterious holes might be used as short cuts through space. Perhaps a practical method is devised to do this within the next few years.

I
N THE 1990s PHYSICS WILL TAKE A GIANT LEAP forward with the emergence of a mathematical explanation of how a black hole functions. When a giant star dies, it collapses, its mass crushed by its own weight until it reaches the state of a "black hole" which has no mass, but enormous gravitational pull on its surroundings. Nothing, not even light, escapes this pull and there has been some speculation that anything entering the hole may somehow lead into another universe.

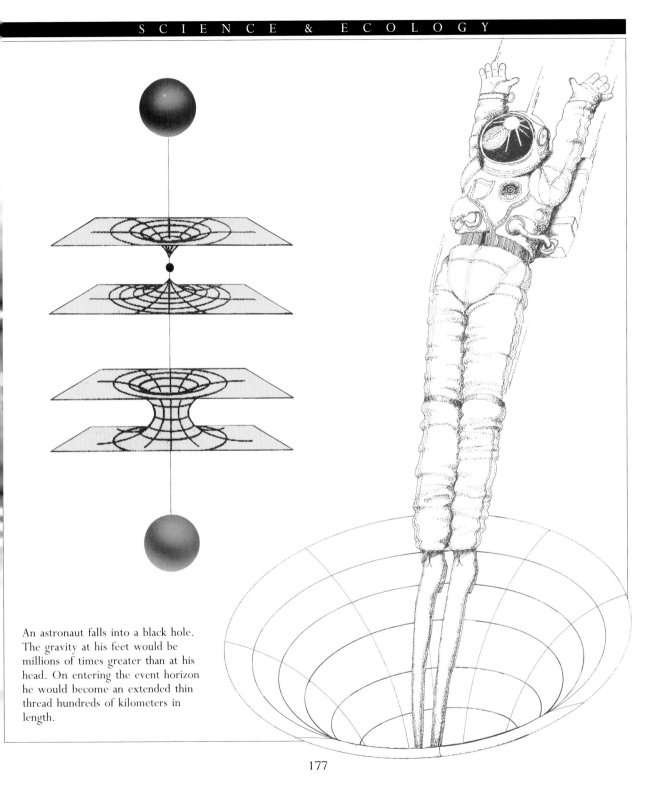

An astronaut falls into a black hole. The gravity at his feet would be millions of times greater than at his head. On entering the event horizon he would become an extended thin thread hundreds of kilometers in length.

A spacecraft approaches a black hole. Around the perimeter of the hole light from stars has been trapped into temporary orbit which makes it appear that there are millions of stars around the event horizon.

Nostradamus indicates that the explanation will be based on new theories of physics proposed after June 1995. These theories may involve a total explanation of how the universe functions – a fundamental advance in the understanding of the nature of matter initiating the Aquarian Age. There may in fact be some more esoteric result from the realization of the functions of the black holes – perhaps not only beginning a new scientific era but opening up mankind's own understanding of the psyche. The phrase "after June" might apply to the year 1997, in which case the number 197 can be interpreted to mean 19th July.

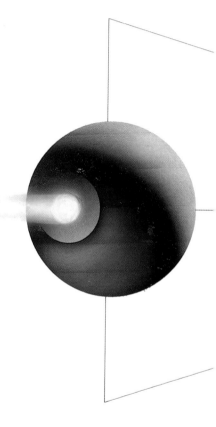

It is fascinating to note the way in which Nostradamus often divides his predictions into two parts – in this case concerned with black holes on one side and Sudan in Africa on the other – but uses similar imagery in both sections. The word "porte" can, if the "t" is taken out, be used instead to indicate the French word "Pore" which means "porous" or full of holes. An interesting theory might be that the universe is full of black holes in the same way as Nostradamus indicates that Sudan is the "sieve of Africa", and somehow these holes work in the same way as the pores in the human body. It has already been established that the planet Earth operates in this way.

From Sudan we can expect to see mass migration from 5th July 1996, as everything passes through the country – the sieve of Africa. In the same year the United Nations becomes concerned with "blood groups" or perhaps groups of blood, in any case certainly a connection with AIDS. The problem to be solved continues as a matter of debate between 1995 and 1998.

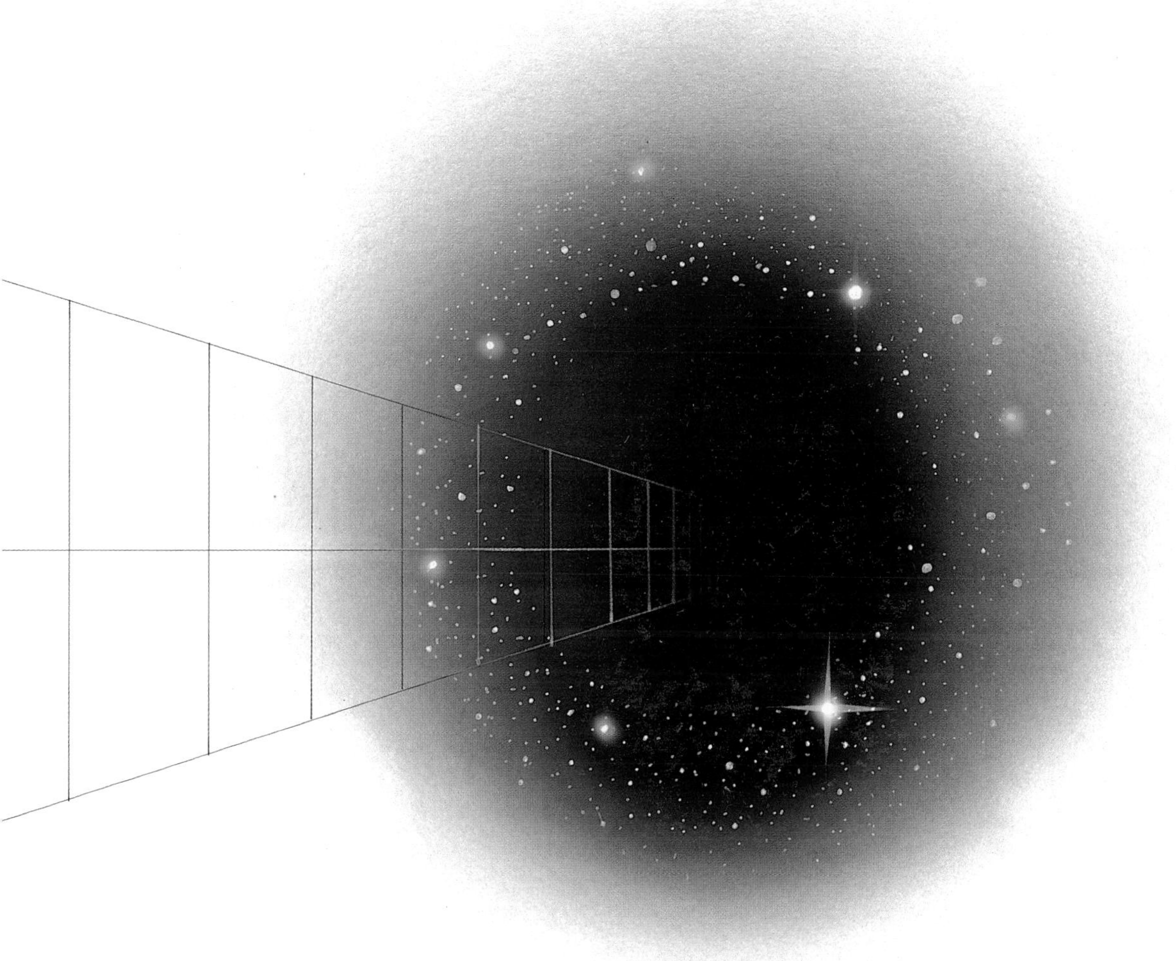

SECTION FIVE

THE SYSTEM REVEALED IN FULL

THE MURDER OF HENRY II OF FRANCE

I N ORDER TO GIVE THE READER a detailed explanation of the decoding system, we must turn to the past – to one of the most famous predictions that Nostradamus ever made – a prophecy made concerning an event that was to take place during his own life – one that came true while he lived, and linked him forever with the fortunes of the royal families of France. This event influences even our world today. First the story surrounding the event predicted.

In the year 1556, Catherine de Medici, wife of the French king Henry II, became deeply troubled by a prediction issued by an Italian astrologer she had known in her youth.

The prediction told of danger, blindness and possibly even death for Henry from any form of single combat during his forty-first year.

Catherine, like many of her contemporaries, was steeped in astrological culture and knew that such a warning could not be ignored. Nevertheless, she needed confirmation from an independent and, if possible, French source – particularly if the King had to be told of the prediction.

Catherine's mind worked in typically methodical fashion.

What could be a better solution than to summon to the capital the new prophet from the French Mediterranean south – one who had no connection with the French Court and – even more importantly – with Catherine herself?

This prophet had only the year before published a book of his own predictions, one of which had been specific about an accident

befalling a royal "lion" in a duel. The prediction had already caused disturbed whisperings in Paris.

So it was that a retired doctor living in Provence, who made his living by writing almanacs, received a royal summons he had long foreseen, a command to attend the Queen.

This month-long journey and its resultant meeting would forever link him with the event which caused the downfall of the Valois royal house and the immense historical changes which issued from it.

The text of the quatrain describing the circumstances of Henry II's death is unusually precise, because Nostradamus already knew when he wrote it that it contained the first prophecy to be fulfilled in *Siecles*, his book of predictions. *The Siecles*, or *Centuries*, were not published in full until after Nostradamus' death, but the quatrain describing Henry II's death in 1559 had been published in 1555.

In its original form, prophecy I.35 is still cited as one of his most extraordinary successes. It has continued to fire the reader's imagination over the centuries, as it was intended to do by the author himself. Compared with many other predictions that he made concerning more distant future events, the Henry II verse is very clear. It is as though he knew when he wrote it that it contained the first of his major prophecies which would come true during his life and that it should be understandable to all who read it.

The event it describes would come about during his own lifetime three years from the time of his journey to Paris. His prediction of it would place him in some danger and ensure that he did not again leave his native Provence.

But all that, as with so much in his life and work, was still in the future.

> *Le lyon ieune le vieux furmontera,*
> > *En champ bellique par fingulier duelle,*
> *Dans cage d'or les yeux luy crevera,*
> > *Deux claffes vne puis mourir mort cruelle.*

I.35

This is the original form of the prophecy, with the archaic "f", instead of the letter "s" which we use today.

Some of the spelling is different, too. For example, *ieune/young* is spelled nowadays as *jeune. Luy/him* is now lui.

In addition, of course, the text is in old French, or Provence. The first task then, is to unlock the coded texts by modernizing the text without losing the essential elements which make up the verse as you see it now.

We change the medieval "f" to "s" and we correct some of the more outlandish spellings by putting the familiar letters in.

What we don't do is lose sight of the old letters. They go over the top of the new ones so that we are still aware of their presence. This is very important as these "left-over" letters are going to show us how to date the prophecy.

Let us work through the verse line by line with the literal English meaning of the line directly underneath.

>   **y i**
> *Le lion jeune le vieux surmontera*
> *The lion young the old will overcome*
>
> *En champ bellique par singulier duelle*
> *In field warlike by a remarkable duel*
>
>   **y u**
> *Dans cage d'or les yeux lui crevera,*
> *In cage of gold the eyes him will blind*
>
>   **v**
> *Deux classes une puis mourir mort cruelle.*
> *Two classes one then to die death cruel*

I.35

Originally Nostradamus predicted two lines of fate for Henry II and the Royal House of Valois. He said that Henry could become the finest king since Charlemagne, healing the wounds between the warring religious factions of Catholic and Huguenot. He prophesied, however, that there was an alternative and tragic path of destiny on which Henry could die from a jousting "accident" which would bring the whole House of Valois to extinction within one generation.

It should be remembered that we are not here trying to translate the verse itself because it was never intended to be translated as such, but decoded. It was designed to remain as a verse simply as a device to divert the attention. All 942 the verses of *Siecles* were written for this reason in this form.

Nostradamus actually told us this himself in his Preface to *Siecles*, stating plainly that he had provided distorted versions of his original prophecies because society in the coming centuries was going to alter so much that the authorities of his time – Church, monarchy and nobility – would not find it possible to believe what he was telling them if the prophecies were too clearly uttered.

Remember, this is still the same verse, even though it now looks much more modern.

The text still appears confused, because the French is confused.

A normal French word like "duel" ends in this verse with an extra "le". This is not a mistake, but deliberately inserted. We will see the exciting use to which they can be put.

Catherine de 'Medici, 1519–1589
Catherine held power as Regent throughout the reigns of her sons, Francis II and Charles IX, only relenquishing that power during the reign of her third son, Henry III.

The young lion the old will overcome
In a warlike field by a remarkable duel,
In a cage of gold the eyes he will blind him,
Two classes one then to die cruel death.

Just why did this verse arouse so much controversy both at the time it was made and three years later when Henry II died (the verse is a prediction of his death, for those who are not familiar with Nostradamus' works)?

Although the verse remains confused, its descriptive imagery is striking. What concentrated interest on the prediction most was the reference to "a lion", for this was an occasional emblem of Henry II.

The prediction of Gauric, Catherine de Medici's childhood astrologer, was that Henry should beware of a single combat during his forty-first year which might bring about blindness and possibly death.

Gauric's prediction is very specific while Nostradamus' seems to skate around the subject. It describes an old and a young lion engaged in a duel in which one will overcome the other in a field of war. There are obscure references to a "cage of gold", blinded eyes, two "classes", then one will die a "cruel death". But there is nothing definite there; no factual statement, no real conclusions, and, above all, no reference to age or indeed any date at all! Concentrating on this text is like trying to hold water in your hands, you can only do it for a few seconds, after which it runs away.

Nostradamus' verse contains dramatic images in abundance – that is his trademark – but not a single detail which could convince the reader that he was prophesying this event at all. And this has often been the failing of the prophet in the eyes of the modern reader. So many interpretations have been made of his work and many of them have simply turned out to be wrong because the literal verse has been taken as the basis for the interpretation. To the cynic therefore, there is nothing reliable upon which he can base his belief. But the real problem is not that we invariably seem to fail in our attempts to gather precise information from the Prophet's verses, but that we have not asked the right questions of his works – or indeed enough questions.

When Nostradamus arrived in Paris, he had a long audience with Queen Catherine, who remained impressed to the end of her life with his prophetic powers, and a briefer conversation with Henry, to whom, it is said, he explained the meaning of the prophecy above.

As will become clear, he could not have explained the *true and secret meaning*, otherwise the King might well have acted differently, history would have been irrevocably changed and none of Nostradamus' other predictions would have come

true. Perhaps this needs a little deeper explanation.

Nostradamus' understanding of the future was that it was irrevocable – there were no "shoulds" or "coulds", nothing conditional – life either happened as it was destined or it did not happen at all. His vision of the future was literally split into two parts; one that was unchangeable, the events and people unaware of what was going to happen, and one that could be appreciated and acted upon. The first period was that time which would elapse from his own life until today, and the second period was from today onwards. Only once a deciphering code was learned would it be possible for mankind to appreciate his own future. Henry II could not, therefore, be allowed to know the true and secret meaning of the verses, for if he did, he might have altered all time to come. Nostradamus believed that only in the late 20th century would mankind possess sufficient intelligence to be able to handle his own future, and that the discovery of the correct code would come at precisely the right time. It is the contention of the authors that this time has now come.

After a stay of some weeks in the capital, during which he had the further delicate task of drawing up horoscopes for Catherine's several children (the ruling house of Valois would not survive beyond her four sons and the last daughter, wife of the Bourbon Henry IV, would die childless), Nostradamus was warned that the magistrates in Paris were making inquiries about his possible use of magical practices. Astrology was permitted, but magic was

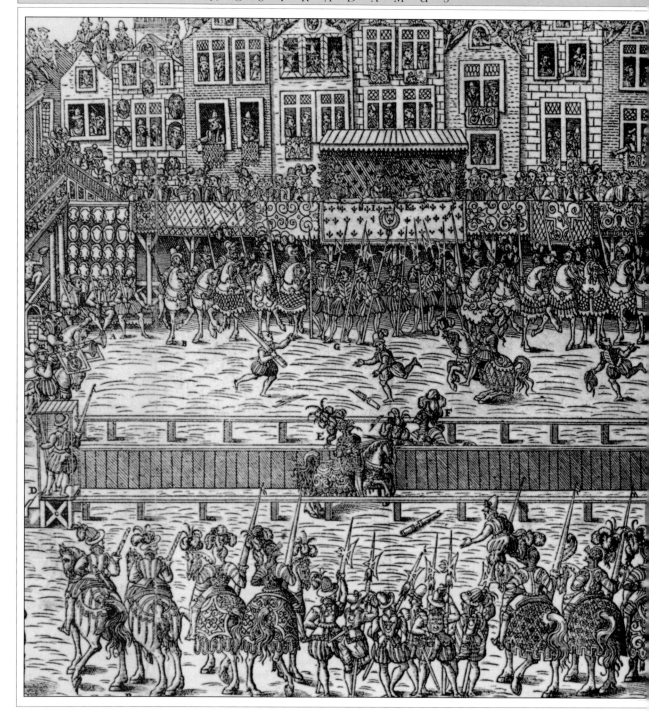

not – a distinction which seems strange to us, but astrology was then regarded as a science.

He immediately left Paris and returned home.

Three years later, on 28 June 1559, a three-day tournament began in Paris to celebrate the double marriage of the King's daughters to Philip II of Spain and the Duke of Savoy.

Henry himself took part, delighting everyone with his skill.

On the afternoon of the third day he jousted with Count Montgomery, Captain of his Scottish Guard. They rode against each other twice, with no decisive result.

In their third encounter, the point of Montgomery's lance passed through the visor of the King's helm, piercing his eye, and Henry fell from his horse.

He lingered on in agony, his doctors powerless, until his death on July 10th.

The French Court and people were stunned. Henry was a vigorous, athletic man who had been expected to live for many more years. His eldest son, Francis, was only fifteen.

This tragic event took on a more disturbing aspect when it was realized that Nostradamus had prophesied the circumstances of Henry's death, word for word, in the edition of *Siecles* published four years before and one year before he had met the King in Paris.

Armed with this knowledge, we, as receivers of the prophecy, can now adjust the wording of the quatrain in line with the historical event.

We left the prophecy in this form:

       y   **i**
Le lion jeune le vieux surmontera
"The lion young the old will overcome"
En champ bellique par singulier duelle
"In field warlike by a remarkable duel"
               y   **u**
Dans cage d'or les yeux lui crevera,
"In cage of gold the eyes him will blind"
        v
Deux classes une puis mourir mort cruelle.
"Two classes one then to die death cruel"
                             I.35

Above: Seventeen years after Montgomery's lance had pierced the eye of the king he returned to France as leader of a Huguenot uprising. He was captured and Catherine, now an older woman as in the painting, had him executed.

Previous page: The tournament in which Henry II received the fatal wound as Montgomery's lance pierced the golden visor of the king's helm. This tragic event marked the beginning of a series of diabolic intrigues, religious persecutions and assassinations which had far reaching effects across the whole of Europe.

In the light of our knowledge of the events we can adjust the text to look like this:

   i   **y**

Le jeune surmontera le vieux lion. En champ bellique par singulier

      y **u**

duelle, lui crevera – "Les yeux dans cage d'or", deux classes, puis une

mourir mort cruelle.

In English then:

"The young man will overcome the old lion. In a warlike field by a remarkable duel, he will blind him – 'the eyes in a Golden Cage'; two training runs, then one will die a cruel death."

In a sense, we are cheating here because we know what happened, but the purpose of the operation is to use this knowledge in order to reveal the code so that we can apply it to events in the future that we do not know by any other means. We leave, as we always will, the old letters in their correct positions above the modern versions of them. The reasons for this will become clear.

In this version, the verse is transformed into straightforward simple prose. One of the two major reasons why Nostradamus' prophecies have always appeared incoherent is the fact that interpreters always went directly for the verses. The tension between these two forms, the visible verse and the hidden prose, creates the confusion for the reader. The other principal reason for confusion will become clear with further examples. Before we get into the actual decoding method we must go deeper into these examples. The reader is requested simply to trust the method for the moment.

So what does this new form of the prediction offer us?

Firstly, it offers a much more complete picture of the event. Continuity is often lacking in any prophecy, but we may suspect that those of Nostradamus and certainly older forms of prophecy, such as those appearing in the Bible, mutilated any form of continuity to avoid detection at awkward times. As a Jew, Nostradamus is simply following a very ancient tradition of his forebears. The repositioning of the words, therefore, offers an opportunity to return to the original prophecy hidden behind the distorted verse.

Secondly, there are the details, always present, often pointed out, but usually, in the verses, not presented with any clarity. In this new prose form everything is very clear.

Henry's opponent, Montgomery, was younger than the King. The lion was an emblem used by Henry. The tournament field could be described as a "warlike field" without actually being a field of war. Montgomery's lance would blind the King in one eye.

Next comes the amazing description "Eyes in a Golden cage" – a reference to Henry himself, *since he was wearing a gilt helmet with a barred visor.*

The phrase "deux classes" can be identified with "training runs", meaning the two previous jousts with Montgomery, before the third in which Henry was fatally wounded.

Nevertheless, despite all the glorious drama of the verse, its exciting imagery deludes us into thinking that it conveys more than it really does. There is not one single hard fact, one name, one date which could be drawn from this prediction to establish the accuracy of Nostradamus. That is not a satisfactory situation and one of the main reasons why so many people have become somewhat cynical about Nostradamus' predictions – how can we believe something that can be interpreted in so many different ways?

The details of the prophecy caused a storm when they were known in Paris. Calls came from the Inquisition authorities for Nostradamus to be arrested for questioning. His effigy burned in the streets.

Perhaps the Prophet was somewhat protected by the influence of Catherine, but had the true meaning of the prophecy been known, Nostradamus could not have escaped torture and the stake. He knew too much. In fact, he knew even more than the authorities suspected.

In order to illustrate this extraordinary degree of knowledge we can look at the first line of the prophecy.

i   y
Le jeune surmontera le vieux lion In English –
   "The young man will overcome the old lion"
   Now look at it again transformed.

Le jeune Mont(gomery) rusera le lion vieux
"The young Mont(gomery) will deceive the old lion"

Everything is the same, except that the verb "surmontera" has become "Mont rusera" – "Mont" will deceive.

The most startling aspect of this transformation is the emergence of part of the name *Montgomery*. This is evidence that Nostradamus knew before the event who the protagonist was going to be. Remember that the prophecy was published four years before the event.

The second piece of information is that he not only "overcomes", but deceives "the old lion".

Does this merely refer to his ability to deceive the king in the joust, so piercing the royal defense and by a terrible misfortune fatally wounding Henry?

Or does it indicate a deliberate intention or even a conspiracy to kill Henry?

Although it was thought at the time to be an accident, later events cast a doubt. Henry had been particularly zealous and cruel in persecuting the Protestant Huguenots of France. Many had been hideously tortured and executed. Montgomery was Scottish, a land where Protestantism was burgeoning fast.

Soon after Henry died, Montgomery left France, but he returned seventeen years later as a leader in a Huguenot uprising. He was captured and put to death by Catherine de Medici in Paris. Was there a stronger reason than simple revenge for Catherine's insistence that Montgomery should die? Henry II, after all, had pardoned him before he died. Nostradamus tells us that there was. Who is "the old lion"? Let's take another look at this line.

Le jeune Mont(gomery) rusera le lion vieux
This then becomes:

i   u   l   y
Le jeune Mont(gomery) rue Henri Rex Valois
"The young Mont(gomery) attacks Henry, the Valois King."

The complete meaning of the line therefore is: "The young man will overcome the old lion. The young Mont(gomery) will deceive the old lion. He attacks Henry the Valois King."

Henry, the "Valois King", is revealed as the other duelist. If we look at the original line of the prophecy, we see that it contains an anagram, making "surmontera" into "Mont rusera", so that we

When Nostradamus gave his private prophesies to Catherine he was very careful as to what he might reveal to the strong willed and often dangerous queen. He could hardly tell her outright that her entire family would not survive her so he concealed his predictions in difficult verses. Now we can see just how accurate he was.

might realize that there is likely to be more of this kind of shenanigans in the same text.

There are four letters appearing above the line. The letter "i" was the old letter in the original "ieune".

The letter "y" appeared in "lyon" and was pushed upwards by the modern "i". Although "lyon/lion" has now disappeared from the new line, the old letter "y" must still be kept above the letter "i" as this will help us to define the date of the prediction.

The substitute "y" is in Valois, not in Henry. A crucial principle of the system is that only one substitute letter may appear in any word. Henry already has a substitute letter – "u". The only other "i" in the new prediction occurs in Valois.

"U" and "i" were present in the line – *Mont(gomery) rusera le lion vieux*. They must be kept to date the text, even though they are not now part of the new line.

So the method is to "dig out" the new text by treating it as an anagram and rearrange the letters in keeping with the information given in the prophecy and include what we know of the historical event.

```
i    u    l    y
j    h    r    i
```

These are the four substitute letters (the letters on the top line) and the letters which have replaced them on the second line. The most obvious point to notice is the word "iuly" or July. The letters "I" and "J" obtain the same numerical value (as we shall see in the Numerical Code later in this section) – 10.

Henry II died on the 10th July 1559.

So now we must take a look at the dating system.

HOW TO USE THE DATING SYSTEM

The system is founded on two principles –

1. – the Numeric Alphabet in which each letter has its own number and

2. – the Substituted Letter Device in which the numbers belonging to the "raised" letters in a line of the text, together with the numbers of the new letters immediately below the raised letters are analysed for dates which support and extend the meaning of the new predictions.

3. – A third aspect of the system is the "time-signal" explained below.

THE NUMERIC ALPHABET

This is made up of the 24 letters of the old French alphabet, excluding the Greek "k" and the Germanic "w", neither of which appear in modern French. Each letter has its own number.

a b c d e f g h i j l m n o p q r s t u v x y z
1 2 3 4 5 6 7 8 9 10 11 12 13 14 15 16 17 18 19 20 21 22 23 24

In the text, the letter "k" is substituted by "c" and "w" by "uu" or double-u.

ROMAN NUMERALS

Three letters also possess numbers from the Latin or Roman numbering system.

I = one, V = five and X = ten.

This is particularly important for "I", whose two values 1 and 9 often apply to predictions of this century.

THE NUMBER 10.

By itself, the number 10 can also signify 1, 1 and 9 (making 10), or even on occasion 19 (1 and 9 again making 10).

NUMBER REDUCTION

Numbers ending in zero can be reduced by deducting the zero. 10 – 1, 20 = 2 etc.

The number 11 attached to letter "L" may be reduced to 2. In most cases either 11 is reduced to one:one for use in the calculation, or if that does not seem to produce relevant information, it is reduced to 2.

NUMERICAL ANAGRAMS

Numerical anagrams are sets of mixed up numbers which emerge from these substitute letter devices in the lines of secret prophecy, which then have to be decoded.

TIME-SIGNALS AND TIME WORDS

Time-words are normal French words, woven inconspicuously into the text of the predictions. They are all words whose meaning is linked with an aspect of time.

Typical examples are "jour/day", "jeune/young" and "encore/again".

Such words in the predictions betray the presence of a date, or series of dates related to the subject of the text. Other words, such as those connected with rank or royalty, often contain dating aspects.

OTHER INFORMATION

A letter/number can signify other information, such as royal lines of descent – Charles the Second, or George the Sixth. Numbers can either be used as they are: 11, 12, 13 etc., or "reduced" by adding them together – 18 = 9, 16 = 7 and so on.

Dating and other numerical information will appear throughout this book under the heading – TIME-SIGNALS.

The reader will find when studying the dating system that the same dates will be confirmed several times through a variety of calculations and different numbers, thus discounting the possibility of simple coincidence.

As a brief practical example we can take a look at the time-signal of the verse we have examined in this section.

TIME-SIGNAL – Prophecy I.35 Line one.

```
i   u   l   y
j   h   r   i
```

The first thing to notice about this arrangement of letters is that the top four letters very nearly represent the word "July".

The missing "J" is the first letter of the lower set.

As will be seen throughout the pages of the book, this kind of formation happens too often to be coincidence, it is the result of the correct application of the decoding system. Henry II dies during July 10th. English words appear from time to time in the secret prophecies. Under the dating system, both letter "i" and "j" are worth 10. So let us dig a little deeper into this collection of letters by setting out their numbers. It must be noted here that we are, of course, deducing the dating system by working backwards from dates that we already have. Again, we are cheating! But it will become clear that this is merely a method which will later allow us to apply the same system to the future.

```
i   u   l   y        1:9   20   11   23
j   h   r   i         10    8    17   1:9
```

These eight numbers hold the dating of the event described by the Prophecy I.35

```
i          1:9
j          10
```
9-1-1 = 7 = the 7th month, July.

July – the month when Henry died – appears in the letters belonging to this set.

```
u      20 + 8 = 28
h      8 − 2 = 6 = the 6th month, June
```
The tournament in which Henry was fatally wounded began on the 28th June.

```
l       11
r       17
```
7 + 1 + 1 + 1 − 10 = 10th day of July (7)

Henry died on the 10th July.

```
y          23     =   5
i          1:9    = 1   9
```

CHARLES IX *(8 years old)*

CHARLES IX *(23 years old)*

Charles IX. Henry's son, called the "savage", or worse, the "black", was a cruel and hated king. He sanctioned the hideous St. Bartholomew's Day Massacre of the Huguenots. It was with considerable public relief that he expired at the age of 24 from a common cold.

The year of the prophecy is 1559

The final confirmation occurs in the letter device in the name of Henri in the prediction.

u   = 20   =   2

henri

The device confirms that the Valois King called Henri whom Nostradamus refers to in the prediction is Henry the Second.

The period of the time-signal is 28th June – 10th July. The tournament opened on 28th June and Henry died on the 10th July.

"Jeune" is a time-word describing Montgomery.

```
j  e  u              n   e
10 5  20            13   5
10 5 + 2 = 7
10        7  =   10th July
```

The left set provides the vital date of the King's death yet again – further confirmation.

The right set is even more remarkable – 13 and 5 appear as the decoded numbers from the two raised letters "n" and "e". 135 is also the verse number. Perhaps this is Nostradamus' complex seal of approval for our solution to the riddle.

So, having run through the total "package" on this verse, we end up with, including dating:

"The young Montgomery attacks Henry the Second, the Valois King, during the period 28th June - 10th July 1559."

If we think back to the original image of the "Vulcan" and his furnace – the image that Nostradamus gave us in his Preface – we can now experience the device first hand – the methods by which he distorted his verses artificially in order to disguise his genius from those whom he knew would not be equipped to accept it. Now that we begin to "melt down" this extraordinary raw material, we find that perhaps we can reconstruct the original prose prophecy – allowing the prophecy to emerge from its hiding place amongst the lines of the verse.

BY SINGULAR DUEL

To give further confirmation of the method to be used in the book we can complete line two of the prophecy.

En champ bellique par singulier duelle
– using anagramatic techniques becomes –

b   i   l

que le chapelet ne lie pas (Mont)gomeri, dur nul — retaining the old letters above becomes then in English —
"as the rosary does not bind (Mont)gomery, the harsh man (is) no more."

Here the intermediate stages of coding have not been included to save space, but the reader can test them if required, using the previously explained system. The most important point is to look for anything that appears unusual. "Duel" is "duelle" in Nostradamus' lines — aberrant spelling gives us a hint that a different prediction is concealed in the text. The "singulier" gives us a last syllable — "lier" which is also the French verb "to bind." By these detective methods we can find the true meaning of the lines.

Nostradamus regarded Montgomery as Henry's assassin. His name emerges in line one and in line two we learn more about the situation. By the time of the making of the prediction, Gabriel Lorges, Comte de Montgomery, Captain of Henry II's Scottish Guard, was no longer a Catholic. The rosary is the portable image of Roman Catholicism — the single most familiar object within the faith. Thus we have — "As the rosary does not bind Montgomery, the harsh man is no more…" The tournament was a perfect opportunity for Montgomery to avenge the Protestants and prevent Henry from committing further crimes against them. As can be seen in the time-signal, the dates are yet again confirmed using the same code.

CATHERINE DE 'MEDICI

HENRY III

TIME-SIGNAL Prophecy I.35, line two —

| b | i | l | 2 | 1:9 | 11 |
| e | t | o | 5 | 19 | 14 |

The number 11 is reduced to 2 before calculation.

2	10	2
5	10	14
2 + 5 = 7	10 10	2 + 1 + 4 = 7

The date emerges as 10th July, twice!

Passing on now briefly to the last two lines of the verse we can conclude our testing phase.

With Line 3 we see the consequences of this act.

y

les yeux dans cage d'or lui crevera
becomes

Catherine lived to see all her sons die before her. By the time Henry III reached the throne she was forced to relinquish her power as Regent. Henry, a universally unpopular, homosexual ruler, was assassinated by a Franciscan monk called Clement, thus ending the royal line of the Valois.

l   **y d**   **c**

(Mont)gomery a rasé u = 20; casque henri X du leve
"(Mont)gomery has brought down the "Second". The helmet raises the indebted Henry."

The Protestant Henry IV who was proclaimed King in 1589 was, in Nostradamus' eyes, historically indebted to Henry II's killer, since it brought about his own succession through the infertility and early death of Henry's sons. (The crossed poles of the letter X uncrossed to signify 11 or 2 is a device often used by Nostradamus to denote royal titles.)

Henry IV was forced to fight for his kingdom before it would yield to him. It was not until 1593 that he was able to enter Paris – hence the reference to his soldier's helmet.

In line three of the verse a rare past tense occurs. This section of the prophecy has now moved past Henry's death in 1559 and concentrates on its historical consequences – the succession of Henry IV, first of the Bourbon line thirty years later.

That succession changed the future of the world, for it brought about the French Revolution and shaped much of modern politics until the East European revolutions in 1989.

The final line of the prophecy contains the most remarkable information so far.

                    v

Deux classes une puis mourir mort cruelle
  becomes

      s   s   p   u   s   u   r
Mort – seul loue a Caterina Medici, veuve, Rex 1 = 2.
"Dead, the one man hired by Catherine de Medici, widow of the King, who is the second."

We may notice the number of substitute letters in this last line – as though Nostradamus wished to securely hide this treasonable message from everyone! This is not surprising as he appears to be saying that Catherine de Medici was herself involved in the assassination of her husband Henry II.

Catherine used Montgomery as her political instrument.

Catherine had borne her husband seven children, including four sons, during the twenty-four years of her marriage. She was a short,

MARY QUEEN OF SCOTS

Nostradamus precisely predicted when the sickly Francis would die and foretold that Mary Stuart, his wife, would be childless. When the King died just before his eighteenth birthday the Spanish Ambassador wrote to Phillip II "These catastrophes have struck the court with stupor, together with the warning of Nostradamus, who it would be better to punish than to allow to sell his prophecies, which lead to vain and superstitious beliefs."

FRANCIS II

dumpy, plain woman, whereas her rival, the King's mistress, Diane de Poitiers, was a legendary beauty and wit, rumored to maintain the King's interest in her by aphrodisiacs and enchantments.

Catherine had often been slighted in this woman's presence, treated as if she were ranked behind her.

But in 1558 an event had taken place which might have set Catherine's mind working on a way to change that state of affairs. Her eldest son Francis had married the young Mary Queen of Scots.

Since Henry had fathered seven legitimate children, she had no reason to suspect that Francis would have any difficulty. Mary was a charming, healthy girl.

By 1559 the entire Court would have known of the three-year-old prediction from her Italian astrologer in 1556, confirmed by Nostradamus in the same year and communicated to Henry himself that he would face blindness and death in his forty-first year.

When the tournament came, could it have been possible that Catherine used Montgomery as her instrument of assassination? Her reputation for intrigue is the most famous in history.

She could trust in her ability to manipulate the teenagers Francis and Mary, rather than the autocratic, harsh Henry who had been in love with another woman for years.

This is the scenario which the last line of the secret prophecy appears to suggest.

When Montgomery returned to France years later to lead a Huguenot rebellion, he was captured and put to death by Catherine's troops in Paris.

By then, Catherine's third son, Henry III, was ruler. She was no longer Regent of France and the folly of a past act might have been very perilous to her then, had the truth come out.

Montgomery, the one man who knew the truth, had to be eliminated.

"Dead – the one man hired by Catherine de Medici, widow of the King."

We can now see perhaps more clearly just how much more complex and fascinating Nostradamus' prophecies are. And this is only the beginning for all we have done in this short demonstration is to decode the basic information from the naked lines of the verse. We haven't yet looked behind the lines into the deeper and almost magical material that lies there.

THE FINAL CODE

U NTIL THIS POINT IN THE BOOK, we have understood hope-
fully the method by which verses can be used to decode
the past, the present and the future – using verses that
start in our past. We have been standing on more or less firm
ground. But now we need to lose our footing altogether and in
order to do this there is a refinement to the coding system that
must be added.

In order to illustrate the refinement we will take verse III.65
once again to illustrate the last refinement of the system. The following decoded and anagrammatically melted-down prediction
concerns the future directly and Europe in the form of Rome, in
particular. Close attention is needed to understand the new refinement of the coding system.

c   p   j
Karol mourra quand l'Europe a l'est du Rhin, Russie seront devenus piles
         s   y p a i f
Age des guerres tue un fer voue. Apres an/ de sac, Rome nuee; cloches/ne
   p   i
sonnent. / Age

"*Karol will pass away when Europe to the east of the Rhine and Russia
have reversed their coin. An age of wars kills the consecrated iron man. After
a year of pillage, Rome stripped bare; the bells no longer ring. Age —* "

In this case we give the time-signal material in full –

Time-Signal

c	p	j	s		y	p	a	i	f	p	i
k	e	s	f		d	r	e	c	e	t	Age
3	15	10	18		23	15	1	1:9	6	15	1:9
	5	18	6		4	17	5	3	5	19	175
3	6	1	9	1	5	6	1	19	6	6	19
	5	9	6	9	4	8	5	3	5	19	1 7 5
	9	91		Dec				Jan	6	196	195
	5	96		94		8	5	193	May		Jan7 or Oct 7.

The meltdown reveals much. First we are told that the Pope – Karol Wojtyla – will pass away in 1995. By that year Russia and the other countries of Eastern Europe will have become market economies. Between 1991 - 1995 there will be a period of conflict involving Rome which will result in the Pope's death. "Europe to the east of the Rhine" includes much of Germany – her postwar capital has been Bonn, which lies on the River Rhine, but perhaps Nostradamus is telling us that once the east and west are merged in a unified Germany, the new capital will once again be Berlin. This would be an apt result of the greater involvement of Western

Germany with her new partner.

Rome will be overrun and looted of her religious treasures between 5th January 1993 and 8th December 1994. Christian churches will not ring their bells on the 6th May 1996. We may assume from this that Christian worship will have ceased, at least temporarily, from that point.

From the time-signal we can pin down the date of the Pope's death as being either January 7th or October 7th of 1995. 7th October is the more likely date as the number 75 appears in the final device and the Pope will reach the age of 75 on the 18th May 1995 – after January 7th.

We will see in other parts of the book that this is a serious and disruptive period for Rome, Italy and countries around the Mediterranean. Commercial shipping in this part of the world is disturbed through conflicts in the south of Europe.

When this verse was first melted down, it appeared to be concerned largely with the existing Pope but also seemed to contain some detail surrounding his life and death. However, as time passed it became clear that there was much more embedded in the verse than this. A whole panoramic vista is opened up by the verse – as though Nostradamus were using these seemingly simple lines to paint a wide picture of the whole state of Europe. Once again, the opening of the Pandora's box revealed an entire nest of goodies. When the initial decoding was done, the changes in Europe and Russia had only just started – the reunification of Germany had not even begun at that time and yet the details were there, lying beneath the surface – staring us in the face! Nostradamus was giving us what he saw as an established fact – the reunification of Germany – to indicate the prospected changes that would take place in the whole of Europe and Russia.

And here we can begin to see the final requirement for predicting the future. The secret is to "key in" certain vital words on a given subject in order to get back details of events in the future.

Using the now familiar verse – III.65 – we chose the following words as our key to the future –

Karol mourra – "Karol will die."

The device, of course, depends somewhat on the instinct of the "operator" for what is important as a feature of prediction. The Pope is clearly a major figure in today's political, social and religious events and so his death must also figure as a substantial feature of change in the future. It would seem therefore to be a vital key to changes to come. Also, the event has not yet occurred. If the prophecy, Nostradamus' original quatrain, has anything to say on the subject of the Pope's death it would have to be speaking to us of our future. The result of this was truly spectacular. The prediction called *The Sack of Rome* – a dramatic title for a dramatic result, for the keying in of this important event – the death of the Pope – opened up a panoramic vista of the way the world will look at the time of this event.

Just like unlocking a door into a fantastic world, our keying-in process takes us through the door as though we really were time travelers – the resulting picture a whole world of hitherto unknown information.

So – to summarize this last but most important feature of the prediction code – we take the key words from the melted-down prophecy – in this case *Karol mourra* – and isolate them. What remains of the four-line verse makes up the rest of the new prediction. If we were to take the words *Nations Unis* instead, we would then find a different prediction which relates to the United Nations involvement in the future. If we wanted instead to find out about George Bush, we would take the letters that make up his name and then the rest of the prophecy would give us the answers surrounding the US president.

Each verse functions as an oracle – with all the twists and turns traditionally resulting from an oracle – the answers very often not being those that we might wish to receive! Keying in the question and then abiding by the rules of the hitherto explained system will inevitably result in answers that give us accurate views of our future. One more addition to be made before we proceed to use the oracle extensively –

MODIFICATION OF THE FUTURE DATING SYSTEM

Dating from prophecies that have already occurred is obviously not difficult as we have the events to verify our instinct and the system we have adopted. Dating into an unknown future is somewhat of a different matter. The system for this, however, is only a slight adaptation of the original system.

To reach a time-signal and a precise date for the future, we must first decode the prediction using all the letters within the prophecy. When we have used up all the letters there will still remain a number of substitute letters which appear at certain points above the lines of the text. These and the letters immediately below them form the basis for our dating system. So far, this is familiar.

However, when we have extracted a prediction clearly describing our future, how can we adopt the dating system so that it will offer us dates in the future which might be seen to apply to the new prediction? Let us look back at the time-signal which we displayed at the beginning of this prediction and explanation section. It is repeated on this page with some additional features of explanation –

Time-Signal

c	p	j	s		y	p	a	i	f	p	i
k	e	s	f		d	r	e	c	e	t	Age
3	15	10	18		23	15	1	1:9	6	15	1:9
	5	18	6		4	17	5	3	5	19	175
3	6	1	9	1	5	6	1	19	6	6	19
	5	9	6	9	4	8	5	3	5	19	1 7 5
	9	91		Dec			Jan		6	196	195
	5	96		94		8	5	193	May		Jan7 or Oct 7.

The vital clue in this case is the frequent appearance of the numbers 9 and 19 in the time-signal chart. We have dropped the numbers of the letters down to a second row by adding together the two-digit numbers. For instance – 15 becomes 6, 23 becomes 5, 17 becomes 8 and so on. When 18 is added together it becomes 9 – one of the special numbers which helps us to reveal year dates. Single digit numbers remain as they are. 1:9 becomes 19 on the dropped row.

We can immediately figure out that the "year" aspects of our dating emerge from the numbers 9 and 19. We then, as the second stage, divide up the dates into sections – trying always to keep track of the sense of the text as we do so. The dates and the words work in harmony to produce greater information. There can be no separation of the two, after all, they only occur in tandem – time and space.

When calculating the year 2000 or 2001 there will be separate notes to the predictions to explain the device.

But still, the system cannot obviously be verified until events start to come true. We are therefore still at a primitive stage of decoding and will remain so until the period of monitoring begins with the publication of this book. This whole process is, by its very nature, is still experimental for everyone using or reading it. It may appear on occasion that arbitrary rules have been applied for slicing up the date cake, but we have to start somewhere for the future really is an infinite dimension. Either we slice somewhere at random or we get no slices at all!

SUPPLEMENTARY DATES.

Inevitably there are one or two restrictions to this "drop-line" system. Since all the numbers result in single digits, except 19, the months November and December (11 and 12) cannot be decoded. Nor can the dates of the month from 11 - 31. The tenth month, October, and the 10th day of the month arise from extending 1 into 10 – this is permissible under the existing code rules.

To go some way towards solving this enigma the original two rows of numbers have been reincluded at the middle of the time-signal as "Supplementary Dates". These include all the original double-date numbers. We can therefore pick out 15th May, 18th October, 23rd April and 19th March as being related to the prediction. The highest day-date number, however, can only ever be 24 as there are only this many letters in the alphabet. Thus we are still left with the day-dates between 25-31 unaccounted for. The only method we can assume for solving this problem is by accepting that on occasions where there are two numbers we simply add them together to get the appropriate dates – 23 and 4, for example, giving us the 27th of the month.

Ultimately, however, when attempting to decode Nostradamus with some perfection we are reliant on one factor – trust, until some of the events have begun to be fulfilled. The authors have tested the scheme to their own satisfaction using the methods on events in their future which have now been fulfilled. But the readers can only do this once the book has reached their hands and been given time to prove itself. Gaps will be filled and further volumes will follow as the system is authenticated.

To my mother for the early years.

ACKNOWLEDGEMENTS

The authors would like to thank everyone at Labyrinth Publishing and of course the Master Nostradamus himself with grateful respect and affection to him who is always one step ahead.

CREDITS

The Publishers would like to thank the following Photographic Agencies for their help in locating photographs: Frank Spooner, Art Directors, Gamma, Popperphoto, Environmental Library, Magnum, and Zefa.

Photographs:

24/5 G. Kearle, 36/7 Pascal Maitre, 40/1 NASA, 44/5 Lochon, 50/1 Eric Bouvet, 54/5 Patrick Piel, 57/8 *Sunday Times*, 60/1 James Nactwey, 65 Iverson (Time), 66 David Rubinger (Time), 68/9 Baitel, 70/1 Patrick Baz, 83 Kerman, 88/9 Don James, 90/1 Bartholomew, 98/9 E. Sander, 106/7 Vlastinir Shone, 109 Evening Standard, 110/11 Syndication International, 112 C. Vioujard, 112/13 Mark Deville, 115/16 Walker, 116 Peter Magubane, 117 Bernet, 118/19 Barry King, 120/21 Rick Diamond, 136/37 Chuck O'Rear, 137 Maggie Steber, 138/39 Sarjkano, 142/43 Ansin, 147 Oldfield, 154/55 Alex Olaa, 156/57 Eliot Elisofon, 158/9 Eric Bouvet, 160/1 Marc Riboud, 165 Arkek Katie, 164 A. De Wildenburg, 167 Oswald Iten, 168 M. Manson, 170/71 Syndication International, 172 Julian Parker, 173 V. Miles.

SHOES

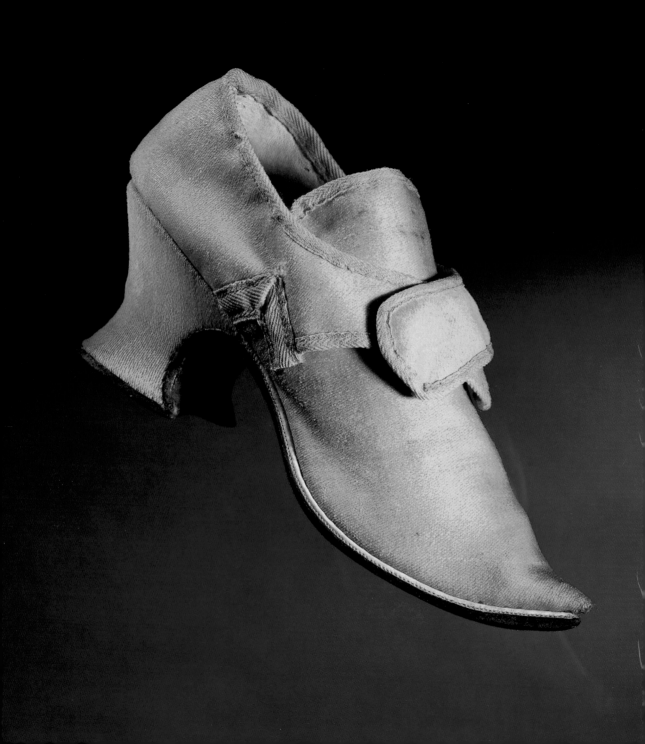

SHOES

LUCY PRATT & LINDA WOOLLEY

LEARNING
RESOURCES
CENTRE

HAVERING
COLLEGE

V&A Publishing

First published by V&A Publications, 1999

Paperback edition published 2008

V&A Publishing
Victoria and Albert Museum
South Kensington
London SW7 2RL

Distributed in North America by Harry N. Abrams,
Inc., New York

Library of Congress Control Number 2007935517

ISBN 9781851775378

10 9   8   7   6   5   4   3
2012 2011 2010 2009

A catalogue record for this book is available from
the British Library.

Designed by Broadbase
New V&A photography by Sara Hodges,
V&A Photographic Studio

Printed in China by Imago Publishing Limited

Front cover illustration:
Photograph by Anthony
Denney, evening pumps by
Rayne, 1950.
Anthony Denney/Vogue © The Condé
Nast Publications Ltd

Back cover illustration:
'Pirelli', printed leather shoe
by Manolo Blahnik. English,
1985. T.487–1985

Spine illustration: Lilley and
Skinner shoe catalogue
(detail). Late 1920s.
AAD5/5 1977

Frontispiece: Woman's shoe;
British (possibly Norwich),
1720s–30s. The latchets
were originally fastened over
the instep with a buckle. The
upper is covered in glazed
worsted and a similar, but
unglazed, material has been
used for the heel.
Circ.511–1928

V&A Publishing
Victoria and Albert Museum
South Kensington
London SW7 2RL
www.vam.ac.uk

Contents

Acknowledgements

We would like to thank the following colleagues at the V&A for their help during the writing of this book: Linda Parry, Clare Browne, Paul Harrison, Amy de la Haye, Ngozi Ikoku, Valerie Mendes, Susan North, Debbie Sinfield, Jennifer Wearden and Helen Wilkinson of the Textiles and Dress Department; Avril Hart, Consultant for the British Galleries Project; Anthony North of the Metalwork Department; Shaun Cole, Charlotte Cotton and Susan Bright of the Prints, Drawings and Paintings Department; Lynda Hillyer, Marion Kite and Audrey Hill of the Textiles Conservation Department; and Clive Errington-Watson of Information Systems Services. The excellent photographs were taken by Sara Hodges, and we are also grateful to Ken Jackson, chief photographer of the V&A Photographic Studio.

We would like to thank the team at V&A Publications: Mary Butler, Miranda Harrison, Clare Davis, Geoff Barlow and Valerie Chandler. We are indebted to Kelvin Ithell of the British Library and Maria Flemington at Ham House. We would also particularly like to acknowledge the support of the following: Jim Roberts, Pamela Pratt, Richard Cross, Robert Chorley, Gus and Daisy.

Finally, we are very grateful to all the designers, donors and other individuals who have made this publication possible.

Opposite: Man's platform shoe, patchwork of snakeskin; British, 1972. By Terry de Havilland.
T.78A–1983

Introduction

I have spread my dreams under your feet;
Tread softly because you tread on my dreams.
(Excerpt from W.B. Yeats, *He Wishes for the Cloths of Heaven,* 1899)

Shoes are one of the most evocative areas of dress. Often beautiful and sculptural objects, they can be powerful indicators of the social and economic status of the wearer. The more elaborate and decorative, the less likely they are to be functional or easy to wear, and these very qualities have often resulted in their survival. Shoes have also been kept for aesthetic or sentimental reasons, and a number have survived by being buried, hidden or simply as an accident of fate.

Focusing on the V&A's outstanding shoe collection, this book explores the development of fashionable footwear from the Middle Ages to the present day. Women's shoes are better represented than men's because these have tended to survive in greater numbers. Some examples are included because of their extraordinary design or links with a particular moment in history, while others show how technical developments have altered methods of construction, resulting in new shapes and styles.

Whether fashionable or functional, the shoe has excited as much comment in the past as it does today. The toes of medieval poulaines grew so long and pointed that laws were passed to limit their size, while women who staggered on chopines – the Renaissance equivalent of the platform sole – were compared to Venetian prostitutes. The beauty of the foot has also been admired. Richly embroidered mules of the seventeenth century and delicate Georgian shoes sought to enhance an elegant ankle or complement the clothes with which they were worn. In the early Victorian era, shoes became so restricting that writers complained of how women were prevailed upon to 'pinch' their feet into tiny satin slippers. Less extreme and more comfortable designs have also made an impact. A simpler style of shoe was adopted during the French Revolution in keeping with the ideals of equality,

and by the end of the nineteenth century the growing popularity of
sports encouraged a more practical approach to footwear.

The twentieth century witnessed the rise of the designer shoemaker. During the 1920s and 1930s names like Salvatore Ferragamo,
André Perugia and Roger Vivier focused the eyes of fashion on jewel-
encrusted heels, chunky wedge soles, surrealistic shapes and
startlingly sleek silhouettes. The designer shoemaker continues to
make an impact. Exploring elements from the past, combining
traditional craftsmanship with technological advances and uniting
function with art, contemporary designers have created innovative
styles which continue to inspire and often surprise. In this book,
creations by Vivienne Westwood, Jimmy Choo, Patrick Cox, Christian
Louboutin, Armando Pollini, Oliver Sweeney and Manolo Blahnik
suggest that shoes of the 1990s will shape the future of footwear
design into the millennium and beyond.

Chapter One

Medieval Gothic and the English Renaissance

Sum men sayd that they wolde wear long pykys [pikes] whether Pope wylle or nylle, for they sayde the Pope's curse wolde not kylle a flye.
(Anonymous writer, continuation of William Gregory's *Chronicle of London*, 1468)

Shoe Fashions in the Middle Ages

Fashions in shoes for the wealthy seem to have changed in the Middle Ages as quickly as they do now, according to material excavated by the Museum of London covering the period of about 1150 to 1450. This is one indicator of the immense importance of textiles and dress in a period when there were few luxury goods available; status and class could be demonstrated by colourful and stylish clothes as well as furnishings and hangings.

Textiles and dress, particularly at the luxury end of the market, were very expensive and the outlay for them constituted a far greater part of a wealthy person's income than it would today. It has been suggested that the large market in the re-making and repair of old shoes may have been one of the main sources of cheap shoes for the poor, almost all of whom seem to have worn footwear of some kind. Shoes are among the articles of dress frequently cited as bequests to the church, as donations to monasteries for example.

Medieval shoes, like all early clothing and accessories, survive only in small numbers and often in very poor and fragmentary condition. Only the sturdiest of footwear remains from this period – except in an ecclesiastical context – leaving us with little evidence of the range of materials available, which originally included leather, cloth and silk. The majority of excavated shoes are made of leather which, given certain conditions, lasts better than most textiles. Although such shoes may retain their original shape they are generally dark and dirty, revealing little of the nuances of colour and the stylishness which may have characterised them when they were made.

Stylistic changes, some made possible by technical advances in shoe-making, can be defined by such features as the height of the quarters, the manner of fastening, the shape of the toe and, more rarely, the addition of some form of decoration. Sometimes hose were fitted with a leather sole, obviating the need for a separate shoe, and this presumably acounts for the many contemporary illustrations in which people appear to be unshod.

Throughout the period shoes were flat, but toe shapes varied from rounded to very pointed. Ankle boots sometimes predominated, while at other times shoes were favoured; style seems to have varied regionally as well. Buskins, a form of long boot, were worn for riding. Long boots were also fashionable footwear in the second half of the fifteenth century. Fastenings included lacing, buckles and latchets. One major change in construction, which made shoes slightly more comfortable, occurred in the late twelfth or early thirteenth century, when the shaped or 'waisted' sole was introduced. The shaping of shoes to fit the left and right foot, from as early as the twelfth century, and the use of good quality, supple leather also contributed to making footwear fit the contours of the foot more closely. In the late fourteenth century, openwork decoration or engraved patterns were introduced.

Fig. 1 below Facsimile from a 15th–century manuscript, showing a court scene with a man wearing fashionable poulaines. Source unknown.

E.1278–1888

The Cordwainers

The guild of shoemakers was one of the earliest in England, issuing its first ordinance in 1272. It was called the Guild of Cordwainers, a name taken from a corruption of Cordoba, the town in Spain from which the best leather, *Cordovan,* came. The Guild was originally established in London's Cordwainer Street. In the Middle Ages cordwainers disputed with cobblers about the latter's use of pieces of new leather in the re-making of shoes. New leather was thought by the cordwainers to be for their use only, and for making new shoes.

The Poulaine or Pike

By the last quarter of the fourteenth century, shoes with pointed toes predominated, reaching their extreme in the much commented-on and derided 'poulaine' or 'pike' (fig. 1 and plate 2). This long, pointed medieval shoe is also known as the 'cracow' after the important cultural centre of Krakow in Poland, to which its origin is sometimes attributed. The poulaine was worn by priests as well as laymen and in *Piers Plowman* (*c*.1377), William Langland describes 'vain priests in the company of the Anti-Christ' as wearing 'pyked shoes'. Shoes with the longest points were cut low on the instep and fastened with buckles or latchets. The toe length could be of in excess of 4 inches (10cms), and was normally stuffed with moss or hair which had the twofold effect of keeping the toe straight and of raising the end off the ground, making it marginally easier for the wearer to walk.

Plate 2 above Men's poulaines. Top (a): Part of a leather poulaine; English, 1370–1400 or 1450–1500. The back part is missing and the method of fastening difficult to determine, so a precise dating is impossible. T.111–1918
Bottom (b): Copy of a 15th-century poulaine; Spanish, 19th century? Considered to be genuine at the time of acquisition, this shoe is now thought to be a very good fake. It was reputedly found in the rafters of a house in Toledo. T.391–1913

There is a charming but probably apocryphal notion that there were pikes or poulaines which were tied right up to the knee (or even the waist) with laces or chains. One of the two written sources cited as evidence for this, the late fourteenth-century *Eulogium Historiarium*, seems to have been misread and regrettably no shoes of this type survive to prove this form of fastening existed, although they are sometimes shown in manuscripts.

The poulaine was popular from about the 1370s to 1400. The fashion was revived in the mid-fifteenth century and became subject to a sumptuary law passed in 1463 in the reign of Edward IV, which stated 'that no knight under the state of a Lord, Esquire, Gentleman nor other person should use nor wear in any Shoe or Boots having pikes passing the length of Two Inches...'. As with all extremes of fashion, the very long poulaine was not standard footwear but worn by a fashion-conscious minority. Styles for women were basically similar to those of men, but without the extremes. Wearing very long pointed shoes as well as walking in long skirts must have largely precluded the wearing of poulaines by women.

The adoption of sumptuous clothes and ostentatiously fashionable shoes reflected the growing wealth of the middle classes. For example, poulaines dating from the fourteenth century have been found in France, which like England was becoming increasingly prosperous at that time. In Amsterdam, however, no poulaines have been found dating from earlier than the late fifteenth century, which coincides with the date of the city's prosperity.

The fashion for shoes with pointed toes, in keeping with the spiky, vertical lines characteristic of fashionable dress in the late Gothic period, had died out completely by 1500.

Pattens

Pattens – wooden-soled overshoes to protect the feet in mud and snow – were in use in the fourteenth century but were apparently restricted to the wealthy. By the early fifteenth century the introduction of a new, cheaper form of patten, which had a composite leather sole and may have been worn without a shoe, made them more widely accessible.

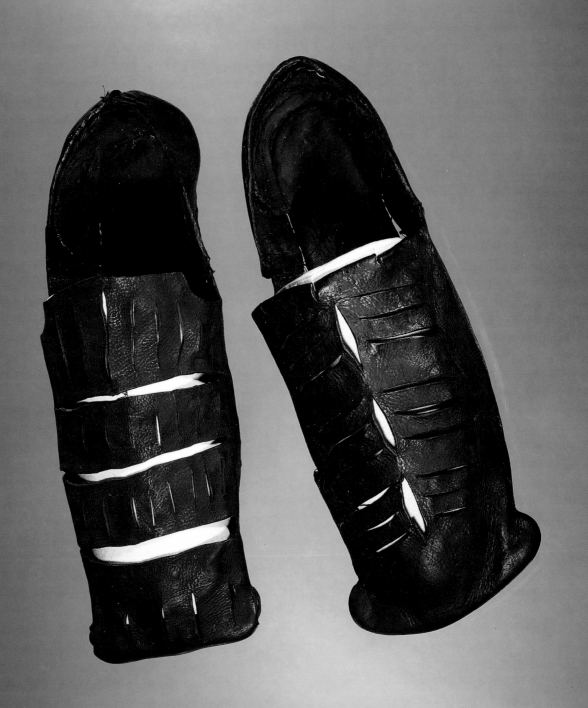

The Renaissance

The spirit of the Renaissance changed political, social and intellectual attitudes, with a different distribution of wealth following the rise of a rich and powerful bourgeoisie who competed with courtly circles in the world of fashion. The emphasis in fashion for men changed from the vertical line of the Gothic period to the horizontal, and this is very noticeable in the case of the shoe.

Many of the aristocrats at the court of Henry VIII (reigned 1509–1547) had acquired wealth through the confiscation of church property during the Reformation, and wanted their dress to project a powerful image. Wealth and physical strength were demonstrated in clothes made of sumptuous imported materials, with wide shoulders and massive padding across the chest. Initially, in the early sixteenth century, the toe changed from pointed to a sensible, broader shape which was fashionable with the wealthy merchant classes. The style became much more exaggerated during the reign of Henry VIII with some soles being more than $6^{1}/_{2}$ inches (17cms) wide. These extremely wide shoes, like the extremely pointed shoes of the previous century, fell under the stricture of sumptuary legislation.

A distinctive style popular in the 1530s and worn by Henry VIII was the lower cut shoe with a strap across the ankle, usually with a buckle, and a square or 'horned' toe (plate 3).

The famous portrait of Henry VIII (1539, school of Holbein), in Chatsworth House, Derbyshire, shows the king in typical aggressive and self-confident pose, feet planted apart (fig. 2). The slashing of his silver brocaded doublet is echoed by the slashed white or cream silk of his square-cut shoes. Silk or velvet shoes were fashionable formal wear, reflecting the popularity of these materials, which were principally imported from Italy. Due to their fragile nature examples have not survived, but the style seen in the portrait survives in the leather shoes shown in plate 3.

Another style of broad-fronted shoe known as the 'high shoe' was so formless that there was no point in having a distinction between the right and left foot. Such shoes were known as 'straights'.

According to French tradition, Charles VIII of France (reigned 1493–98) had six toes on each foot and special shoes were made for

Plate 3 Slashed leather men's shoes (not a pair); English, *c.*1510–30s. Found in a Plague Pit in London. T.412–1913; T.413–1913

him with wide ends. It is possible, therefore that a congenital royal deformity started the new fashion.

Shoe Decoration

The vogue for puffs, panes and slashes characterised the dress of Henry VIII and his court, which vied for supremacy in fashion with the court of the French king, Francis I (reigned 1515–47). Slashed patterns in shoe uppers, with vertical, horizontal and diagonal cuts through which the brightly coloured lining could be glimpsed, reflected this fashion. The slashing also softened the solid appearance of leather, while making the shoes more supple. It may have derived from Swiss mercenaries, who incorporated the slashing as a form of decoration in imitation of the sword slashes their clothes received in battle. In France, slashing on shoes was attributed to the need to accommodate the bandaged, wounded feet of Francis I's soldiers, who fought in the Italian wars. The Germans took up this look with particular fervour, and other nations, including England, copied it in a less extravagent way.

During the 1540s there was a return to a more natural, rounded or almond-shaped shoe, which continued beyond the end of the century. Slashed decoration also remained popular. In a famous portrait in Hampton Court Palace by an unknown artist (c.1540–48), a young man dressed all in red, except for a shirt with blackwork embroidery, wears red silk or velvet shoes with rounded toes, cut high at the ankle, slashed diagonally, and studded with jewels.

Women's shoes

Women's dress was less flamboyant during this period, although embroidery and slashed decoration were favoured. Women wore similar shoe styles to men, presumably following male fashions. A charming portrait by Holbein (c.1540), in the Ashmolean Museum, Oxford, shows a woman wearing square-toed shoes cut low at the front and sides, with a strap fastening across the instep.

The 1554 inventory of Queen Mary Tudor (reigned 1553–58) included payments for the making of 38 pairs of velvet shoes lined with satin and with scarlet soles, two pairs of buskins and three pairs

Fig. 2 above Portrait of Henry VIII. School of Holbein, *c.1539*. Several portraits show the king in this characteristic stance. Said to have been copied from a fresco formerly in the Palace of Whitehall. The Devonshire Collection, Chatsworth. Reproduced by permission of the Chatsworth Settlement Trustees: photograph Courtauld Institute of Art

of velvet slippers lined with scarlet. Boots were not fashionable wear for men or women at this period and the buskins listed here were presumably used for riding. It is evident from these entries that huge quantities of shoes were made for the rich and powerful at this time. These were mostly in luxury materials which were not durable, and this is even more vividly demonstrated in the case of Queen Elizabeth I's wardrobe.

The Reign of Queen Elizabeth I (1558–1603)

'When your Posterity shall see our picture they shall think we were foolishly proud of apparell', wrote R. Verstegen in *Antiquities Concerning the English Nation* (1605). Queen Elizabeth, like her father before her, indulged in what in modern terms would be called power dressing. Her portraits bear witness to the sumptuous array of clothes and jewels she owned. For the first twenty-two years of Elizabeth's reign, Spanish fashion, which had prevailed since the marriage of Mary Tudor to Philip II of Spain in 1554, continued to influence the shape of English dress. However, the decoration and exaggeration of certain features were uniquely English.

Men's dress lost the assertive shape which it had acquired during Henry VIII's reign. Shoes retained the more natural, rounded or oval-shaped toe which fitted in well with the romantic, almost feminine look of clothes, such as pointed doublets and padded trunk hose which emphasised the hips.

In *Queen Elizabeth's Wardrobe Unlock'd* (1988), Janet Arnold details both the materials available and the changing styles for the wealthy which were favoured during Elizabeth's long reign. Until 1564 all Elizabeth's shoes, like those cited in Mary Tudor's inventory, were made of velvet. By contrast, one of her servants, Ippolyta Tartarian, had only leather shoes. In 1562 she was given twelve pairs of leather shoes, two pairs of Spanish leather shoes, and one pair of leather pantobles.

Elizabeth had her first pair of leather shoes made in 1564 and in 1565 another three pairs. By 1575 more leather than velvet shoes were made for the queen: 'for xxiiij paire of velvett Shoos Slippers and Pantobles stitched wtih silke Lined with satten and in the Soles with skarlett two paire of Slippers of Tufte Taffata lyned with velvet, xxxiij paire of Spanish lether shoes and pantobles of sondrie colours and fashions'. This seems to have been an early example of fashions filtering up through the classes rather than down.

Although the queen's favourite colours were black and white, her leather shoes were made in a wide range of colours, including tawney orange, green, white and 'ashe', and her velvet and satin shoes included colours such as black, crimson and 'murrey'. As well as making new shoes, the queen's shoemakers 'translated' or re-made old shoes. There are also references to pinking, embroidery and the 'perfuyming' of her shoes by a man called John Wynneyard in 1572.

Terminology

Shoe terminology is often confusing, especially when the words describing a single style have varied linguistic origins. Additional complications occur at a time when terminology in documents was inconsistently spelt and clerks no doubt had their own idiosyncracies in recording items. The terms mule, pantoble (variously spelt) and chopine (also variously spelt) all describe forms of backless shoes or slippers. Writing in 1589 in the *Art of Poesie*, George Puttenham referred to: 'these high corked shoes or pantoffles [pantobles] which now they call in Spain and Italy shoppini [chopines]'.

It was never noted that Elizabeth I had mules in her wardrobe, although her servant did have mules made, and Janet Arnold has suggested that the terms mule and pantoble were probably interchangeable.

In 1591, Peter Johnson made the queen three pairs of pantobles 'of the new fashion layed on with silver lace'. The new fashion perhaps refers to arched heels or to open toes, as he also made 'two paire of Spanyshe lether pantobles open at the Toes, laid on with silver lace'. It is possible, therefore, that the chopines seen in plate 5, which have trimmings of

Plate 4 below Kid leather chopine; Italian (Venetian), *c.*1600. Mounted on wood with decoupé decoration and figured silk underlay.
T.48A–1914

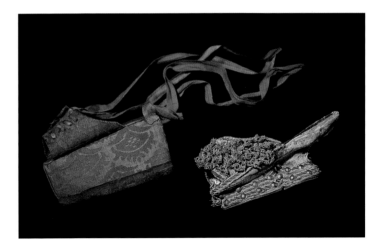

gold lace, may be similar to the queen's pantobles. The origin of an embroidered chopine or pantoble of about 1600, now in the Ashmolean Museum, Oxford, is thought to be Italy or England.

The Chopine

Like the poulaine, chopines were the subject of satire and of moral censure by the church. They are condemned as early as 1438 by a priest in Spain, mentioned in the second act of Hamlet and, as late as 1653, derided by Dr John Bulwer in *Artificial Changeling:* 'What a prodigious affectation is that of chopines where our ladies imitated the Venetian and Persian ladies'.

The chopine was one of the most extreme and artificial styles of footwear ever created. A fairly modest example is shown in plate 4. It could reach a height of over 18 inches (50cms), but this extreme seems to have been confined to Italy and possibly Spain. It probably originated in Venice and was first worn by prostitutes, but was then adopted by fashionable Venetian aristocrats. The style derived from the Turkish bath shoe which kept the feet of the wearer out of the water. In a painting by Vittore Carpaccio (c.1495–1500) in the Correr Museum, Venice, two seated courtesans wear chopines – concealed by their dresses but clearly visible in outline – which look as big as dinner plates. The chopine was originally a form of overshoe, but the modified later versions could be worn as either over-shoes or on their own. Sometimes Elizabeth I had pantobles (chopines) made to match her shoes, but they are also listed separately which suggests that she may have worn them without a shoe inside. This illustrates the development of an originally utilitarian item of dress to one purely of fashion.

Although a small number of chopines survive from the late sixteenth to the early seventeenth century, very few other types of fashionable shoe survive from this period, particularly in England. However, the Ashmolean Museum in Oxford has an example of a pinked white leather shoe with a heel and latchet fastening of about 1600 (fig. 3), and Queen Elizabeth I can be seen wearing a pinked shoe in portraits of the 1590s.

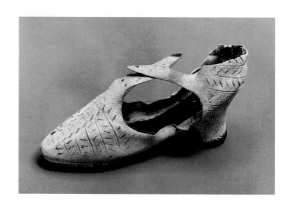

The Development of the Heel

The general trend in Elizabeth's reign for both men's and women's shoes was towards a narrow bluntly pointed toe and a gradual increase in the thickness of the sole. During the last quarter of the century the latchet fastening began to replace the slip-on type of shoe.

The development of the shoe with heel and arched sole, which was to be a central feature of seventeenth-century fashionable footwear, began in the sixteenth century. It developed from the wedged shoe and the chopine. Examples with arched wedges, which date from 1545, were found on the wreck of the Mary Rose ship. High heels and arches are not mentioned in Queen Elizabeth's warrants until 1595. In *Queen Elizabeth's Wardrobe Unlock'd,* however, Janet Arnold cites a reference by June Swann to a monument to Mary Carewe in Hascombe Church in Devon, dating from 1589, which features a shoe with a curve up under the arch.

Queen Elizabeth I is shown in an engraving of c.1593–95 wearing wedge-heeled shoes. In 1595, Peter Johnson made the first pair of shoes for her described as having high heels and arches. These probably had heels made of wood like those requested by Dame Margery in *The Shoemaker's Holiday* by Thomas Dekker, 1599: 'Prithee, let me have a pair of shoes made; cork, good Roger; wooden heel too'.

Fig. 3 above White suede girl's shoe; English, *c.*1600. Large open sides and latchet fastening for ribbons; pinked and slashed decoration. The lower pair of lace holes on the tongue were for a decorative rose. Ashmolean Museum, Oxford

Chapter Two

Heels, Buckles and Bows: The Seventeenth Century

> All repute
>
> For his devices in hansoming a sute,
>
> To judge of lace, pinke, panes, print, cut and plight,
>
> Of all the Court, to have the best conceit.
>
> (John Donne, *Satyres, Epigrams and Verse Letters,* ed. W. Milgate 1967)

James I (reigned 1603–25)

The early years of the seventeenth century saw considerable growth in trade, including that in luxury goods such as silks and lace, and a relative economic stability in spite of growing political and religious division. However, James I's court, unlike that of Elizabeth I who had kept a tight reign on her courtiers, was riddled with scandal and disorder and dominated by James' posturing favourites.

The Jacobean fop was narcissistic and spent vast sums on his wardrobe. With a more pronounced emphasis on the leg, both stockings and shoes became elaborate and colourful and played a far greater role in fashion than previously. Decoration by slashing along the uppers to show the stocking or coloured shoe lining continued until about 1615.

The Heel

The development of a proper heel with an arched sole was the dominant feature of shoes in the seventeenth century. It completely altered the posture of the wearer, encouraging both men and women to carry themselves in a way which set off the flowing lines and affected manner of the Baroque period. The raised heel was at first low and rounded but was to grow to a height of two to three inches, with a square base made of leather or wood.

Plate 6 left Miniature of
Richard Sackville, 3rd Earl of
Dorset. Isaac Oliver, 1616.
Sackville was described
as a 'licentious spendthrift'
and had a vast wardrobe.
His shoes have the
contemporary fashionable
heel, large side openings
and large exotic gold rose.
721–1899

All shoes were now made as 'straights', which June Swann has suggested was due to the technical complications of making mirror-image lasts which would differentiate right from left for shoes with heels.

The Toe

The rounded toe continued to be fashionable for the first decade or so of the century, but between 1610 and 1620 the square toe began to dominate and remained fashionable to the end of the Cromwellian period, that is, until about 1660. Portraiture was popular in the seventeenth century and, together with engravings, literary references and other documentation, provides a great deal of information about fashion, including footwear, which is particularly invaluable where no examples survive. William Larkin's portrait of Lady Dorothy Carey (c.1614), in Rangers House, London, depicts her wearing white shoes with blunt toe, medium high heel, large open sides and latchet fastening obscured by a large gold rose. Such shoes were worn by both men and women, and in 1618 the Chaplain to the Venetian Ambassador in London commented that ladies attending the masques 'all wear men's shoes (or at least very low slippers)'.

Latchet Fastenings, Ribbon Ties and Roses

Shoes with latchet fastenings had begun to replace the slip-on shoe in the last quarter of the sixteenth century and continued into the seventeenth century. The ribbon ties fastening the latchets over the tongue grew large enough to become decorative features in themselves, and large bows or rosettes began to adorn the front of the shoe.

From about 1610 magnificent court roses, such as those seen on Lady Dorothy Carey's shoes in the portrait mentioned above, were very fashionable. In *The Devil's Lawcase* of 1618, John Webster refers to 'overblown roses to hide your gouty ankles'. A wonderful portrait of Richard Sackville dated 1613 and, like the Carey portrait, now in Rangers House, London, is attributed to William Larkin and shows Sackville wearing shoes with a huge rose and embroidery matching that of his doublet. The shoes are very similar in style to those worn by Lady Carey in Larkin's portrait of the same period.

A miniature of Sackville (plate 6), dated 1616, shows him wearing a less elaborate, but still very fashionable outfit. The blunt, almost square-toed shoes have wide side openings, which were a notable fashion feature at this time for both men and women. The large gold roses adorning the shoes are typical of the period and could be very expensive. They are listed as separate items in Richard Sackville's inventory, which included '59 item one paire of Roses edged with gold and silver lace' and '110 item one paire of greene Roses edged with gold lace'.

Charles I (reigned 1625–49)

Dress became more refined during the reign of Charles I. Braid and lace replaced the cruder decorations of slashing and paning, and the display of jewellery was less ornate. At the same time, France became the fashion leader in Europe and superceded Spanish influence, although England modified French style to suit its own national taste.

Men's footwear, not surprisingly, was considerably influenced by military dress, since this was a period of unrest and warfare through-out Europe, including the Civil War in England (1642–49).

The knee-high boot dominated footwear in the reign of Charles I, and from about the 1620s to the 1690s it was fashionable for both indoor and outdoor wear. A portrait of about 1618 (School of van Somer), housed in the Tower of London, shows Charles, then Prince of Wales, wearing white knee boots with turn-down top, a blunt-pointed toe and low heel, in soft, slightly wrinkled-looking leather, with spur and spur leather. This wrinkled look was already much admired, as confirmed by the *Return from Parnassus* of 1606: 'One that more admires the good wrinkle of a boot, and the curious crin-cling of a silke stocking'. Fashionable boots could be made to look extremely decorative and elegant, and were very costly.

Charles I had twenty pairs of riding boots made in 1634–35, which cost the large sum of £24. The wide range of items listed in Philip Massinger's play of 1632, *The City Madam,* illustrates the comparative costs of such boots with the shoes for a poor man: 'a pair of shoes for the swineherd...cost 16 pence'.

Unless strictly for practical use, fashionable boots were made of fine supple leather to give an easy fit around the leg. They were made very

Fig. 4 above Portrait of Henry Rich, 1st Earl of Holland. Studio of Daniel Mytens, *c.*1632–3. The soft wrinkled leg boot was fashionable aristocratic wear in the reign of Charles I. The boot has a decorative butterfly spur leather and a lace trim at the knee. Flat goloshes were worn over the boots to add protection. National Portrait Gallery, London

long but were turned over below the knee, either in a double fold or in a cup or bucket shape. In the 1640s bucket tops became very wide, and when turned down fell almost to the ankle. Heel spurs were attached to the foot by large, butterfly-shaped spur leathers which covered the instep. Boots were also lined with inner boothose to protect the stockings from the rough or greasy surface of the leather. The tops of the boothose appeared above the boots and were usually trimmed with a border of lace or embroidery (fig. 4), focusing attention on the knee as roses (worn at the knee as well as on the shoe) had done earlier in the century.

More functional and heavy jackboots, made of hard black leather, were worn for fighting. A few examples of such boots survive, including an example in the Northampton Museum with blocked toe and turned-over top.

There is, however, little evidence that this fashion for boots so widely embraced by men affected women's footwear and, as previously, women wore boots only for riding.

Chimney Shoes

Shoes are often associated with good luck, and although it is still not entirely clear why, they are often found concealed in buildings – a practice which has continued for centuries. They were thought to ward off evil spirits, or at least in some way to keep the building and its occupants safe and lucky. Usually concealed in the chimney but sometimes in the rafters or under the floorboards, this hidden footwear has been a particularly fascinating source of information. The shoe seen in fig. 5 is likely to have been found in a chimney, judging by its blackened appearance. Its blunt toe, small side opening and latchet fastening for ribbon ties suggest a date of the 1640s to 1650s. Probably not an example of high fashion wear, although it has fashionable features, it is a sturdy shoe for outdoor wear. Its well-worn state could indicate that it was working-class country wear. It relates closely to a 'chimney shoe' of about the same date in the Northampton Museum, which came from a house in Stowmarket, Suffolk. The poulaine shown in plate 2b is reputed to have been found in rafters in a house in Toledo in Spain, and thus may be another example of the phenomenon of footwear concealed to protect a property and its occupants.

Mules and Slippers

Mules (later in the century referred to more often as 'slippers') continued to be fashionable for both men and women throughout the seventeeth century. Surprising numbers survive, principally from the second half of the century, perhaps because they were not subject to the hard wear of other shoes.

A man's mule (plate 7), now sadly faded from its original salmon pink – a particularly fashionable colour in the seventeenth century for both men's and women's dress – is the earliest seventeenth-century example in the V&A's collection. The pronounced square toe and heel shape suggest a date of the 1650s. Silk and velvet mules and shoes were very fashionable. They were often embroidered, reflecting the vogue for domestic embroidery which burgeoned in the second half of the sixteenth century and throughout the seventeenth century. After the Reformation, when ecclesiastical embroidery had ceased to be required for the church, embroidery came into its own in dress and furnishings, as the middle classes spent money on both building and furnishing their houses and on lavishly embroidered clothes. Interestingly, surviving mules from the seventeenth century do not reflect the great interest in naturalism in England, being generally embroidered with stylised patterns in metal thread. It may be due to the slightly more durable quality of metal thread that these have survived rather than lighter weight mules of silk with silk embroidery, although it is possible that the latter was considered too flimsy to be used even for shoes for indoor wear.

Both women's and men's shoes had moderate or high heels, and a velvet mule (plate 8) with medium heel and square, slightly over-hanging toe is a typical example of luxury indoor wear for women of about the 1650s to 1660s. A similar mule of embroidered velvet, which was worn by Queen Henrietta Maria, in the collection of Northampton Museum, is dated to between 1660 and 1665. It has a slightly higher and narrower heel and the addition of a woven strip round the top.

Fig. 5 above 'Chimney' shoe of darkened brown leather; English, 1640s–50s. Very worn, perhaps belonging to a working-class woman. Has fashionable features of side opening, blunt toe and latchet fastening for ribbons. 692–1897

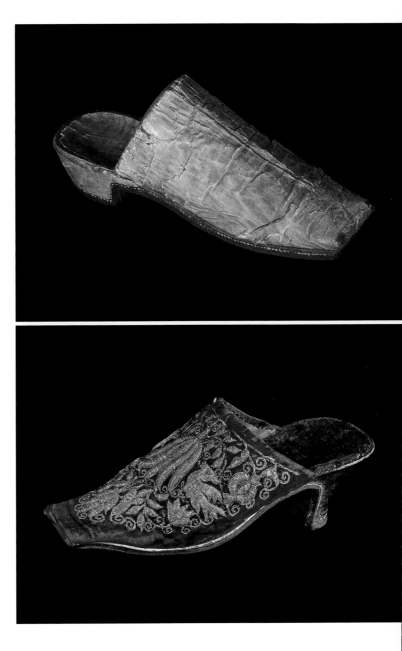

Plate 7 above right Watered
silk man's mule, originally
pink; English, 1650s–60s.
193–1900

Plate 8 right Velvet mule
for a woman; English,
c.1650s–60s. Embroidered
in couched and raised gold
thread. T.631–1972

Both mules have white kid rands (narrow strips of leather) which became a distinctive fashion feature of women's shoes from this time until about the 1760s. Prior to this date darker, inconspicuous rands had been used.

The forked toe, fashionable from the 1660s to 1680s, may be seen as a more elegant, modified version of the sixteenth century 'horned' toe. A small number of examples survive, including the woman's mule in plate 9. Randle Holme's *Academy III* of 1688 records that 'Shoes according to the fashion of the Toes or Noses are sometimes round, others square, then forked, and others turned up like a hook'.

The Restoration and the Influence of French Fashion

The introduction of French fashions for men coincided with the return of Charles II to England in 1660, and the subsequent restoration of the monarchy. Louis XIV (1643–1715) had made Paris the capital of the civilised world and, given Charles II's French background, it was inevitable that French fashions should come to dominate in England. Boots, with their Civil War associations, disappeared as fashion wear but were retained for riding. For English men, black and brown were the most common colours for footwear, but white was used for ceremonial and court wear.

The long square toe seems to have become particularly fashionable on Charles II's return from exile, although examples had appeared in the 1650s. The red sole and heel, a fashion of the French court, also became more common in England from this period.

Buckles and Bows

A portrait of Charles II by J.M. Wright (1661), in H.M. the Queen's Collection, shows him enthroned in his coronation robes. He wears white leather shoes with shallow square toe, high red heels and red sole, but notably a buckle fastening over a high tongue. This innovation had been noted a year earlier by Samuel Pepys in his *Diary* on 22 January 1660, in the much-quoted remark: 'This day I began to put on buckles to my shoes'. Although not widely adopted as a fashion immediately, buckles were to become a prominent feature of men's and women's shoes until the French Revolution (fig. 6b).

Plate 9 opposite Woman's silk mule with forked toe; English, 1660s–70s. Embroidered with raised work in silk and silver thread. T.860A-1974

The buckle was an adaptation of the latchet tie. Although essentially a method of fastening, buckles were always treated as separate items from the shoe itself, and as jewellery to be preserved and transferred from one pair of shoes to another. This has resulted in the survival of pairs of shoes without their buckles. The latter have generally also been preserved separately, and cannot usually be matched up with any particular pair of shoes.

The fashion for buckles seems to have come in at about the same time as the mode for absurdly wide ribbon bows, which Louis XIV's court favoured. In 1660, Louis XIV was presented with a pair of shoes with high red heels and bows 16 inches (40cms) in width, and several portraits of Louis' court in the 1660s show the court wearing shoes with huge bows. Sometimes both buckles and ribbons were worn on the same pair of shoes, thereby maximising their fashionable appeal. Multiple ribbons and ribbon ties were worn alongside buckles throughout Charles II's reign, but subsequently buckles predominated until the French Revolution. In the seventeenth century, buckles remained small and set off the decorative tops of high-tongued shoes, such as seen in fig. 6b.

Fig. 6a far left Engraving of French female négligé costume. After J.D. de St Jean, 1693. Depicts high heeled mules. 26363–10

Fig. 6b left Engraving of French male costume. After J.D. de St Jean, 1695. Depicts square-toed, high-heeled shoes with high tongue and small buckle. 26363–17

Femme de qualité en deshabillé negligé

Homme de qualité en habit de Teckeli

Women's Shoes: the Long Square Toe

The long squared-off toe was popular for women from the 1660s to the 1680s. A pair of women's shoes of this style in the V&A retains the latchet and ribbon tie fastening (plate 10). Buckles were in vogue for women as well as men but adopted less assiduously, probably because they rubbed against the hems of their dresses. The shoe shown here has a small side opening. Openings were diminishing in size by this time and are no longer the conspicuous fashion feature that they had been earlier in the century. In the eighteenth century they disappeared altogether.

For men's shoes, the side opening seems to have disappeared earlier, particularly for sturdy outdoor wear, as noted by Randle Holme (1688): 'Close shoes as such as have no open in the sides of the latchets, but are made close up like an Irish brogue. They are to travel with in foul and snowy weather'.

Overshoes: the Slapsole

Overshoes of various forms were in use in the seventeenth century, worn to protect flimsy shoes and boots. Clogs and pattens were the usual forms of protection, worn over shoes to keep the wearer's feet out of the mud. There were also flat-soled versions with just a toe-cap, known as goloshes, worn over both shoes and boots. A small number of shoes survive which were made with the flat golosh sole attached. These were known colloquially as 'slapsoles': the heel on the golosh was not attached to the shoe, and this caused the undersole to slap up and down as the foot flexed in walking. Two slapsoles (not a pair) from the V&A's collection, the larger seen in plate 11, are particularly interesting as they are of very similar styles but different sizes. They may perhaps have been made for a special occasion for an adult and child or very young woman. In these two examples the heel is actually attached to the sole, which would have made walking considerably easier than in a 'true' slapsole. Other collections, including those at Northampton Museum and the Museum of London, have examples of slapsoles, and there are also versions in other European collections. It seems likely that they were not actually much worn and were a fashion extreme rather than of any genuine practical value.

The Pointed Toe

Pointed shoes for women marked the first real divergence between shoe fashions for men and women, probably developing from the tapered square. For about the last quarter of the seventeenth century, the pointed toe was an entirely feminine fashion and the high heel (particularly pronounced on French shoes) which accompanied it assisted in the fashionable deception that women of quality had tiny feet. Towards the end of the seventeenth century the pointed toe on women's shoes became upturned, a fashion described by Randle Holme (1688), as 'hooked'.

Leather was commonly used for working women's shoes. To a lesser extent it was also used for women's fashionable outdoor wear, but was not as common as the more exotic materials such as velvet or silk. A rare surviving pair of fashionable women's leather shoes, of about 1700 (plate 12), shows the contemporary style of pointed, slightly upturned toe with white rand, red leather heel and latchet and ribbon fastening.

Plate 11 above Woman's kid 'slapsole' shoe with lines of silk ribbon decoration; Italian? 1670s. The stacked leather heel is attached to the golosh sole with a rounded piece of leather; slapsoles usually have unattached heels, from which the name derives. HH 519–1948; Ham House, Richmond, Surrey

Plate 12 opposite Leather woman's shoe with pointed toe; English, *c.*1700. White vellum rand, red leather heel and latchet, and ribbbon fastening. The ribbon is a modern addition. 1124–1901

Chapter Three
Taste and Elegance: 1700–1750

The Cupula-coat allows all the freedom of motion; the graceful walk, the majestic step, not to mention the beauty and splendour of the foot which plays visibly within the circle and ravishes the eye of the watchful beholder. (*The Whitehall Evening Post,* 1747)

At the beginning of this period the gentry advertised its wealth and status through sumptuous clothes and accessories. As the century progressed, however, wealth generated by the growth of trade increased the prosperity of the middle classes. They were keen to imitate their superiors and one of the ways in which they sought to elevate their social status was through wearing fashionable dress and stylish shoes.

New forms of entertainment such as assemblies, as well as the development of pleasure gardens and spas, offered opportunities for members of respectable society to place themselves before the public gaze. The motions of walking, dancing and sitting down at such events or places might reveal a fine shoe beneath a flowing gown, or the sparkle of a buckle as it caught the light. The wide-hooped petticoats which came into fashion also provided an opportunity to show off the feet. Elegant footwear therefore became more prominent in the language of display.

The Fabric of Fashion

The Weekly Journal, of 1 May 1736, commented: 'The ladies shoes were exceeding rich, being either pink, white, or green silk, with gold or silver lace and braid all over, with low heels, and low hind-quarters, and low flaps, and an abundance had large diamond shoe-buckles'.

Throughout the first half of the eighteenth century, the colours and materials of fashionable women's shoes often reflected the elegance of their gowns. Fabrics ranged from delicate silks to sturdier materials,

Fig. 7 above Detail of a pair of blue, ivory and green brocaded silk shoes; British or French, *c.*1740. The date is suggested by the low heel and rounded toe, although the silk is much earlier, dating from 1705–20. The shoes would have been fastened with a buckle.

T.443&A–1913

such as leather and wool, for everyday wear (see Frontispiece and plate 1). The uppers and soles would be cut out separately and then sold on to the shoemaker who adapted them to the shape of the last. This helps account for the asymmetrical positioning of the fabrics on many surviving shoes (fig. 7). They were usually lined with kid, silk or canvas, and the combination of fragile materials forming the upper called for a great deal of skill at the hands of the shoemaker:

It is much more ingenious to make a Woman's shoe than a Man's: Few are good at both, they are frequently two distinct Branches; the Woman's Shoe-Maker requires much neater Seams as the Materials are much finer. They employ Women to bind their shoes and sew the Quarters together, when they are made of Silk, Damask or Callimanco (R. Campbell, *The London Tradesman,* 1747).

It is, however, rare to find a shoe which exactly matches the damask and brocaded silk designs of the dress. It would have been too complicated and costly for most women to acquire matching shoes for every gown. Moreover, as shoes were usually viewed from some distance and glimpsed beneath the hem of a skirt, it would not have

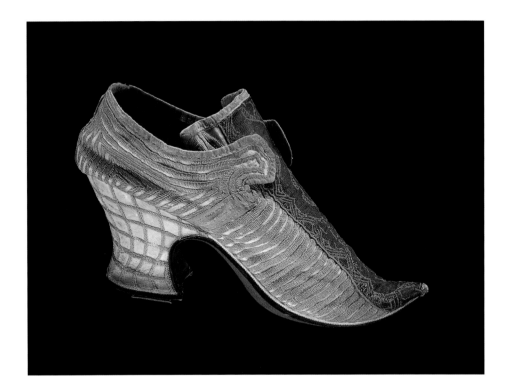

mattered if the pattern was slightly different. This might explain why the shoes in fig. 7 can be dated to the 1740s from their style but are covered in a much earlier silk. The woman who wore them probably had a dress of similar colours and asked the shoemaker to hide the outdated bird design under the latchets, leaving the floral decoration on the toe which would have blended in with a silk of this period.

Richly trimmed or embroidered shoes could, on the other hand, be used with a number of different garments. The criss-cross and parallel lines of applied decoration on the shoes in plate 13 resemble the designs on quilted petticoats which were worn with open-fronted gowns. Broad bands of silver-gilt braid decorating the front of the uppers became very popular in the 1730s and 1740s (see plate 13). They were known as 'laces' and could easily be added to or removed from the shoe to suit the costume or occasion. In a painting attributed to Thomas Gibson (fig. 8), Henrietta Howard, Countess of Suffolk,

Plate 13 above Woman's silk shoe; British, 1720s–30s. Decorated with silver-gilt braid and embroidery. Faint pencil markings delineating the parallel stripes and lattice design are still visible in places. The toe curves upwards, rather like the prow of a ship. 230–1908

wears 'laced' shoes to match the braid on her stomacher and skirts. When the heroine of Samuel Richardson's novel *Pamela* (1740–41) believes she is returning home from her position as a favoured maid, she removes the 'lace' from her shoes, with the intention of replacing it with plain buckles more suited to village life.

Heels, Toes and the Art of Movement

The shape of the stylish English lady's shoe, with its thick, waisted heel and prow-shaped toe, varied very little during the early eighteenth century (plate 13). Although they look more sturdy than some of the slender tapering styles then fashionable in France, they cannot

Fig. 8 below Painting of Henrietta Howard, Countess of Suffolk. Attributed to Thomas Gibson (early 18th century). Blickling Hall, Norfolk. National Trust Photographic Library/John Hammond

have been particularly easy to walk in. If the heel was placed too far under the instep, or sloped at an abrupt angle, the foot was likely to fall backwards (plate 14). Moreover, the higher the heel, the more the weight of the body would be thrust forward onto the balls of the feet, causing considerable strain. Despite such impracticalities, women were expected to walk smoothly and it is little wonder that carriage and posture became such an art. Dancing masters taught the virtues of graceful movement, and children practised walking in shoes, hoops and wigs from an early age.

By the 1740s a greater variety of styles, including blunter toes and broader, lower heels, were coming into fashion, but this does not mean that shoes were necessarily more comfortable. They were still made as 'straights' which forced the toes into unnatural directions and caused distortions, despite the common practice of frequently changing the shoes from one foot to the other. The flatter, more shallow shapes also offered little protection against the hazards of stony ground and unpaved streets. Dr Camper, writing in the 1770s, argued that shoes curved up like the front of skate irons (see plate 13) at least prevented the wearer from bruising her feet on loose stones and cobbles.

An elegant ankle was much admired in a man. Although his black or brown leather shoes tended to be more practical than women's footwear, the dark tones would have set off

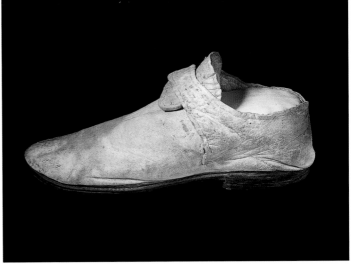

Plate 14 left Ribbon-tied woman's shoe with vandyked tongue; English, *c.*1720. Covered in Spitalfields brocaded silk dating from 1715–20. The sloping heel and the pressure of the foot has caused the back of the upper to extend over the sole. The ribbon tie is not original. T.446–1913.

Plate 15 above Man's mule slippers (not a pair) of silk brocaded with metal thread; British, 1710–20s. T.8–1922; T.9–1922

Plate 16 right Man's dress shoe with rounded toe and long latchets for a buckle; British, 1740s–50s. The low, stacked heel appears to have been originally coloured blue. T.151–1937

the glistening buckles and pale stockings with which they were often worn. Lighter and brighter colours were reserved for court, special occasions and extravagant dressing (plate 16). The Prince of Wales donned a pair of 'white shoes' for his wedding day in May 1736 and *Mist's Journal* of 1727 describes a young dandy of the day sporting red heels about town. The squared blocked toe, fashionable during the reign of George I (1714–27), had virtually died out by the end of the 1720s. It was replaced by a rounder shape and the term 'old square toes' came to be used in mockery against the older generation. The whole style of a man's shoe gradually became less heavy and heels dropped to about an inch (2.5cms) in height, as in plate 16.

Throughout the eighteenth century a gentleman was often most at ease in his nightgown and 'slippers' (plate 15). He wore them to relax privately in his home, receive visitors and sometimes even as a sign of informality out-of-doors. Cut in the form of a mule, they often matched the rich materials of the nightgown, as described in an early eighteenth-century advertisement: 'Taken from a Gentleman's House ...A flour'd Saten Night gown, lin'd with Pink colour'd Lustring, and a Cap and Slippers of the Same' (quoted by John Ashton in *Social Life in the Reign of Queen Anne*).

Boots: for Jockeys or Gentlemen?

Boots were largely reserved for riding, hunting, travelling and military use. Pehr Kalm, a Swedish botanist who visited England in 1748, noted how anyone walking in town wearing boots would always carry a riding whip as a sign that he had ridden in. A growing interest in horse-racing, however, led to the rise of the jockey boot (see plate 35a) as an item of fashionable clothing. By the 1730s they were becoming an increasingly familiar sight. Ending just below the knee, they had a turned-down top of a softer or lighter coloured leather and were pulled on using leather or string loops. Although dashing to the eye, such styles were not always approved of, particularly indoors. The popular press loved to poke fun at the young sparks who wore boots, likening them to 'jockeys', 'footmen', 'grooms' and even 'pickpockets' as they strutted about the streets or congregated in boxes at the theatre.

Buckles and Ribbons

Gold or silver buckles often gave the finishing touch to a shapely foot (fig. 9). They fastened the latchets of the shoes over the tongues and were one of the few pieces of jewellery worn by men. Making beautiful buckles became a highly skilled craft at which the English silversmith and jeweller excelled. Exquisitely carved designs, glittering pastes and precious stones reflected the status of the wearer as well as the occasion. Cheaper and plainer versions were made of steel, brass and pinchbeck. A gentleman often possessed several pairs of buckles which he could transfer between shoes to suit his needs. He might also wear matching knee buckles to fasten his breeches at the sides, as in fig. 9.

Although many women wore small square or oblong buckles, some still preferred to fasten their shoes with ribbon ties (see plate 14). This was probably a practical consideration. Hooped petticoats helped raise the skirts above the ground but the prongs and sharp edges of a buckle might easily become ensnared in the flowing lengths of a gown. Men had to be cautious too, and the various hazards which might befall them are well illustrated in a poem by Soame Jenyns:

Thin be his yielding sole and low his heel,
Nor need I, sure, bid prudent youths beware
Lest with erected tongues their buckles stare,
The pointed steel shall oft their stockings rend
And oft th' approaching petticoat offend.
(*The Art of Dancing,* 1730)

This satirical note might also have had something to do with the size of men's buckles, which reached enormous proportions after 1730. Some were so large that they covered a man's instep and half of his foot.

Sole Protectors

Pattens (plate 17) were often worn to lift the shoe out of the dirt and damp. Despite their beneficial qualities, the wooden sole and iron ring must have made them very heavy and uncomfortable. Gentlewomen sometimes found occasion to use them, but because of their functional appearance they were more generally associated with

Fig. 9 above Portrait of the Prince of Wales; later George III (r.1760–1820). British, *c.*1750. He is wearing large silver buckles on his shoes and his breeches are fastened at the side with a matching knee buckle. w.35–1972

the lower classes and country people. In his poem *Trivia* of 1712, John Gay wrote of working housewives 'clinking' through the wet London streets on pattens and Pehr Kalm noted how women of farming families '...wear their *pattens* under their ordinary shoes when they go out to prevent the dirt on the roads and streets from soiling their ordinary shoes' *(Kalm's Account of his Visit to England,* 1748).

Leather overshoes, known as 'clogs', were the elegant alternative to pattens (plate 18). They were often covered in fine materials or decorative leather stitching, to complement the richness of the shoe. Curved and shaped to fit neatly under the arch, they would have supported the foot, perhaps making the high heels easier to walk in. But the thin leather soles of the clogs offered little protection from the dirt of the roads or unpaved streets. The lack of wear on the soles of surviving pairs suggests that they were worn in dry conditions; inside the house, hackney carriage or sedan chair. Clogs are therefore generally linked to luxurious lifestyles or to those who wished to imitate the fashions of their betters. In 1725 Daniel Defoe published *Every-Body's Business, is No-Body's Business,* a pamphlet on the social embarrassment caused by well-dressed serving maids. To highlight the problem he described how a country girl, aspiring to dress like her mistress, kicked away her 'high wooden pattens' for 'leather clogs' when she became a London maidservant.

Plate 17 left Patten with wooden sole and iron ring; British, 1720s–30s. The heel socket and latchet fastenings would have helped secure the patten to the woman's shoe. It is likely that this example was worn by someone of genteel birth as the latchets are covered in velvet, an expensive material. T.43–1922

Plate 18 opposite Woman's shoe of brocaded Spitalfields silk with latchets for a buckle; British, late 1730s to early 1740s. The leather clog is partly covered in velvet and the sole is similar in shape to the base of a chopine. T.274A&C–1922

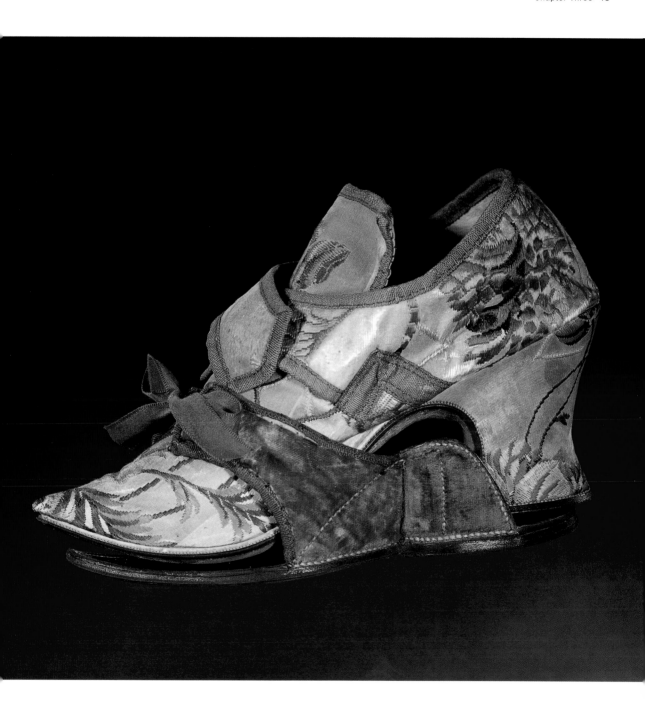

Chapter Four

The Revolutionary Shoe: 1750–1795

In England, Fashion, it is true, shifts like the weather cock, with every breeze;
but in France, it keeps one continual whirl like the fliers of a jack.
(*The Fashionable Magazine,* August 1786)

The growth of prosperity during this era produced a wider market
than ever before for luxury goods, including fine clothes and shoes.
The fashion-conscious kept up with the latest styles through observa-
tion, letters, and by means of the popular press. From the beginning
of the century journals had carried descriptions of new styles of dress,
but frequently with a satirical or moralising edge. The 1750s saw the
beginnings of illustrated descriptions of fashion which had no other
intent but to inspire and inform.

During the third quarter of the eighteenth century French and
Italian shoe styles quite literally reached their height. High and brittle
heels made some shoes positively unstable while buckles grew in size
and extravagance. From the 1780s, however, a taste for simplicity
began to prevail in Britain, a movement given further impetus by the
reaction to social and political events in France. More practical styles
of footwear, such as boots, became increasingly popular, as if to meet
an increasingly energetic society's need for less formal costume.

'Tott'ring every step they go': Women's Shoes 1750–65

Despite Anglo-French hostilities, the British often looked to Paris as a
source of inspiration. Rococo styles were never adopted in Britain
with the same enthusiasm as they were in France, but they did make
some impact, particularly during the 1750s and 1760s. Many lamented
the 'frivolous', 'ridiculous' and sometimes 'indecent' fashions which
they claimed were corrupting English dress. Such criticisms do not

Plate 19 opposite Buckle-
fastened woman's shoe;
British or French, 1750s–60s.
The 'French' or 'Pompadour'
heel measures 4 inches
(10.5cm) in height and is
covered in silk damask. The
upper is covered in brocaded
silk woven in Lyons dating
from the 1730s. T.423A–1913

Plate 20 left Woman's shoe; French, German or Italian, 1750s. Decorated with couched straw 'splints', flowers and leaves embroidered in silk, and scalloped edges of silver-gilt thread. The latchets are tied over the low tongue with silk ribbon and the broad heel is covered in satin. T.69A–1947

Plate 21 opposite Pair of woman's shoes with floral designs painted onto kid; Brussels, 1760s. The curving heel is covered in silk satin and the latchets would have been fastened with a buckle over the tongue. 270&A–1891

Fig. 10 below Detail of a lappet in Flemish (Brussels) bobbin lace; Brussels, 1740s–50s. T.316–1971

seem to have prevented women from adopting the precariously high and sensuously curving 'French' or 'Pompadour' heels (plate 19). Named after Madame de Pompadour, an official mistress of Louis XV, they were narrow-waisted with a very small, tilted base. A heel of such dramatic height, positioned directly under the instep, would have made the foot look petite – but beauty had its price. Perhaps the poet Francis Fawkes was exaggerating when he described women 'tott'ring' on these heels (*His Mistress's Picture*, 1755), but they may well have hindered the wearer from walking firmly in an attempt to alleviate the agony suffered by her toes.

Not all heels would have been so uncomfortable, and a huge variety of shapes continued to prevail, 'some as broad as a tea-cup's brim, some as narrow as the china circle the cup stands upon' (*The London Chronicle*, 1762). Although shoes of brocaded silk and wool remained popular, more unusual materials were occasionally used, such as ornate straw-work (plate 20) and richly decorated leather. In 1767 Lady Mary Coke bought six pairs of painted leather shoes from a shop in Brussels. Those in plate 21 are possibly very similar, as the design

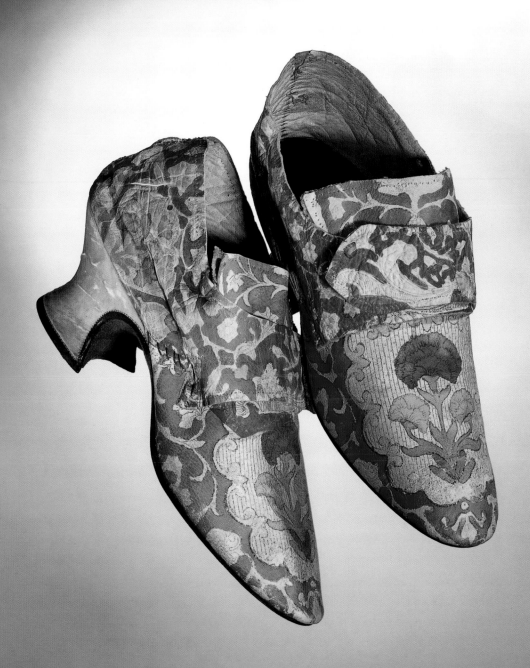

on the toe, with its vertical lines, scalloped edges and flowering plant closely resembles the patterns on the Brussels lace lappet in fig. 10.

High-heeled mules, commonly known as 'slippers', became increasingly popular for indoor wear (plate 22). In 1772, a commentator in *The London Magazine* marvelled at how well women danced and how firmly they walked in this type of shoe. The name 'slipper' also applied to a type of 'slip-on' shoe without fastenings (see fig. 11). Often very fragile and finely decorated, they were best set off by an elegant ankle. In *The Life and Adventures of Sir Launcelot Greaves* (by T. Smollett, 1762), Sir Launcelot holds forth against the pretensions of rich yeomen whose families ill-advisedly followed this fashion: '...their wives and daughters appeared in their jewels, their silks and their satins, their negligees and trollopees; their clumsy shanks like so many shins of beef, new cased in silk hose and embroidered slippers'.

The Influence of Italy: 1760s–80s

By the middle of the century, increasing numbers of wealthy and influential Englishmen were undertaking the Grand Tour of the continent. Young men who had travelled in Italy introduced the term 'Macaroni' to signify anything particularly stylish and elegant. The word also came to be linked with fops, who dressed extravagantly in tight-fitting clothes and low-cut shoes weighed down by enormous buckles.

The Italian influence on women's dress, however, was rather more subtle. The slender 'Italian' heel with its wedge-like extension under the instep (plate 23) gained in favour during the late 1760s. Made of wood and usually covered in a white or cream material to contrast with the colour of the upper, they were extremely elegant. The toes were often embroidered in silver-gilt threads, spangles or foils, and *The Fashionable Magazine* of 1786 included 'fancy patterns' for shoe vamps very similar to those in plate 23. The delicate form of the shoe would have accentuated the shapeliness of the leg, complementing the shorter styles of dress which were popular in the 1770s and 1780s (see plate 24).

Although stylish, they were highly unstable. Heels became so thin and high that they required the reinforcement of a metal spike down the middle to prevent them from snapping. This would have made them impractical for walking on cobbles, and it seems hardly surprising that their emergence coincided with the more widespread paving of streets. There were of course other styles to choose from but, according to Dr Camper, all were equally injurious to the foot:

...from our earliest infancy, shoes, as at present worn, serve but to deform the toes and cover the feet with corns, which not only render walking painful, but, in some cases, absolutely impossible...We bestow reasonable compassion upon the fate of the Chinese women, who dislocate their feet in obedience to the dictates of a barbarous custom, and yet we ourselves have submitted complacently for ages to tortures no less cruel (*The Best Form of Shoe, c.*1770).

Fig. 11 left Silk satin woman's 'slipper' with pointed tongue and high, slender heel; French or Italian, 1770s–80s. This shoe is very similar in style to those worn by the woman in plate 24. T.215–1916

Plate 24 opposite JACK OAKHAM throwing out A SIGNAL for an ENGAGEMENT. Hand-coloured print, British (London), May 1781. Private collection. Reproduced by kind permission of Mrs Pamela Pratt.

Buckles: an Extravagance

Shoe buckles for both men and women grew in size and extravagance. They reached their extreme in the enormous Artois style of
1777. Some were so large that the latchets wore out very quickly and
had to be replaced. Buckles displaying sparkling pastes set in exquisite patterns (fig. 12), Wedgwood cameos and silver-gilt embroidery all
created dazzling effects. One writer was so struck by the appearance
of her lover that she recorded in *The Lady's Magazine* of 1784: 'His
buckles totally covered his shoes and almost blinded me with their
brilliancy'.

Even the lower classes kept up with the fashion for larger buckles.
Although they were often made of cheaper materials, as wealth
increased and new manufacturing processes boosted supply such
luxuries were affordable to more and more people. *The Gentleman's
Magazine* of June 1777 observed: 'All our young fops of quality, and
even the lowest of our people in London, wear coach-harness
buckles, the latter in brass, white metal and pinchbeck'.

The Natural Form

By the mid-1780s, more natural styles had become fashionable in
English dress. Many women adopted a simpler style of shoe to accompany their flowing gowns of silk gauze or fine muslin. Often made of
plain leather, with medium-sized heels and pointed toes, they were
meant to make the foot look graceful. *The Lady's Magazine* of May
1785 remarked that whereas high heels were dangerous and low ones
unflattering, 'a heel about an inch and a half high, will make the
wearer tread firmly, and will not deform the leg'. Although some
shoes were still fastened with buckles, slippers (similar to those in
fig. 11) became increasingly fashionable. This was probably because
they were simpler in style and less likely to become entangled in the
longer gowns.

Many men also preferred to replace the buckle with ribbon ties.
Until then shoe-strings had been disliked in genteel society, perhaps
because of their associations with the labouring classes. Their re-
emergence is probably linked to the general move towards more
informal and comfortable styles of dress. During the second half of

Fig. 12 below Men's and
women's buckles. Top (a):
Man's buckle with silver
decoration mounted onto
iron; British, 1780s. The
chape is inscribed with the
maker's name: 'Bingham'.
T.357:1–1998
Bottom left (b): Square silver
buckle, man's?, inset with
paste stones; British,
c.1780. 945A–1864
Bottom right (c): Round silver
buckle, woman's, inset with
paste stones. British,
c.1780. 974A–1864

the century men's shoes became lower cut, a fashion which shifted the buckle nearer the toe (see plate 24). A large and heavy buckle would weigh down the front of the foot causing the heel to slip up over the back of the shoe when walking. A ribbon tie which lightly but firmly secured the shoe to the instep was far better suited to an active life of work or pleasure. They were also worn by London fops with some of the more extravagant fashions of the day, as a satirical poem in the June 1786 issue of *The Fashionable Magazine* suggests:

The Men, precious creatures, in high and stiff capes,
Strut with all the erectness of newly-train'd apes;
While ribbands, which might for their necks form a noose,
Are idly transferr'd to tie only their shoes.

Sporting Styles

The English gentleman so devoted himself to country pursuits that he wore sporting dress for much of the day. Boots became more and more popular in town as well as on the country estate, although their presence was still not always welcome inside the house. Fanny Burney's heroine, Evelina, is certainly dismayed by the appearance of the brash Lord Merton, who 'came shuffling into the room with his boots on, and his whip in his hand' (*Evelina,* 1778).

By the 1780s, however, the fashion for boots was so widespread that foreigners identified them as a characteristic of British dress. Young French dandies took to wearing them, much to the dismay of critics like Louis-Sébastien Mercier who expressed his disapproval of the prevailing vogue for Anglomania in his *Tableau de Paris* (1782–88), bemoaning the 'ton parmi la jeunesse de copier l'Anglois dans son habillement (fashion among the young to copy English dress)'. The most popular style was still the jockey boot (plate 35a), re-named the top boot, possibly to dispel any associations with the working classes. Some were so close fitting that they were difficult to remove without assistance.

Women also began wearing fashionable clothes inspired by country styles. During the 1780s the riding coat as well as the boot became fashionable for walking costume, and the impropriety of women

(who never rode) strutting about the streets in half-boots, great coats
and neckcloths excited much comment, particularly as they looked so
masculine. Even pattens (plate 17) gained a certain fashionable status
in the spa town of Bath where, according to Betsy Sheridan's *Journal*
of 1789, 'We Ladies here trot about in Pattens, a privilege granted no
where else to genteel Women'.

The Revolutionary Shoe

Reactions to the French Revolution strongly influenced developments
in English dress. Shoe styles were gradually becoming simpler during
the 1780s, but events in France acted as a catalyst, speeding up the

processes of change. Conspicuous symbols of wealth, such as extravagant shoe buckles, were not in keeping with the ideals of liberty, equality and democracy advocated by the newly elected French National Assembly. The authorities in Paris encouraged donations of buckles to the *caisse patriotique,* established during the autumn of 1789. Enthusiasm for French fashions, as well as a degree of sympathy with the early stages of the Revolution, also hastened the decline of the shoe buckle in Britain. Of course they did not disappear overnight, and heavy clumsier versions continued to be worn for court and evening dress well into the next century. But decreased demand in Britain, combined with the loss of the once flourishing export trade to France, meant that by 1791 there were large numbers of bucklemakers out of work in the Birmingham area. According to the Dutch fashion magazine, *Kabinet van Mode en Smaak,* in April 1792:

English fashions can hardly be seen; everything is in the French taste, which gains more ground, because of the general desire of the Ladies to visit France...Despite all the petitions of the Birmingham manufacturers to the Queen, the Princesses and the Prince of Wales, shoe buckles refuse to come into fashion again.

Many women's shoes (also known as slippers) followed the French fashion for broad, flat heels, a low V or U shaped throat and long pointed toes (plate 25). In the early 1790s 'sandle shoes', which were tied on with criss-cross ribbons, also became fashionable (a later example is shown in fig. 13a). These were inspired by the French *cothurnes* or *sandales* which formed part of a distinctive style of 'revolutionary' dress, modelled on the clothes of classical antiquity. Nancy Woodforde, a country parson's niece, acquired a black and yellow pair in 1792, but she probably chose them for their charm rather than their associations with the Revolution, which was rapidly moving towards a bloody climax.

The 'Terror' of 1793–94 and the downfall of the monarchy reawakened latent hostility towards French dress and manners. The Parisian fashion magazines fell silent, and the few depictions of clothing which did emerge were largely in the form of caricatures. During these years dress in Britain and France developed along quite different lines.

Chapter Five

Classicism and Romanticism:

1795 to the mid–1830s

The model of fashions which used to be dispatched every week from Paris, to reign without controul [sic] in all the toilettes in Europe, is no longer sent abroad to give the law in dress…To that well-conducted legislation, which formerly regulated with so much propriety the colour of a ribband, the size of the shoe, the thickness of the waist, the most complete anarchy has succeeded. (*The Lady's Magazine,* March 1797)

By the mid-1790s significant differences had emerged between French and British shoe styles. The latest Parisian modes could not, however, be ignored for long and the re-establishment of communications after the end of the Terror revealed the classical tastes of the new Republic. A simpler style of dress developed that extended to footwear; indeed some shoes were so basic they could be produced at home. Even the continuous wars with the French had an effect, as boots with military associations became popular and trimmings derived from army uniforms appeared on footwear. Although practical and utilitarian styles flourished during the Napoleonic period, the Romantic movement of the 1820s and 1830s inspired greater exuberance in the dress of both sexes. Subtle changes in footwear, such as squared toes and new colours, reflected these developments.

The Classical Line and Gothic Ornament: 1795–1815

The disruption of links with France during the mid-1790s had a considerable impact on women's costume in Britain. Whereas French dress favoured a pure, classical style, the British tended to combine neoclassical influences with lavish romantic ornament. Such variations are reflected in many shoes of this period. Although the 'slipper' retained its low-cut shape (plate 26) and 'sandle shoes' (fig. 13a),

Plate 26 opposite Woman's shoe of cut and punched leather with pale kid underlay; British, 1797. The overshoe is of a similar design and has a spring loop which would have fitted around the 'small Italian' heel (see the heel in plate 23 which is almost identical in shape). Shoe: 1126–1901; overshoe: 608C–1884

loosely based on Greek or Roman styles, remained popular, their decorative features were often very 'unclassical'. Cut-out patterns with coloured underlays reminiscent of the slashed designs on Tudor shoes became fashionable, and some slippers had matching toe-pieces to protect them out-of-doors (as can be seen in plate 26). There was also a short phase of higher heels, and in June 1797 *The Lady's Magazine* announced that 'Small Italian heels are again coming in with the rising generation' (plate 26 and fig. 13a).

By the end of the 1790s, however, Parisian styles were again exerting their influence on British taste. Once the Terror had ended and a reasonably secure government was established, French fashion magazines began to reappear. Descriptions of the latest classical styles were much admired, and the silhouette of British gowns gradually narrowed, becoming simpler with greater unity of design. Shoes were kept deliberately plain to preserve the pure lines of this fashion. Some were decorated with small bows or delicate patterns, but these generally harmonised with the details on the dress to create an elegant and uncluttered effect (see plate 25b and fig. 13b). Colours ranging from olive and lilac to orange often matched those on the pelisse, sash, hat, gloves or border of the pale muslin gowns, as described in *The Lady's Magazine* of 1799: 'Grecian dress; Round gown white muslin...fastened round the waist with a yellow girdle, having a border of purple flowers embroidered on it... Head-dress...with fillets of lilac and yellow. Lilac shoes'.

During the early years of the nineteenth century, classical influences remained strong (plate 27a). Fashion magazines, on both sides of the channel, frequently referred to Grecian slippers or Roman sandals, and some shoes were simple enough for women to make their own. The Honourable Mrs Calvert, for example, recorded in her *Souvenirs* (1808) how she had spent two hours with 'a master'

Fig. 13a below left Fashion plate showing walking dresses of 1797. Hand-coloured engraving; French, 1797. The woman on the right is wearing 'sandle' shoes: low-cut slippers fastened with ribbons which cross around the ankle and lower leg. Both women are wearing shoes with small, possibly 'Italian' heels. 298734.4

Fig. 13b below Fashion plate depicting a classical-style gown with yellow shoes stencilled in black; British, 1801. Hand-coloured engraving and stipple engraving, by H. Mutlow, from *The Lady's Magazine*. See plate 25b for a similar shoe. E.2044–1888

Plate 27 right Women's slippers. Bottom (a): Leather with a silk bow and low, wedge-shaped heel; British, 1810. This shoe is typical of the simple, yet elegant styles which were prevalent during the early nineteenth century. It was worn by a Mrs Grawshaw on her wedding day, 7 February 1810. The inner lining is inscribed with her maiden name, Miss E. Brown.
T.193–1914

Top (b): Leather, ornamented with vandyked and scalloped leather trimmings; British, c.1812. Although the basic shape is the same as in (a), the ornate decoration and the square throat cut higher on the instep show how shoe styles were changing.
T.479–1913

learning the 'Science' of shoe-making, and expected 'to make very nice shoes' herself. By 1812, however, a taste for greater ornamentation had again begun to interrupt the purity of the neoclassical line. So-called 'Gothic' styles inspired by Medieval, Tudor, Elizabethan and Stuart costume flourished in English dress, and ornate decoration adorned many shoes. Square-throated slippers were slashed across the front in a second brief revival of Tudor styles, and cutwork trimmings echoed the vandyked edgings on early seventeenth-century dress, as in plate 27b.

Masculine and Military Styles: 1795–1835

The long-toed man's shoe received much comment in the popular journals of the late 1790s. In October 1799, *The Lady's Magazine* commented: 'If ever, in some centuries to come, the little hat, stuffed coat, and long-toed shoe of a modern fine gentleman should be discovered in some museum of antiquities, or to survive upon the stage, they would no doubt give birth to many learned doubts and extra-ordinary *speculations*'. Although low-cut, bluntly pointed slippers were fashionable in the 1780s, they had never reached such extreme

Plate 28 left Top (a): Man's shoe with velvet upper, rounded toe and wedge-shaped heel covered in leather; British, 1805–10. The ribbon tie (not original) fastens high over the instep. T.440–1988

Bottom (b): Woman's leather shoe, probably worn with walking dress; British, 1806–11. The round toe, wedge-shaped heel and latchets tied well over the instep are almost identical to those in (a). AP.1–1912

Fig. 14 below Bottom (a): Lace-tied woman's leather shoe with a raised sole; British, 1805–20. The laces are not original. Circ. 818–1920 Top (b): 'Promenade' or 'Carriage clog' with a raised cork sole and square toe; British, *c.*1825–35. The leather straps and toe cap would have fitted over the woman's shoe or boot, helping to protect the fragile silks and kid leathers of the upper from dirt and damp. T.460–1920

proportions. Fops were caricatured in their beribboned shoes, and the 'peaked' toe was compared to the fourteenth-century poulaine.

At the same time, however, more practical and comfortable shapes continued to gain in favour. By the beginning of the nineteenth century many men had adopted the higher-tongued shoe with rounded toes and latchets tied well over the instep (plate 28a). Women also began wearing similar styles (plates 28b and 31) and in January 1808 *The Lady's Monthly Museum* noted that black velvet lace-tied shoes were 'the newest Mode' in walking dress. Some designs combined shoe and patten in one (fig. 14a), raising the foot off the ground, yet passing as sufficiently elegant to be considered genteel. Although they remained popular for men, such styles were not to the taste of every lady. James Devlin, in his publication *The Shoemaker* (1840), describes how the 'woman's tie shoe' went out of fashion because of 'the tying being a trouble' and 'the shoe looking too masculine for the chaster taste of the wearer'.

Fig. 15 above Parisian fashion plate showing fashionable men's dress of 1827. Hand-coloured engraving; French, 1827. The figure on the right is wearing Hessian boots with shallow, square toes.

E.1159–1974

During the period of the Napoleonic wars the army became more socially visible, and military costume influenced fashionable dress. The Hessian boot (fig. 15), originally associated with the light cavalry, was popular from 1795 until about 1830. Reaching to just below the knee, Hessians were cut with a peak at the front which was decorated by a tassel. Worn with pantaloons, they brought the glamour of military uniform into civil life. As an anonymous cavalry officer wrote in *The Whole Art of Dress* (1830): 'it is impossible to dress a fine leg, more especially of a short person, to greater advantage than in a Hessian'.

Wellington (plate 35b) and Blucher boots, named after the allied commanders at Waterloo, also appeared at this time. The former was similar to the top boot but without the turn-over top, while the Blucher was a half-boot laced over the tongue. Lacking adornment, both could be worn under trousers or pantaloons without spoiling their line. Some styles of Wellington had 'stockings' attached and were used as a substitute for dress shoes (plate 35b). *The Whole Art of Dress* explains: 'This boot is invented, doubtless, for the mere purpose of saving trouble in dress; for without attending to silk stockings or the trouble of tying *bows,* you have merely to slip on the boots, and you are *featly* equipped in a moment'.

Boots also became increasingly acceptable for women. By 1804, half-boots with front lacing and ribbon trimmings (plate 29) had started to appear in fashion illustrations for 'walking' or 'morning' dress. Many were still made of leather, although hardwearing alternatives were also available due to the huge increase in raw cotton imports towards the end of the eighteenth century and new processes of mechanization in the textile industry. Cotton jean became particularly popular (seen in plate 29b): *The Ladies Monthly Museum* of July 1812 remarked that 'jean demi-bottes' along with other items of dress would 'suit the parade as well as the picture gallery – equally cool for both purposes'. Although women's boots tended to be more delicate than men's, they were also adorned with decorations borrowed from military uniforms. In 1815 Elizabeth Grant described, in her *Memoirs of a Highland Lady* (1797–1827), how she had walked out in Edinburgh, 'like a hussar in a dark cloth pelisse trimmed with fur and braided like the coat of a staff-officer, boots to match, and a fur cap set on one side'.

Romanticism: 1825–1835

The Romantic movement inspired some of the most flamboyant styles of the nineteenth century. By 1830 puffed sleeves, tiny waists and bell-shaped skirts had reached such exaggerated proportions that women were compared to 'ants' and 'bottle spiders' (see plate 30). Shoes did not alter quite so dramatically, but the more compressed line of the dress extended to the shape of the toe, which became square after 1825. Heels also disappeared, perhaps to compensate for the increasing height of head wear and hairstyles. As skirts increased in width they also became shorter, focusing attention once again on the foot and ankle. Brightly coloured silk boots or slippers complemented the richness of the gown, sometimes matching the sash or long fluttering ribbons worn with the hat (see back jacket; plate 29a; plate 30). A wide range of colours was available with evocative names such as 'canary yellow', 'palm-leaf green', 'marshmallow blossom' and walnut-tree brown'. Even the black satin shoes which became increasingly popular for evening dress were not always left unadorned:

Some of our fashionables have made exchange in the slipper, lacing it up the front with coloured ribbons. Black satin shoes made in this manner, and laced with green or rose-colour, are very becoming to the foot; the rosettes are worn larger than they were, and ornaments in various styles will be probably introduced for dress shoes (*The World of Fashion,* October 1834).

Due to their fragility, silk slippers were probably reserved for indoor wear, evening dress or special occasions (see back jacket image). Kid shoes and boots tended to be more economical as they lasted longer, but they were also often very thin (plate 29c). 'Promenade clogs' and 'carriage clogs' therefore became an essential accessory for fashionable women wishing to keep their feet relatively dry and dirt-free (see fig. 14b). According to an 1830 trade advertisement of W. Jackman of Oxford Street, London, some were 'peculiar for their lightness and neat appearance, not being distinguishable from the boot or shoe' (*Townsend's Monthly Selection of Parisian Costumes,* 1830).

Changes in men's clothing were less dramatic, but the general style of their dress altered in line with women's fashions. Along with fuller

Plate 29 opposite Women's ankle-length boots. Top (a): Side-laced ankle boot of watered silk with a flat heel and square toe (see plate 30); British or French, 1830s–40s. T.517–1913
Middle (b): Striped cotton jean half-boot with low, stacked heel and rounded toe; British, 1812–20. The boot is laced up the front and trimmed with a silk rosette. T. 509–1913
Bottom (c): Kid half-boot with low, stacked heel and rounded toe; British, 1815–20. The boot is laced up the front and trimmed with a silk rosette. T.435–1971

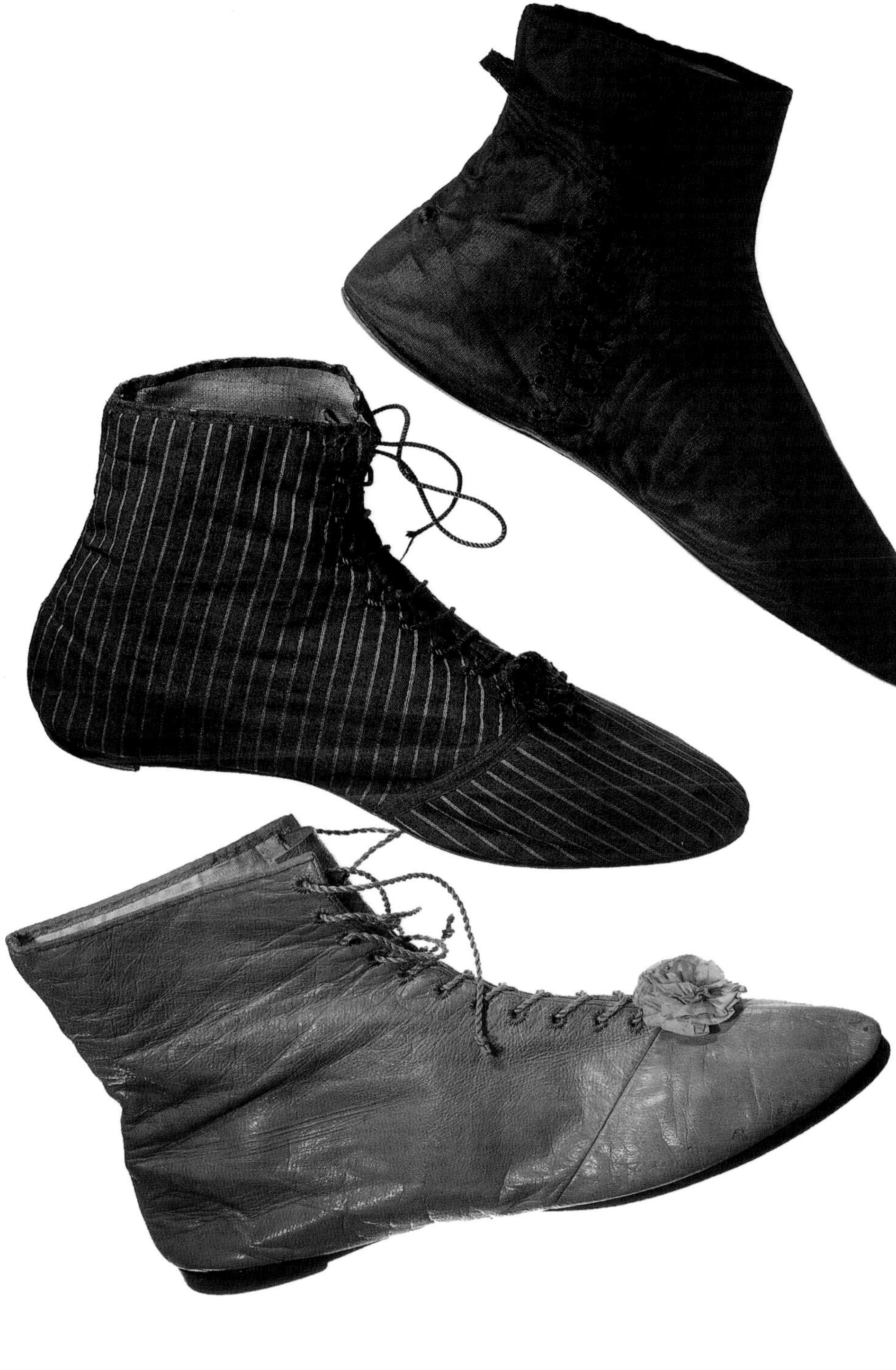

coat sleeves, nipped-in waists and padded coat fronts, men also adopted the shallow, square toe, as seen in fig. 15. Although Wellingtons, Bluchers and lace-tied walking shoes predominated for everyday wear, leather 'pumps' worn with formal evening dress closely ressembled the general shape of women's slippers (see back jacket image and plate 33) with the same long, low and narrow line; according to Prince Pückler-Muskau, who visited London in 1827, they were 'as light as paper'.

Ideals of Beauty: 1800–1837

Men's and women's shoe styles during this period reflected the prevailing ideals of beauty, which equated delicate bone structure with gentle birth and fine breeding. Great attention was paid to the size of the foot and this was sometimes carried to such extremes that the author of *The Whole Art of Dress* remarked: 'frequently in company I have heard the chief beauties singled out among good-looking individuals, were their feet; because, perhaps, they have been rather small and cased in a neat pump'. Narrow half-boots and slippers min-imised the size of the foot, not always with comfortable results: pinching shoes, aching imprisoned feet, toes folded one over the other, bunions, corns and inflamed joints were com-monly cited ailments. Sometimes, even the most rigorous efforts failed to have the required effects. Captain McDonough's *The Hermit in London* (1819–22) described one stout lady's 'sandal' lacings as 'so tight that they crippled her, from which ribbons crossed her ankle and cut it at angles backwards and forwards'.

Neatness was admired as it indicated good taste and gentility. A delicate female foot encased in a close-fitting silk shoe looked

1.*Chapeau de gros de naples. Robe en Chalys.*
2.*Capote en gros de Naples. Rodingote de gros de Naples à petits quadrilles.*

elegant and refined, suiting the ideal image of a woman. New standards of perfection were set for men, and George Beau Brummell achieved lasting fame for his efforts to establish restraint, simplicity and cleanliness in dress during the early nineteenth century. He reputedly paid such meticulous attention to the shine on his boots that their brilliancy was the envy of the finest London dandies. Captain William Jesse, who cultivated Brummell's acquaintance in 1832, remarked that he even insisted on his servants polishing the soles so that the edges would not be neglected. By the 1830s several publications, such as *The Whole Art of Dress* (1830) and *Hints on Etiquette* (1836), had appeared, advising men on the finer points of good dressing, including what they should wear on their feet.

Despite such ideals, badly made and ugly footwear received much comment. James Devlin in *The Shoemaker* (1840) remarked on how many shoemakers were failing to make proper use of a recent technical improvement – the re-introduction of lefts and rights. The development of the pantograph in the early nineteenth century, combined with the return to flat shoes, meant that it was easier to make a mirror image pair of lasts. Shoes cut to the form of the right and left foot therefore gradually began to replace 'straights' (see the red shoe in the back jacket image), although women were slower to adopt them than men. In theory, this development should have ensured a closer-fitting shoe, but according to Devlin the reality was very different. He complained of how the 'light shoe' or 'pump', fashionable throughout the 1830s, 'sits often so loosely along the quarters, and in a most inelegant and injurious hollow curved line...making the foot appear thick and clumsy'.

Plate 30 opposite Fashion plate showing fashionable women's dress of *c*.1832. Hand-coloured engraving; French, *c*.1832. The woman on the right is wearing olive-coloured boots which match the trimmings on her hat and are similar in style to the boot in plate 29a. The woman on the left is wearing black slippers with ribbon ties which closely resemble the style of the yellow shoe shown in the back jacket image. E.1058–1959

Chapter Six

Shopping for Shoes: 1700–1835

> So you'll measure me, please, for shoes – and shoes
>
> That will wear for years and years;
>
> And you'll make me a pair that shall fit me well,
>
> Of leather and thread, and – tears.
>
> ('Leather and Thread and Tears: A Ballad of Boughton Fair', from
>
> Thomas Wright, *The Romance of the Shoe,* 1922)

Men and women seeking to purchase fashionable footwear had several options at their disposal. Although the actual methods of shoe-making remained largely unchanged until the mechanization of the 1850s, output and retailing rapidly increased to meet the demands of an ever-widening consumer market. By 1700, the origins of the modern shop had emerged: Daniel Defoe, in his book *The Complete English Tradesman* (1726), noted how London shopkeepers were spending large amounts on fitting out their shops with shelves, shutters, 'boxes', glass doors and 'sashes'; 'a modern custom...and wholly unknown to our ancestors'. Shoes were often made and sold under the same roof, but as the century progressed some enterprising shoe-makers extended their businesses and began selling their footwear on separate premises. To differentiate between bespoke and ready-made shoes, the former were usually inscribed with the customer's name (see plates 23 and 27a).

People who lived in the provinces often depended on fashion-conscious local shoemakers with London contacts and suppliers. They could also shop by proxy, relying on a friend, relative or trusted retailer to purchase shoes for them. Some even gave commissions to friends travelling abroad, as made-up items could pass through customs as personal clothing and were exempt from the high duties

Plate 31 opposite Woman's leather shoe with a low heel and latchets to fasten over the instep; British, 1810–20. The label on the insole reads 'Borsley Maker, Hanway House, Hanway Street, Oxford Street'. From about 1750 shoemakers began to use labels for advertising purposes, attaching them to both ready-made and bespoke shoes. T.385–1960

levied on imported goods. *The Letters and Journals of Lady Mary Coke* record how she purchased several pairs of shoes on behalf of a friend in this way, during a visit to Brussels in 1767: 'I went to several Shops, and remembering your having said you wish'd for some painted leather shoes, I bought six pair, which I shall present you with, when I return to England'.

From the 1750s onwards a huge variety of ready-made boots, shoes, pattens and clogs were sold in 'Shoe Warehouses' (see the label in plate 25c). Sometimes warehouses were a sales outlet for a single shoemaker, but more often they served as agents and distributors for a variety of suppliers. Anyone with ready money was welcome to shop there, although they proved particularly popular with the middle classes, offering as they did a wide range of fashionable goods at a reduced cost. Traditional bespoke shoemakers accused these dealers of foisting inferior goods on the public, but shoe warehouses continued to expand despite the protests. They became so widespread that *The London Chronicle* of June 1765 enquired: 'Have we now any shops? Are they not turned into warehouses? Have we not the English warehouse, the Scotch warehouse, the Irish warehouse, the shirt warehouse, the stocking warehouse, the shoe warehouse, the hat warehouse, nay, even the buckle and button warehouse?'.

One of the more traditional ways of purchasing shoes was at markets or fairs. A great shoe-trading event in the seventeenth, eighteenth and nineteenth centuries was the annual 'Boughton Green Fair' in Northamptonshire, when hundreds of prospective customers, rich and poor, poured in from miles around to sample the wares of the renowned Northampton shoemakers. Itinerant salesmen and pedlars also continued to travel from village to town, supplying the countryside with a whole range of goods; they often brought with them buckles and ribbons and sometimes even ready-made shoes.

Chapter Seven
Towards the Modern Age: 1837–1914

Fig. 16 below The Queen
Victoria and Prince Albert
Polka. Baxter Print; British,
c.1840. Both wear flat,
square-toed shoes: Victoria's
are of ivory satin with a bow
and ribbons round the ankle,
while Albert wears patent
leather shoes with a small
metal buckle. The print
employs the contemporary
convention of depicting the
feet as impossibly small,
creating tiny, delicate feet for
Queen and Consort.

E.828–1959

The really well-dressed woman deals in no gaudy confusion of colours – nor does she affect a studied sobriety; but she either refreshes you with a spirited contrast, or composes you with a judicious harmony. (Lady Eastlake [Elizabeth Rigby], *The Art of Dress, The Quarterly Review*, March 1847)

Queen Victoria's accession in 1837 coincided with a change in mood and a more sober taste in dress. Rapid industrialisation was taking place, and the middle classes in Britain and most of Europe had emerged in society as a dominant force in political, economic and social life. Middle-class values and the virtues of hard work and respectability were embodied in the domestic lives of Victoria and Albert, whom she married in 1840. Women's dress portrayed the ideal of modest gentility embodied in the Romantic movement of the later 1830s and 1840s, with its tendency to sentimentalism and nostalgia.

By the late 1850s men's clothes reflected a more relaxed and easy line in keeping with a work-oriented lifestyle. After 1850 a few more practical forms of dress such as separate jackets and skirts also presaged women's more active future roles.

Toes and Heels: 1830s–1850s

The gentility of the early Victorian period was reflected in women's shoes, which continued in shape as before (see back jacket), but in more subdued colours. Small hands and feet were associated with gentle birth and suited the contemporary ideal image of women. The foot when it was seen beneath the dress was expected to look small and delicate (fig. 16). Mary Merrifield, in *Dress as a Fine Art* (1854), complained of 'poets and romance-writers' who encouraged women to 'pinch their feet into small shoes'.

Toe shapes for both men and women were square and shallow at the beginning of the period, but by the 1850s they had become deeper for men and thus more practical. Few women's shoes had heels in the 1830s, but by the middle of the century heels had come back into fashion. The delicate but extremely impractical heel-less shoe, usually made of satin, was still popular, with black or white favoured for formal wear. Satin pumps of the kind shown in the back jacket image, although tied round the ankles with ribbons, must have offered little support to the foot.

Generally the height of heels on men's shoes settled at a modest one inch (2.5cms), which is still the norm to the present day. Reflecting the move towards practicality, engendered by a more active lifestyle, the sturdy Oxonian or Oxford shoe became popular for men. This style subsequently became a mainstay of men's shoe fashion and, as described by J. Sparkes Hall in *The Book of the Feet* (1848), it 'laces up the front with three or four holes; the vamp comes well above the joint; seam across the instep. The best shoe for walking'. Shoes or pumps with a low heel and ribbon tie continued to be worn at court or as dress wear, in conjunction with knee-breeches (plate 33).

Plate 32 below left Pair of women's shoes or slippers of linen; British, 1840s–50s. Tongue and upper decorated with silk trim and glass beads. Inscribed inside: 'MARSH Ladies and Childrens Shoe Manufacturer, 148 Oxford Street, opposite Bond Street'. T.734:1&2–1997

Plate 33 below Man's ceremonial or court patent leather shoe with decorative ribbon tie; German, shown at the Great Exhibition of 1851. After the first few years of Victoria's reign, buckles on court shoes (like those seen on Prince Albert's shoes in fig. 16) were abandoned briefly in favour of ribbons. T.257–1963

Boots for Men and Women

Boots were still more commonly worn than shoes by men throughout the nineteenth century, and were regarded as more formal for day wear (plate 35). In 1840, James Devlin (see chapter five) observed, 'At present we are emphatically a booted people; so are the French and the Americans'.

Half-boots were popular for men from the 1830s (plate 36c) right up to the Depression of the 1930s. They were more appropriate than long boots for wearing with trousers which, except for more formal occasions, were replacing breeches. After the middle of the century, long boots were rarely worn other than for sport or by the military. For women, half-boots were popular from the 1830s until the 1870s when shoes again predominated. Usually the crinoline completely obliterated the foot, but occasionally the modest boot peeked out beneath it. Side-laced boots with a flat heel were worn by fashion-conscious women. By the 1840s they were made in a range of materials, including leather, which was much more appropriate for country and outdoor wear than lightweight cloth or silk, such as that used in the boots shown in plate 29a.

Plate 34 below Man's elastic-sided boot; British, mid-19th century. Canvas upper with domestic embroidery. T.24–1936

The elastic-sided boot, a prototype of which was presented to Queen Victoria in 1837 by J. Sparkes Hall, who had patented it, was the result of experiments made with india-rubber cloth (plate 34). By 1846 Sparkes Hall was promoting his 'elastic sided boot', which had 'a cloth upper with a toe cap of black leather'. Gussets of elasticated material were inserted at each side of the boot obviating the need for other fastenings. Elastic-sided boots were popular, but laced and buttoned styles were also fashionable. Side-buttoned boots were popular for men from the 1830s, but adopted more slowly by women. There is a mention in 1858 of 'boots of kid, buttoned at the side' for women.

Other styles for men included Bluchers, with open tab front and lacing, and Alberts, cloth-topped boots with side lacing, which were a short-lived fashion introduced in the 1850s. In Dickens' *Pickwick Papers* (1837), Sam

Plate 35 left Men's long boots: Top (a): Leather jockey or top boot with a turn-over top and cloth straps; British, 1820s–30s. This style, which became popular in about 1730, altered very little over a long period, although the shallow, square toe in this example was fashionable during the first half of the nineteenth century. By 1830, top boots had become almost entirely a sporting fashion; similar styles are still worn today for riding. T.599–1913

Middle (b): Wellington (opera boot), leather and patent leather; British, 1840s. Worn under trousers, it would have looked like a pump with a stocking. T.499–1913

Bottom (c): Model boot, leather and patent leather with cloth straps; British, about 1888–90. By Annesley of Brighton. Model boots and shoes were made to show off contemporary styles (such as the rather pointed toe in this example), and the skill of the shoemaker. They were often shown at International Exhibitions and were not intended for wear. T.449–1920

Plate 36 right Top (a):
Woman's model boot, patent
leather and glacé kid with
cork sole; British, 1865–70.
By George Newton. Boots
with curved tops and
tassels, usually cut high
above the ankle, were often
referred to as 'Polish' or
'Hungarian'. T.420–1920
Middle (b): Woman's boot,
patent leather and kid with
decorative stitching; British
or French, 1850s. AP.39–1860
Bottom (c): Man's boot,
patent leather and
snakeskin; British, shown
at the Great Exhibition of
1851. AP.41–1860

Weller had to clean boots described as 'hessians, halves, painted tops, wellingtons' (plates 35 and 36c). Queen Victoria's interest in outdoor life encouraged the wearing of sturdier footwear by women of the higher classes. Named after the queen's Scottish home, Balmorals were boots which laced at the front and were worn by both men and women.

From about the middle of the nineteenth century, increasing numbers of fairly substantial leather boots were being made for women, often with beautiful decorative details such as contrasting coloured leathers or decorative stitching (plate 36). Men's half-boots of leather were plainer, but could also be made in contrasting colours, although these were generally more subdued than colours used for women's boots. The range of materials for uppers for men's boots and shoes increased, and included snake-skin from about the 1850s (see plate 40) and crocodile or alligator skin in the 1870s.

The stylish Empress Eugénie, who had married the French Emperor Napoleon III in 1853, was a fashion setter, whose clothes and appearance were commented on frequently in the British press. She was probably responsible for the introduction of the shorter skirt which led to a greater emphasis on stockings and shoes. *The Letters of Sir William Hardman* (1862) record that 'The girls of our time like to show their legs...it pleases them and does no harm to us; I speak for the married, not single men'. This trend was not, however, wholly approved of, and it is reported that the Emperor Franz Joseph of Austria, when assisting his Empress and Eugénie into his carriage, remarked quietly but pointedly to his wife, 'Be very careful, Madame, you are showing your feet'. However, the fashion persisted and in 1869 *The Ladies Treasury* commented 'Much more attention is paid to boots and shoes since the introduction of short dresses'.

Paris remained the centre of fashion in Europe until the Franco-Prussian war in 1870. Frivolous boots of silk and satin with high heels were imported from France, although French styles were also imitated by British shoemakers (plate 37). By about 1860, chemical aniline dyes had become widely available, providing a range of bright and often gaudy colours which added vibrant splashes to women's clothing. However, these faded quickly.

Mass Production and the Beginning of Large-scale Retailing

Shoes were being mass-produced by the middle of the nineteenth century. The sewing machine had become proficient for sewing cloth by the 1850s, and a machine for sewing leather was in use by 1856. Other machinery was developed for sewing on soles and for riveting. An example of the increasing impact of mechanization on shoe production is the firm of C. & J. Clark, which bought three treadle machines in 1856 and in 1858, and imported machines for cutting

soles from America. Leading shoemaking towns, such as Northampton, were quick to introduce equipment, although most encountered considerable opposition in the early years. Although mass production meant that cheaper footwear became available in greater numbers, handmade shoes retained a particular cachet, as they do now, and men who could afford to continued to buy them. Lilley & Skinner, founded in 1842, were amongst the first shoemakers to combine both wholesale and retail trades, selling their wares through other retailers, and they were to become pioneers of machine production in the shoe trade after the middle of the century.

The Return of the Heel for Women

'As for thin shoes, except for dancing they appear to have vanished from the female toilet', it was noted in *Punch* in 1859. Heels, in fashion again for women's shoes by the 1850s, were initially low, but increased in height to as much as $2^{1}/_{2}$ inches (6cms) in the 1860s. *The Lady's Magazine* in 1858 refers to 'elastic-sided boots for daywear and evening shoes with or without small heels and rosettes'. Six years later the same magazine described fashions in both boots and shoes as 'For day, with high pegtop heels. The toes nearly square; large rosettes. Evening shoes and boots, white for white dresses, blue or pink with dresses of those colours. Heels 1 inch; large rosettes'.

The low-cut slip-on shoe (plate 38) with a small heel was a forerunner of the court shoe which was to develop fully in the 1870s (see

Plate 38 opposite Pair of women's shoes, satin trimmed with silk ribbon, low heel; British, 1850s–60s. T.562&A–1913

Plate 39 right Woman's mule, low heel, satin with bead decoration; French, 1890s. T.305A–1977

plate 41), and variations of which have continued to be worn ever since. This style was much easier to wear than earlier fashions, and was an indicator of the greater freedom and mobility that some women began to demand as the century progressed. Many women's shoes continued to be made as 'straights' and this tradition was to persist until about 1900.

During the second half of the 1860s, the fashion for crinolines faded out and heavy corseting along with the back bustle came into fashion. These, combined with fashionable high-heeled boots (seen in plate 37), gave the wearer a characteristic posture known satirically as the 'Grecian bend', a name which also applied to the corset itself (fig. 17). *The Queen Magazine* for 14 October 1871 commented on the dangers of high-heeled boots:

Everyone who has noticed the height to which the heels of women's boots is now carried, must have marvelled much how the wearer could maintain her equilibrium, walking on stilts is nothing to it. It may be questioned how far the Grecian bend has become fashionable from a certain power it gives the wearers of the high heel to balance themselves.

Fashionable Casual Wear

The wearing of slippers indoors by women was necessitated by the fashion for boots. Following other shoe styles, heel-less mules or slippers were in fashion in about 1850; by the later 1850s some had heels and from the 1870s onwards the mule with heel was very popular (plate 39). Embroidery, bead-work, canvas-work and tapestry were all used to decorate slippers and mules, as seen in plates 32 and 39.

Men wore mules and carpet slippers. To demonstrate their domestic skills, women could embroider the ready-made uppers of slippers and other footwear for their menfolk (plate 34) as well as for themselves. Patterns for these were readily available, although the results were not always that attractive as the colours produced by chemical dyes, which were much favoured for the embroidery, were very gaudy. Other slippers were far more stylish (plate 40).

In the last quarter of the nineteenth century, there was an extraordinary variety of dress for women which reflected social change and the accelerating pace of fashion. Although the traditional role for women

Fig. 17 below Engraving of a woman in walking dress. From *English Woman's Domestic Magazine*, volume VI–VII, 1869. With a back bustle and high heels, the woman is shown bent forward from the waist in the so-called 'Grecian bend' stance. NAL. PP.19.F

Plate 40 opposite Man's slipper, snakeskin, lined with quilted silk; British, 1850s–60s. AP.6–1868

201.—WALKING TOILET.

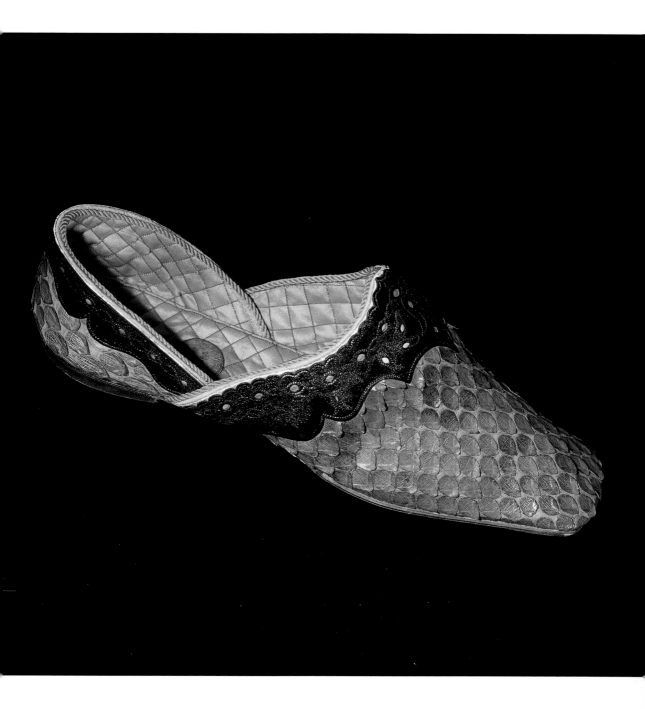

was being re-evaluated, there was still a reluctance to relinquish entirely the protected position they had always enjoyed. Fashions mirrored this ambiguity. There were several major changes in the line of fashionable dress during this period, including the long narrow line of the later 1870s and early 1880s, and an exaggerated bustle shape in the mid-1880s. By 1890 a change to a more horizontal emphasis was shown through fashions for leg-of-mutton sleeves and a stiff flared skirt. Also developing at this time were the more practical tailor-made costumes of matching dress or skirt and jacket. Clothes adapted for sportswear were increasingly in demand. Shoe styles reflected these conflicting attitudes, ranging from the completely impractical to more utilitarian and masculine forms.

Men's footwear, not surprisingly, was generally more sober and practical, reflecting prevailing styles of dress and lifestyle, but details in styling and materials gave them a fashionable edge.

Men's Shoes and Boots

Boots prevailed as fashionable footwear for men, often with stacked heels of about 1–1¼ inches (2.5–3cms) high. Elastic-sided boots (see plate 34) continued to be worn until nearly the end of the century. From 1876 there were indications of the more pointed toe, which developed after 1885. *The Gentlemen's Magazine of Fashion* in 1884 stated that 'modern trousers are close and small bottomed and require narrow pointed boots', and in 1885 *The Tailor and Cutter* described the bottom of trousers as 'cut well up on the boots to show the fancy patent buttoned boots which are now much worn' (fig. 18).

From about 1885 until the end of the century, the fashion for pointed toes showed the influence of American styles. The most extreme point was called 'the toothpick'. From the late 1890s and for the first decade and a half of the new century, the prevailing line for the toe was long, with a small number having the spade-shaped Continental toe. By 1910 the Bulldog or Boston toe had also arrived from America, where it had been fashionable since the late 1890s.

In the last quarter of the century Oxfords and Derbys were the most popular practical lace-ups, and from about 1905 the brogued shoe came into more general use.

Illustration of British Costume,
SUMMER 1885.

Fig. 18 above Man wearing narrow trousers and pointed-toed boots. Plate from *Tailor and Cutter,* volume XX, 1885.
NAL. PP.42.B

Shoes Return to Fashion for Women

'The fashion of shoes instead of boots is quite a revolution in female toilets', reported the *Englishwoman's Domestic Magazine* in 1874, and by 1883 the same magazine was declaring 'Boots are scarcely ever seen in town on well-dressed women'. The rather broad and rounded toes favoured by both men and women in the 1870s (plate 41) were succeeded by the female fashion for more pointed toes in the 1880s, already popular in Paris. As the century drew to a close, leather again became fashionable for women's shoes and some masculine styles, including the Oxford, were worn for walking.

In contrast to these practical examples, the heels of stylish shoes reached an extreme of $6^{1}/_{2}$ inches (16cms) in the 1890s (dubbed the 'naughty nineties') although, unfortunately, this extreme is not represented in the V&A's collection. One fashionable high-heeled shoe with buckle was called the Cromwell, in the mistaken belief that buckles were favoured in the Cromwellian period (plate 42 and fig. 19). Other styles were called after women in the public eye, including the Langtry, named after the actress Lily Langtry, which was popular in the late nineteenth to early twentieth century. Court shoes, some with bows and often beaded, remained a constant feature throughout the period.

Although there had been reactionary movements against restrictive women's clothing since the 1850s, the ambiguous attitude towards women and their clothes was reflected in the Edwardian period. Until the outbreak of the First World War, the majority of women were still wearing full-length skirts, tightly laced corsets, boned bodices and high-heeled shoes, as confining as any nineteenth-century fashions. Although the very high heel disappeared and was even stated to be 'highly objectionable', both boots and shoes continued to have heels of between 2 and $2^{1}/_{2}$ inches (5–6cms), including the Cuban heel (fig. 19), which first appeared in 1904.

Plate 41 below Women's court shoes with low heels. Top (a): Shoe with tapestry-woven upper and small decorative buckle; British, 1870s. The upper was imported from Turkey. From the time of the Crimean War (1854–56), Turkish styles of dress and materials had influenced aspects of fashionable dress in Britain.
T.583–1913
Bottom (b): Ribbed silk shoe with bow; British, 1870s.
T.33D–1932

Overshoes, Country Wear and the Influence of Outdoor Sports

Overshoes were worn by women to protect the flimsy footwear of the 1830s to 1850s. The patten was flat with square toes to match the shoes and had velvet or patent covered leather straps. One form of overshoe made of patent leather and hinged across the ball of the foot was listed on a trade card of 1835, and an example of this type, shown at the Great Exhibition of 1851, is now in the V&A. Overshoes or goloshes of rubber, mainly worn by men, were available for bad weather or outdoor wear and, after the 1830s, soles of india-rubber began to be used for boots. In 1874, Francis Kilvert noted in his diary that he bought a pair of 'ten shilling gutta-percha-soled elastic boots' from Decks of Salisbury.

Shoes with spats and gaiters were fashionable outdoor wear for men and women. Short gaiters or spats which covered the ankles were fashionable for town wear from the 1870s. Sometimes they were made of the same cloth as the trousers but more often of light grey or fawn boxcloth or canvas, with side-buttoning and fastening under the instep with a buckle or strap (plate 43a). In the countryside, cloth and leather gaiters buttoned higher up the leg, like those worn for some sports, gave extra protection.

Plate 42 above Woman's shoe, suede with medium heel and buckle; British, 1905–10. This shape of heel is sometimes described as a Louis heel. T.149–1960

Fig. 19 opposite Advertisement for women's shoes, 1911. V&A Textile and Dress Archive

Plate 43 opposite, right Top (a): Man's boot with gaiters; British, c.1900. T.6A–1970 Bottom (b): Women's boot with gaiters; British, c.1910. From the 1890s until about 1920, it became acceptable for women's boots and shoes to show the foot's natural size, contrasting with the impossibly small sizes that were 'de rigueur' previously. T.147–1960

Some more practical forms of dress had begun to emerge in the nineteenth century as a result of the increasing popularity of sport and leisure activities. Croquet became popular and a magazine (name unknown) of 1867 explained the immense attraction for men: 'One of the chief reasons of the pleasure men take in the game is the sight of a neatly turned ankle and pretty boots'. Tennis was played by women in a blouse and shorter skirt, thus drawing more attention to feet neatly clad in patent leather pumps. A lady wearing 'cycling dress' in the 1890s with knicker-type, knee-length trousers, wore long leggings or boots with buttoned gaiters. Similarly, boots or shoes with cloth gaiters were worn for golf by women in the early 1900s, with a jacket and a skirt which was as much as 6 inches (15cms) off the ground.

Boots and shoes worn by men for sports such as shooting and golf were generally brown, with tan and white favoured in some circles for sportswear. This was adopted in the fashionable two-tone shoe style of the 1930s and 1940s, sometimes known as the 'co-respondent' shoe and seen in plate 50.

Chapter Eight

Austerity and Glamour: 1914–1939

The spirit of practical common sense which has prompted the adoption of suitable attire for the project in hand, is quite naturally also influencing modern dress of every description. (*Fashions for All,* December 1916)

The First World War brought about new attitudes towards dress. Although women had already begun to rebel against unhygienic and restrictive clothing, war conditions were a catalyst for swifter change. By 1916 a significant number of women were participating in the war effort, undertaking a wide range of duties from driving ambulances to replacing male labour in the factories. The work demanded functional, hardwearing and comfortable footwear. Pictures of elegant and stylish shoes still graced the pages of fashion magazines, but as the war continued it was the lower-heeled and sturdier models which filled the advertising spaces (fig. 20). Shoe manufacturers such as Delta, Lotus and Manfield & Sons increasingly emphasised the 'dependable quality', 'wear', 'comfort' and 'splendid service' of their products rather than their chic appeal or decorative qualities.

As the war progressed, extravagance in dress was generally viewed as unpatriotic and even distasteful. Fashion magazines still encouraged women to look stylish to help keep up morale, but they were careful to distinguish between what they portrayed as vanity and innate self-respect. Shoes were described as 'quiet but distinctive', and black remained a dominant colour as so many women were in mourning. Although official restrictions were less stringent than in the Second World War (1939–1945), shortages of materials and a luxury tax on clothes did bring about a degree of economy. 'Cloth-top shoes' became popular in 1918 due to the scarcity of leather, and the magazine *Fashions for All* gave instructions on how to make 'pretty

June, 1916

Manfield
& SONS

**SPENDING
WISELY**

228 & 229
PICCADILLY
LONDON. W.

Branches through
out London and
United Kingdom

There is no point in buying
common footwear, and pre-
tending it is economy. That
does not conform to the
spirit of the times, nor
assist either the labour or the financial position.

Sound value put into a tasteful form—such
as Manfield's standard lines offer—is the true
note of economy. The footwear procured
should give lasting service, and be a source of
pleasure so long as it lasts. No one is called
upon to look unattractive, but to purchase
carefully, and to use such purchases to the
best advantage, is the plain duty of all.

An example is given to illustrate the argument (L622, 13/9), but
it is merely an example,
for Manfield's entire
stock is made up of
styles of equal value
and distinctiveness.

Write for Catalogue.

Fig. 20 above British shoe
advertisement, 1916. From
Fashions for All, June 1916.

NAL. PP.7 AAW

shoe ornaments' from an old pair of paste buttons surrounded 'by a frill of coloured tulle to match the frock' (January 1917).

The Winds of Change

The end of the war brought gloomy prospects for the British shoe industry. Many of its skilled workers had been lost, the economy was in recession, and America had taken a lead in the manufacture of machine-made footwear. Shoe styles altered very little and some companies re-advertised pre-1914 models under different names in an attempt to dispose of old stock. Although the situation was slow to improve, signs of change had appeared by 1920. Hemlines had risen during the years of the war and the new simpler cut of women's clothes gave shoes an even greater prominence. Fashion magazines stressed the importance of smart footwear and pointed out that the wrong shoes could spoil the effect of an outfit. The short-fronted toe became fashionable as it made the foot look smaller (plate 44a), T-bars were introduced and heels increased in height. Chequered designs and appliqué trimmings adorned many shoes, and black was often combined with white or grey in styles worn for half-mourning. There was also a huge range of ornaments to choose from, and iridescent bead insects, gauze butterflies and ornate paste buckles could transform an ordinary shoe into something new and distinctive:

Time was, not so long ago, when women's shoes were for the most part utilitarian, the majority of them boasting but a demure black bow, or plain steel buckle of modest dimensions. Of late years, however, with the increasing variety of material and design in footwear, has come also the greater prominence of the buckle or ornament, and to-day these exist in a profusion greater than ever before (*The Footwear Organiser*, January 1920).

By October 1921 several palatial shoe shops had opened in the West End, and the introduction of stylish new designs increased demand for British footwear abroad. High-heeled shoes with cut-

away straps and elongated toes emphasised the elegance of a shapely ankle, and small decorative buckles known as 'fastenettes' provided a chic alternative to the button side fastening (seen in plate 44a). The increasing popularity of novelty designs also infused many styles with a sense of fun. Celluloid heels were produced in tortoise-shell, mother-of-pearl and clouded gold effects, and some were even hand-painted with brightly coloured figures, flowers and birds.

The latest shoe fashions were not to everyone's taste; an article entitled 'Sensible Shoes for Sensible Women. A Challenge to the Industry. By "An Average Woman"' stated that: 'there is a large and an

Plate 44 opposite Left (a):
Patent leather woman's
shoe, decorated with
interlaced leather; British,
1918–20. The bar-strap has
two button side fastenings
and the toe is short and
rounded. T.291-1970
Right (b): Man's shoe
decorated with interlaced
leather; British (Rushden,
Northamptonshire), *c*.1925.
Made by the COX-TON Shoe
Company. The name was
derived from those of the
two company directors: Mr
Cox and Mr Newton. T.53-1996

Plate 45 opposite, below
Patent leather woman's
shoes with intaglio
decoration and grosgrain
underlay; Italian, late 1920s
to early 1930s. Based on
the traditional Scottish
ghillie. Three tabs project
from either side of the instep
but in this instance the
metal, twisted cord is
threaded through eyelet
holes and not loops. They
have low heels and square
toes. T.491&A-1974

ever-increasing number of women, who...prefer health and comfort
to appearance, and could not under any pretext be induced to
squeeze their feet into...idiotic, high-heeled, unhygienic footwear'
(*The Footwear Organiser,* July 1921.) The writer described the 'almost
insurmountable difficulties' involved in finding a sensible shoe with a
moderate heel that fitted well, looked neat and was moderately
priced. Like many others, she refused to 'crib, cabin and confine' her
feet in styles that bore no relation to their size or shape, and protested
against the 'heavy, ugly shoes with exaggeratedly square toes and
thick soles only suitable to wear on ploughed fields'.

Although such complaints were often met with surprise or dis-
missed, the predicament of the 'average woman' did improve. The
growing popularity of sports, and women's more active participation
in them, increased demand for comfortable, stylish footwear. By the
late 1920s sporting dress had entered the realm of haute-couture and
flat, lace-tied shoes, such as ghillies (see plate 45), appeared in *Vogue*
magazine alongside more formal high-heeled designs.

In Full Swing: 1924–27

As hemlines rose towards the knee, shoes and stockings became focal
points of fashion (fig. 21). In March 1926 British *Vogue* announced:

...shoes are such a perpetually intrusive and interesting subject in this mode
that spot-lights the feet and legs that there is always more to be said. For the
tailored suit or dress there is the Oxford with its high Cuban heel; for the more
formal costume there is still the Oxford, this time with a high spike heel. For
those whose ankles are not impeccable there is the less trying high-cut pump
or the even more flattering one-strap shoe.

New ranges of footwear captivated the public eye and designs
changed radically from one season to the next. Although the bar shoe
prevailed, 'low-cut' Oxfords with slender, tapering heels became
increasingly fashionable for day as well as evening wear. Daring
colour combinations and bold decoration also created new and striking effects, particularly when worn for dancing. Colourful beadwork
complemented the beaded fringes on evening dresses, and gold kid
ornamented with distinctive motifs (plate 46a) reflected the vogue for

'Oriental' designs. Some shoes were even hand-painted to match the gown (plate 46b), and several footwear companies offered a dyeing service.

Men's shoe styles changed very little compared to the transformations taking place in women's fashions. Black or brown laced shoes continued to predominate and boots remained popular, although they gradually fell out of favour for smarter wear. Many styles were lightly brogued but flamboyant footwear was still frowned upon and etiquette strictly followed. Even shoes of the wrong colour could excite comment, and one etiquette book exclaimed: 'I actually saw a man in the Carlton Hotel entrance hall one night last summer, wearing brown shoes, a dinner jacket, and a straw hat. He was presumably an American, but even so...!' (G.F. Curtis, *Clothes and the Man, 1926*).

Despite prevailing attitudes, the shoes manufactured by the COX-TON Shoe Company (plates 44b and 47) show that there was a market for bold colours and innovative designs. They were displayed at the London International Shoe and Leather Fair in 1925, and may have been intended for the American buyer who was more liberated in his choice of clothing. However, as the decade progressed, the popularity of sports and outdoor pursuits encouraged a more relaxed approach towards dressing in Britain. The Prince of Wales led the way in promoting less formal styles, and his love of golf enabled him to indulge these tastes in the public eye. He was a resplendent figure on the links, and among the many fashions he helped to popularise were two-tone brogues with fringed or shawl tongues.

Thirties Glamour

As the twenties drew to a close, more subtle colour combinations and sleeker designs shaped the style of women's shoes. The tailored look of the 1930s and long sinuous evening gowns demanded an even simpler covering for the foot, and British *Vogue* (March 1935) advised

Fig. 21 above Fashion plate from *The Drapers' Organiser*; British, February 1925. The women's afternoon and evening gowns are worn with T-bar shoes (right) and court shoes (left). NAL. PP.9.T

Fig. 22 opposite Shoe advertisement; British or American, 1930s. V&A Textiles and Dress Archive

its readers, 'In planning a wardrobe remember that as clothes make the woman, so accessories often make the clothes'. High-heeled bar and lace-tied shoes remained popular, but clean, elegant lines with discreet trimmings now became the focus of fashion (fig. 22). Dark colours such as 'fir green', 'Havana brown', navy blue and black predominated for daytime wear, complementing the tweeds, flannels and more sombre shades of the tailored garments. Richly coloured velvet (plate 46c), crêpe de Chine and satin shoes were fashionable for evening, often matching the luxurious fabrics of the dresses. Gold or silver piping added elegance to the simplest style, and cut-away lamé shoes set off the glamour of fluid neoclassical-style gowns.

By 1935 sports, fitness and rambling clubs were promoting a greater awareness of physical health, which extended to the well-being of the foot. Manufacturers and beauty editors warned against the dangers of wearing high heels, and set out the ailments caused by rigid or tight-fitting footwear. Although many formal day and evening shoes

remained high-heeled, they were now designed to give the foot greater support. Flatter heels and rounder toes became popular, and many shoe designers experimented with flexible 'ortho-paedic' soles. Leisure wear such as open-toed sandals, previously restricted to the resort, became acceptable elsewhere. In May 1936, for example, *Vogue* ran a feature on smart daytime dresses designed by Edward Molyneux, Jacques Heim and Robert Piguet which included peep-toed shoes with cross-over straps and sling-back heels.

Increasing freedom in dress also resulted in exciting and inno-vative ideas. In the late 1930s wedge heels and platform shoes swept into fashion, popularised by the Italian designer, Salvatore Ferragamo. Wedges had already been seen on 1920s rubber bathing shoes and resort sandals, but Ferragamo brought this style up to date with modernistic designs, 'spool' heels, and layered cork soles. He also designed extraordinary platform-soled sandals inset with mosaics of gilded glass, encrusted with jewels and covered with rainbows of coloured suede (plate 48). Roger Vivier and André Perugia created equally dazzling styles and soon British *Vogue* was tempting its readers with bulky cork

Plate 46 opposite Women's evening shoes. Bottom (a): Leather T-bar shoe decorated with painted motifs; Monaco, *c.*1925. By A. Rambaldi. T.313–1975
Middle (b): Silk satin court shoe with a hand-painted bird motif and beaded ornament; British, 1922. Worn with a matching dress and headband. Made by Stead & Simpson Ltd; the painting was executed by the Misses Parkin. The heel is also painted, and the long pointed tongue is very similar to that in fig. 11. T.737B–1974
Top (c): Velvet shoe with silk satin covered heel and diamanté ornament on the bar-strap; British, *c.*1930. Made by Rayne Shoes Ltd. T.145:1–1997

Plate 47 right Men's shoes made by the COX-TON Shoe Company. Left (a): Shoe of marbled suede with gilt leather decoration; British (Rushden, Northamptonshire), *c.*1925. T.53–1996
Centre (b): Leather shoe with applied gilt leather decoration; British (Rushden, Northamptonshire), *c.*1925. T.56–1996
Right (c): Leather shoe with applied gilt leather decoration; British (Rushden, Northamptonshire), *c.*1925. T.59–1996

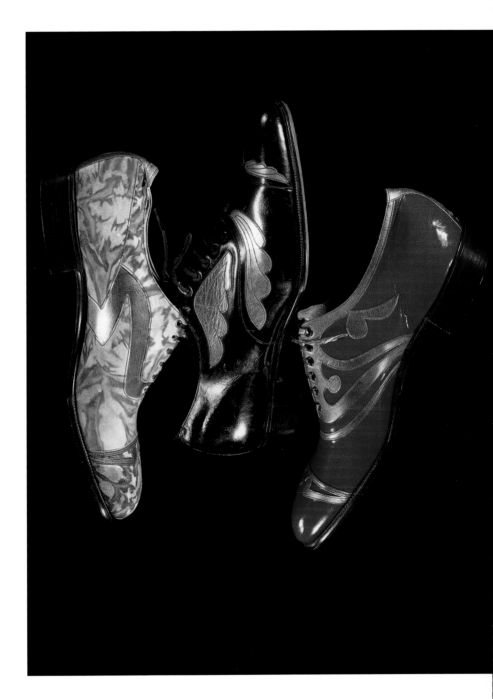

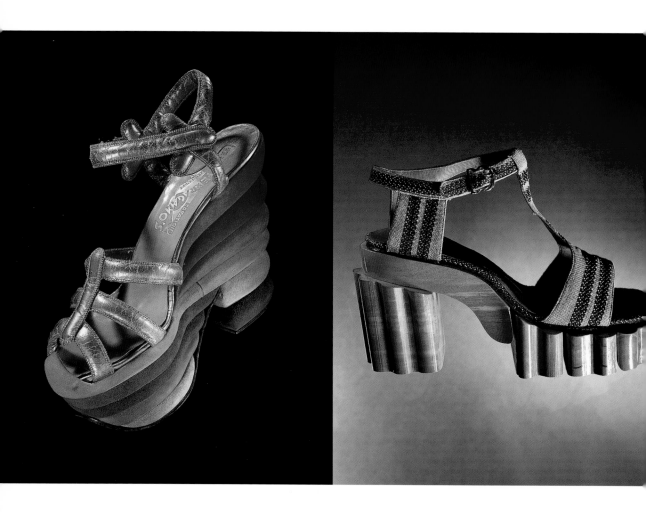

Plate 48 opposite, left
Woman's platform sandal
with padded kid straps;
Italian, 1938. By Salvatore
Ferragamo. The sole is
composed of cork layers
covered with various
coloured suedes. Given by
Sra. Wanda Ferragamo.
T.84–1988

Plate 49 opposite Woman's
sandal with striped canvas
upper and wooden platform
sole; British, *c.*1938. The
front part of the sole is
hinged to give more flexibility
when walking. Part of a
beach outfit, worn with
matching jacket, shorts and
bathing cloak. The insole is
stamped with gilt lettering:
'BUNTING Paris, established
1913 London'. T.301E–1971

Plate 50 right Left (a):
Man's 'two-tone' shoe;
British, late 1930s. Made by
Saxone. Brown leather and
white suede upper with a
pointed toe and low, stacked
heel. T.112–1985
Right (b): Woman's 'two-tone'
court shoe; British, mid to
late 1930s. White buckskin
and brown calf with punched
decoration. T.271–1977

wedges, 'corkscrew heels', hinged soles (plate 49) and chunky 'cut-out clogs': 'It's no sin to call a shoe clumsy, these days. It's a compliment. If you haven't already worn a platform or a wedge sole, do have a pair or two of autumn shoes with this new thick look. Have them to wear chiefly with your street or sports clothes' (October 1938).

Changes in men's footwear were less dramatic. A few new styles developed, such as the casual moccasin, and sandals became more acceptable for summer wear. Two-tone sports shoes continued to offer a flamboyant alternative to traditional Oxford and Derby styles, and by the late 1930s a wider variety of colours and designs was available (plate 50a). Women's shoes also followed this trend (plate 50b), and a Lilley & Skinner advertisement of May 1935 proclaimed: 'You must, of course, have at least one pair of "white and – " shoes. They can even make you look spring-like in your old pleated skirt and jumper, and are invaluable later on to wear with light-weight frocks'.

Chapter Nine

Forty Years of Innovation: 1939–1979

Proper cleaning prolongs the life of leather – and that is now an affair of national importance. Your shoes can last the duration if you pay a good price for them, keep them well polished, correctly treed and regularly mended. (*Vogue,* June 1941)

The Second World War: Women's Shoes

When the war began in September 1939, women were still wearing fashions strongly influenced by Paris. The French capital ceased to be the centre of fashion when it fell in 1940, and Britain turned to New York as well as its own designers for inspiration.

Fashion of the war period was described as 'dictated fashion' and 'purposive but not expressive' by C. Willett Cunnington in *English Women's Clothing in the Present Century,* written from the immediately post-war perspective of 1951. These comments do not allow for the ingenuity of women who, with home dress-making skills and details such as bright make-up, scarves and colourful shoes, could make an outfit expressive of personality and style.

Wartime austerity prevented any complete expression of fashion in Britain, but some innovative and subtly elegant styles of footwear were produced as well as large numbers of practical, flat shoes without any stylish pretentions. Although more serviceable, modest and sturdy than before, the fashionable shoe for this period can nevertheless be seen as a continuation of 1930s styles. Toes which had been rounded became blunter and even square, and the peep toe, regarded as both frivolous and potentially 'dangerous', was banned for fashion shoes until after the war. The wedge heels made fashionable in the 1930s, and also found in modified form on sensible walking shoes, came into much more general use during the war.

Wedges made of cork and wood, harking back to the materials used for the wedge-heeled shoes of the late sixteenth century, replaced the high heels of the 1930s.

Wartime restrictions in the United States were generally less draconian than in Britain; however, shoe designs were under strict limitations and the height of heels was limited to one inch (2.5cms). In Britain two inches (5cms) was the maximum height allowed. Flat shoes and wedge heels complemented the prevailing styles of tailored suits, influenced by military uniforms, and the wide-legged slacks or boiler-suits worn for work or leisure.

British haute couture designers, including Hardy Amies, Norman Hartnell, Digby Morton, Victor Stiebel and Molyneux were closely involved in producing prototype Utility designs for mass production. These were first featured in fashion magazines in March 1942. The Utility scheme had to comply with the 'Making up of Civilian Clothing (Restriction)' orders introduced in spring 1942 which, amongst other things, restricted amounts and types of material used, and fixed prices.

The limitations on style and decoration, dictated both by lack of the usual resources (principally leather) and a sensibility as to what was appropriate for wartime, were balanced by the use of bright and interesting colours, as in a shoe advertised in *Vogue* in 1941: 'High leather shoe, wine, blue, green or black uppers; blue, wine or red wedge and platform sole; zip side fastening. 49/6'.

Inferior grade leathers were disguised with bright hues. Indeed, leather was in such short supply by 1941 that shoes were amongst the commodities traded on the black market. Cheap materials, both natural and synthetic, were utilised on a much larger scale than previously. In addition to low-grade leather, these included cork, wood (as mentioned earlier for heels) and rubber. Strong fabrics, such as canvas, were used for uppers, crêpe was used for soles, and plastic for straps. Many shoes were made of multi-coloured suede remnants and some were made of felt (plate 51). Raffia sandals with cork soles and heels were worn on the beach or for leisurewear. For a short period in 1943 wooden-soled shoes, rated at only two coupons in the ration book, were introduced to 'eke out the nation's leather' (Cunnington). Some

Plate 51 above Pair of women's Utility shoes or slippers; British, early 1940s. Felt and canvas, with wedge heel covered in cotton showing the use of colourful but cheap materials for wartime shoes. The sole is made of a grey composition material, with the Utility mark 'CC 20126 S/W2 4' stamped on it in blue ink.
T.21–1979; T.21A–1979

were hinged across the sole to make walking easier, as certain pattens had been in the nineteenth century.

Extracts from the instructions relating to rationing appeared in the national newspapers on 3 June 1941, explaining the premise of rationing as follows:

Rationing has been introduced, not to deprive you of your real needs, but to make more certain that you get your share of the country's goods – to get fair shares with everybody else. When the shops open you will be able to buy cloth, clothes, footwear and knitting wool *only if you bring your Food Ration Book with you.*

The following extract from the Rationing Table of 1941 shows how shoes were rated compared to other articles of clothing:

Men and Boys	Adult	Child
Coat or jacket, or blazer like garment	13	8
Trousers (other than fustianor corduroy)	8	6
Pair of slippers or goloshes	4	2
Pair of boots or shoes	7	3
Pair of leggings, gaiters or spats	3	2

Women and Girls	Adult	Child
Dress or gown, or frock – woollen	11	8
Overalls or dungarees or like garment	6	4
Pair of slippers, boots or shoes	5	3

Initially the allowance was 66 coupons a year per person but in spring 1942 it was reduced to 60 for 15 months, that is, approximately 48 coupons per year.

Men's Shoes

Fashions in men's shoes continued during the war much as they had previously. In keeping with the spirit of the time, they were modest and practical (plate 52). Men at this time generally had fairly conventional attitudes to clothing, and since large numbers of them were in military uniform, restrictions on footwear did not have the same implications for them as they had for women.

As in the 1930s, men's trousers had a wide leg and to complement this look shoes were heavy duty. Brogues were correspondingly sturdier in the 1930s and 1940s than they had been before. Black was still considered appropriate for town, although brown laced leather shoes were increasingly popular. Suede, previously thought to have 'raffish' connotations, was becoming more acceptable. Two-colour sports shoes were also in fashion. Boots were less fashionable than previously and mostly worn by older men. Gaiters and spats were still in sufficient demand to warrant their listing in the rationing coupons table of 1941.

Plate 52 right Pair of men's Oxford lace-up shoes; British, *c*.1945–50. The instep of the sole has the Utility mark 'CC V3282'.

T.150&A–1980

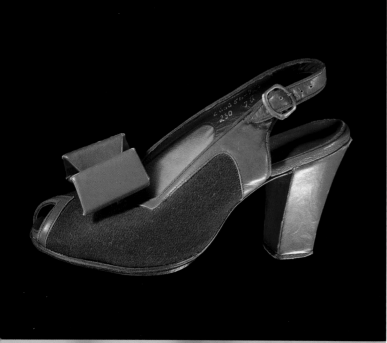

Plate 53 above left
Woman's shoe with peep-toe
and leather bow; British,
*c.*1947. T.153–1973

Plate 54 left Woman's shoe,
black suede peep toe,
'pearl' ankle strap;
American, *c.*1945–50.
Inscribed inside: 'c.h.baker
california "too smart for
words"'. T.283–1975

Once the war was over (1945), seven styles of demobilisation ('demob') shoe became available. Representing styles popular at that time, all were lace-ups with five pairs of eyelets, as in the Utility shoe shown in plate 52. They included three Oxfords, two Derbys and one brown suede shoe.

Women's Shoes: 1947–1950s

A transitional period in shoe styles for women came after the war, with a return in many respects to the styles of the 1930s. Although rationing continued until 1952, a release from the restrictions on style led to the re-introduction of more frivolous and feminine pre-war styles, such as the peep-toe and high heels (plates 53 and 54). Snub toes were back in fashion and decorative details, such as bows, were added. Ankle boots were also fashionable in the late 1940s, perched on a high, narrowish heel. Sandals with wedges or platform soles were popular summer wear. The sturdy shapes of wartime shoes were thus refined but did not immediately change into the radically pared-back lines characteristic of 1950s and early 1960s high fashion shoes (plate 58).

Men's Shoes Post-war

Rationing and Utility during the war had discouraged extravagence, but although rationing continued after the war, new styles were appearing from 1947. However, traditional lace-ups continued to be the most popular form of men's footwear. In the late 1940s American fashions, notably the 'Zoot Suit', were already appearing in British shops, but it was not until the 1950s that, for the first time in British history, a separate youth culture with its own fashions became established alongside mainstream design. Shoe styles, like other elements of dress, were part of this change. Graduates of the newly established Royal College of Art Fashion Design course in London did not move into couture but into the boutique market. Mary Quant, a fine arts graduate of London's Goldsmith's College, received her only formal training for the fashion world at evening courses in pattern cutting. She opened her first boutique, 'Bazaar', in 1955.

With the fashion for tapered trousers in the 1950s, fashionable shoes generally became narrower at the toe also, corresponding to the fashion of the preceding decades for wearing chunky shoes with wide trousers. The long pointed toe was an import from the United States, where it was worn in Harlem by black and Hispanic youths. The extremely long Winklepicker was originally worn by working-class youths, and can be compared to the fifteenth-century poulaine (plate 2a), although the 1950s version never reached the extreme length of its medieval antecedent. The style became more widely accepted and Winkle-pickers were also produced by mainstream shoe designers (plate 55).

A complete antithesis to the narrow pointed shoe was the thick, crêpe-soled Brothel Creeper, with strap or buckle fastening, worn with even narrower trousers ('drainpipes') than those of more mainstream fashion. This style became known as the 'Edwardian' or 'teddy boy' look. The more conventional-looking Desert boot, introduced in 1950, was a refined version of the suede, crêpe-soled boots made in Cairo during the Second World War for officers of General Montgomery's Eighth Army, which fought in the North African desert. It, too, was adopted by British youth and worn by 'Mods' in the 1960s. Desert boots have subsequently become a 'streetstyle' classic.

By contrast, a more upper-class 'preppy' look was imported from the United States in the 1950s in the form of the Loafer, a casual slip-on shoe worn by men and women, which became particularly popular in the 1960s.

High Heels

The first New Look suit, 'Bar', designed by Christian Dior in 1947, shows the model wearing the characteristic jacket with nipped in waist and wide, flowing skirt. The ensemble is completed by hat, gloves and shoes with pointed toes and narrow high heels, an early version of the stiletto heel (fig. 23).

Although the fashion world turned again to Paris after the Second World War, the Italians had also become a force to be reckoned with in shoe design. They competed with French designers to slim down

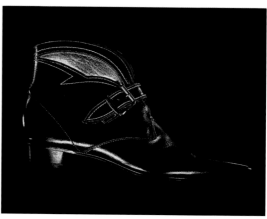

Plate 55 above Man's winklepicker ankle boot; British, *c.*1959–60. Made by Olivers. Leather with gold leather inserts and decorative stitching. T.68A–1978

Fig. 23 opposite New Look outfit, 'Bar', 1947. By Christian Dior. © ADAGP. Paris and DACS, London 1999.

the heel as much as was physically possible. It is not clear who produced it first, but Roger Vivier, Dior's shoe designer, is usually credited with making the first true stiletto in 1954 or 1955. Described as the *talon aiguille* (needle heel), it was reinforced with steel to prevent it from snapping.

In spite of Marilyn Monroe's famous comment, 'I don't know who invented the high heel. But all women owe him a lot' (quoted in *The Sex Life of the Boot and Shoe,* William Rossi, 1976), the stiletto was bad for both wearer and environment, notoriously gouging holes in wooden floors. Stilettos appeared on court shoes and pumps, and the style, although continuing into the 1960s, peaked in about 1958 when Dior introduced the T-strap and wedge toe.

In the 1960s, the centre of the fashion world shifted from Paris to London for both haute couture and streetstyle. Designer shoemakers came into prominence in the 1960s, including Richard Smith who, with Mandy Wilkins, started Chelsea Cobbler in 1967 and later opened a boutique with the same name. Smith created innovative and extravagent designs for a wealthy young clientele, including a pair of cream leather shoes with 'butterfly wings' (*c*.1971), worn by Tolhita Getty and given to the V&A by Mr Paul Getty Junior in 1974.

Classic Men's Shoes

Ankle boots, already back in fashion in the 1950s, remained at the forefront of men's fashionable footwear in the 1960s. The simple but stylish Chelsea boot with elastic sides, first produced in the late 1950s and initially regarded as rather Bohemian, sold in large numbers. It returns to fashion from time to time, including a period in the 1970s, and is a direct descendant of the nineteenth-century elastic-sided boot. The Beatles popularised the Chelsea boot, and made famous another type of ankle boot with side-zip and Cuban heel, which was daringly high for the time. The Desert boot of the 1950s remained popular in the 1960s and 1970s and is now, like the Chelsea boot, regarded as an all-time classic.

Traditional men's shoes continued to be produced, and the beautifully hand-crafted British brogue remained desirable for the discerning male customer. Another classic, worn for formal and evening wear

and based on earlier models (see plate 33), was the low-heeled pump. This continued to be made by established firms specialising in hand-made bespoke footwear, such as John Lobb, and the V&A collection includes a pair worn and given by Cecil Beaton (later Sir Cecil Beaton), dating from around 1960.

Classic and Dashing Designs in Women's Shoes

At the top end of the market, the court shoe remained the classic style for town wear. Since the 1950s, British court shoes had been regarded as the finest in the world. Edward Rayne was one of the leading post-war designers of such traditional styles, which remain in demand for a discerning clientele (see plate 58). The stiletto and other contemporary styles were also included in his range of footwear.

Plate 56 below Selection of heels by H. and M. Rayne Shoes Ltd. V&A Textiles and Dress Department: Rayne archive

Plate 57 right Man's 'space' boot, patent leather with zip fastening; French (Paris) 1967. Part of the 'Cosmos' outfit by Pierre Cardin, Autumn/Winter 1967. T.703D–1974

From the late 1950s lower heels became fashionable and toes longer, giving a foretaste of the revival of 1920's styles which occurred in the 1960s. At the beginning of the decade, toes became square and heels thicker. Designers such as Roger Vivier and Charles Jourdan produced examples of this type in silk for evening wear, often lavishly decorated and made to match couture ensembles (see plate 59).

The choice of materials for shoes underwent radical changes in the 1960s, partly due to a steep rise in leather prices. Plastics and other synthetics with 'wet-look' finishes complemented the 'space-age' geometric look promoted by fashion designers André Courrèges and Pierre Cardin (plate 57). Courrèges' 1964 'Space Age' collection included flat-heeled, shiny white boots with square toes, which came halfway up the thigh. Mary Quant, one of the most influential British

Plate 58 opposite Women's shoes; British, 1950s–70s. By H. and M. Rayne Shoes Ltd. Far left (a): Green leather sandal, high heeled, *c.*1977–8; Left (b): blue satin 'stiletto' shoe with diamanté trim, *c.*1963; Right (c): Pink leather high-heeled mule, 1979; Far right (d): brown crocodile leather 'stiletto' shoe, late 1950s. V&A Textiles and Dress Department: Rayne archive

Plate 59 right Women's evening shoes. Left (a): Silk shoe with diamanté-studded perspex heel; French, 1967. By Charles Jourdan. T.113–1988 Right (b): Silk satin shoe, trimmed with paste-studded band; French, *c.*1965. By Roger Vivier. T.224B–1976 Bottom (c): Silk satin shoe, with applied gold braid, pastes and sequins; French (Paris), 1952–54. By Christian Dior, Paris. T.147–1974

designers of the period, adopted this idea using injection-moulded plastic. Amongst other styles, she designed square-toed boots cut away at the ankle and bearing the Quant trademark – a daisy – on the heel. Clear plastic shoes were introduced by designers, including the American Herbert Levine, and Roger Vivier. Vivier and other top Parisian designers were by this time responding to new demands and seeking a niche for themselves in the youth market. Vivier's low-heeled Pilgrim pump with silver buckles first appeared in 1962 to accompany the cutting-edge Parisian couturier Yves Saint Laurent's 'Mondrian' collection. It was the most imitated shoe of the 1960s, being sufficiently versatile to appeal to both traditionalists and those looking for new styles.

The mini-skirt burst onto the fashion scene in the mid-1960s, and for the first time a great expanse of female leg was exposed. Boots, both long and short, were the ideal accessory to complement the mini-skirt. André Courrèges and Mary Quant, both of whom have been credited with introducing the mini-skirt, did much to promote the fashion for boots. These became the major fashion feature of the 1960s, initially teamed with the mini-skirt but later in the decade with the maxi-skirt. 'Biba' (the trademark of the designer Barbara Hulanicki and the name given to her boutiques) became synonymous with a wide range of clothes, including long boots in a variety of materials. These were dyed in a wonderful array of sludgy colours ranging from pinks and chocolate brown to plum and subtle mauves (plate 60).

In complete contrast to the rage for boots, very feminine shoes were also in vogue, produced from the early 1960s. Low-heeled pumps, bar shoes, and slightly later shoes with ankle straps became available in a range of mouthwatering colours. These styles, harking back to fashions of the 1920s, were based on ballet and tap-shoes. Like the boots, these were often worn by leggy girls in mini-skirts, most famously by Twiggy (Lesley Hornby), the British model who is so closely identified with the youth fashions of this era.

Fashion in the 1970s was a melting pot of styles. The statement 'Be yourself in fashion and you can live nine lives at once'(*Vogue*, March 1974), captures the mood of the time. At the traditional end of the market, classic shoes for both men and women continued to be

Plate 60 opposite Pair of boots, canvas with platform heel; British, 1969–70. By Biba. T.67&A–1985

produced, while street fashion increasingly diversified. 'Pyschedelic' was a term in current coinage, used to describe subcultural and fashionable styles from around 1967. In the context of clothes and footwear, Art Nouveau revival styles were combined with dayglo colours, which were seen in abundance. Elements of ethnic styles, including Afro-Caribbean and Asian, were incorporated first into hippy fashion and then more widely adopted. The creativity of the early seventies encompassed new fabrics, finishes and shapes, often taking old styles such as platforms and wedges and re-working them. Toes were generally blunt or square.

An advertisement in *Vogue,* May 1971, for three styles of knee-length boots by Chelsea Cobbler – one made of bright towelling patches, the second of cotton Madras check, and the third wedge-heeled with bright stars on lilac canvas – sported the caption, 'What's a nice boot doing in a fabric like this?'. This encapsulated the 'unconventional' aesthetics of the new fabrics and designs, which no doubt made them instantly attractive to the young. Knee or thigh-length boots remained bestsellers, the latter worn with hotpants which were popular from about 1971.

Platforms

From about 1967, shoe designers started to re-introduce the platform shoe, which had gone out of fashion in the late 1940s. In the context of street fashion, platform shoes and boots, worn with bell-bottomed trousers by both men and women, rose to alarming heights by the mid-1970s. Particularly in the setting of the more theatrical rock music performances, such as those of Elton John and David Bowie, they were sometimes as high as 6 or 7 inches (15–18cms). Wedge shoes, teamed with outfits by designers such as Bill Gibb or Zandra Rhodes, made a more subtle fashion statement. Heels and soles were often made of textured fabric, cork or rope, as well as crêpe rubber and leather-covered plastics or wood. Canvas espadrilles, perennial leisurewear, now sported wedge heels and were laced high up the leg. One of the most popular styles of the decade was the mule with uppers in a variety of materials, including patchwork suede, canvas and leather.

Platforms were popularised for women mainly by Barbara Hulanicki (Biba) and for men by Terry de Havilland (see page facing Acknowledgements). He also made women's shoes, and became known for his sparkling, metallic leathers inspired by lurid futuristic concepts. His motto 'Cobblers to the World' vividly expressed the attitude of contemporary young designers, who had scant respect for conventional society but did respect traditional craftsmanship. The high-heeled ankle boot, last in vogue in the late 1940s, was revived in the mid-1970s and stayed fashionable into the 1980s. Peep-toed platform shoes also reflected a more romantic revival from the pre and post-war periods.

An advertisement for real leather, again in *Vogue* (March 1974), suggests that the time had come for the craze to diminish, advocating a more conventional, elegant style: 'Pine green snakeskin shoe with the new, narrow toe, higher, thinner heel and not a sign of a platform'. The oil crisis and subsequent world-wide financial depression led to the advent of more conservative styles from the mid-1970s. Flat and heeled brogues were adopted for smart day-time fashion. Wedges became low at the end of the decade and rather like a clog.

The subcultural movement of punk, with its anarchic, nihilistic attitudes, was particularly influential in the 1970s. Footwear worn by punks ranged from an extreme stiletto for women to chunky crêpe-soled shoes, extreme Winklepickers, and heavy, utilitarian Dr Marten boots (DMs), worn by both men and women. The emphasis was on practicality and aggression. Initially considered outrageous, the influence of punk was soon felt in mainstream and high fashion styling. Vivienne Westwood and Malcolm Mclaren were seminal in the development of this look, bringing it to a wider market.

In sharp contrast with the 'unhealthy' look cultivated by the punk movement, a section of society in the late 1970s coveted a more comfortable and healthy lifestyle. For the first time sturdier shoes like the DM (ironically, in view of its previous associations with punk) as well as sportswear made major inroads into the fashionable dress of both sexes. Sophisticated styles remained in demand too. A healthy and well-tended foot was appropriate to show off the elegant, strappy and bright high heel (plate 58a and c) which had returned by the end of the decade.

Chapter Ten

Shaping the Future: 1980–1998

The shoe is probably the most important of all fashion accessories. You can spend any amount of time and money trying to emulate the glossy pictures in fashion magazines but if your shoes don't match the outfit the image is lost. (Gillian Rowe, 'Getting a foot in the door', *The Guardian*, 22 May 1986)

Dressing for Success

During the image-conscious eighties, fashion was a vital symbol of success. It became chic to flaunt expensive designer wear and many accessories were emblazoned with logos. One of the most powerful icons of status was the man's Gucci loafer with its bold double 'G' motif and band of red and green canvas ribbon. It came to represent the new ease with which wealth was displayed, although cheap imitations and over-exposure eventually weakened the power of the image. The growing popularity of jogging and 'working out' also encouraged a trend for 'designer' sportswear. The name on the trainer had to be Adidas, Puma, Nike, Fila or Reebok and every season saw changes of design which had more to do with style than improving athletic performance. Often trainers were not even worn for sport; women office workers in Manhattan started wearing them with business suits and manufacturers increasingly directed their sales at 'street-cred' conscious urban youth.

The 1980s also witnessed the rise of the female 'power-dresser', whose large shoulder pads demanded 'needle-heel' court shoes to complete the expression of authority. According to advertisements and fashion pages of the day, high heels clicking down the corridors of power were no longer the signal for men to 'swoon' but rather to 'shake'. They were popularised by the shoe designer Manolo Blahnik, who removed the stiletto from its 1970s associations with sex and even prostitution. He imbued the style with extravagance and glamour and his stalagmite-style heels, linguine-thin straps and long

Plate 61 opposite Leather 'mock croc' platform-soled shoes; British, 1993. By Vivienne Westwood. Fastened with silk ribbon laces, which pass through ghillie-style loops and cross over and around the ankle. Worn with a lace blouse, blue velvet cropped jacket, tartan kilt, white rubber stockings and a shocking pink feather boa. Heels: 12 inches (30cm) high. Given by Mrs Vivienne Westwood.

T.225:1&2 –1993

elegant toes inspired one fashion writer to eulogise: 'If Christian Lacroix is the wit and fantasy-maker of fashion, then Manolo Blahnik is the heel and soul' (*Observer*, 7 August 1988).

Although youth sub-cultures such as punks and skinheads continued to rebel against the dictates of conventional dress, a number of their motifs were incorporated into mainstream fashion. The Dr Marten boot (DM) is a prime example of this trend. Introduced into Britain during the 1960s as work wear, skinheads incorporated the 16-eyelet cherry-red DM into their aggressive look, and other designs later became a component of punk style. By the early 1980s, however, the DM had been elevated to the international catwalks. Japanese designers Yohji Yamamoto and Rei Kawakubo accessorised their collections with chunky DM black leather shoes, turning a functional product into a high fashion icon. DMs subsequently became accepted as streetwear for a wider youth market, and during the late 1980s were paired with flouncy feminine clothing in a defiant gesture of feminist assertiveness. Today they are a versatile product, worn as much for comfort as for style by a socially diverse market.

Recycling and Retro-chic

During the recession of the early 1990s fashion shifted away from conspicuous consumption. Haute couture, high-investment goods continued to sell well, but the brash, invasive designer label was no longer all important. Sub-cultural and ethnic clothing styles became increasingly fashionable, and many designers profited from the burgeoning interest in ecology. Chunky cork sandals by Birkenstock and shoes made from leather substitutes which allowed the foot 'to breathe' became the ultimate in trendy 'natural' footwear. The desire to return to the great outdoors, or at least to look as if you did, boosted sales of hard-wearing hiking boots such as Timberlands, Caterpillars and Rockports. Growing concern for the environment also encouraged some shoe manufacturers to diversify into producing ranges of footwear made from recycled materials.

Whilst the eclectic range of styles continued to increase, each season witnessed discernible trends. The seventies revival in 1992–93, for example, brought back what has been referred to as the 'Old

Plate 62 opposite Brocaded silk shoes; British, 1996. By Manolo Blahnik. The floral design is similar to patterns on early 1750s silk. Given by Mr Manolo Blahnik.

T.158:1&2–1996

School' variety of trainer. The Puma Clydes and Adidas Gazelles, as worn on the playing field in the 1970s, were heralded as the new cult sneaker. Supermodel Kate Moss declared she owned five pairs, and fashion designer Helmut Lang accessorised his 1993 Winter collection with Stan Smith trainers with the logos painted out.

Despite their associations with aching limbs and twisted ankles, platform shoes also made a sensational comeback in the early 1990s. Vivienne Westwood first re-introduced the platform onto the catwalk in 1984, when her models fought over who should wear the three pairs of 6 inch (15cm) soles that Patrick Cox had designed for the show. She was, however, ahead of her time. The high platforms which formed part of her 1985–86 'mini crini' collection did not make a particularly favourable impact on the general public. By 1992, however, other designers were following her example and chunky soles featured prominently in collections by Yves Saint Laurent, Jean-Paul Gaultier, Prada and Karl Lagerfeld for Chanel. Newspapers and magazines ran full-page features on the return of the 'skyscraper sole' and platforms were cited as an ideal partner to the new, long, pencil-thin skirts. Despite the growing popularity of platforms, it was still Westwood who produced the most outré designs. She challenged convention yet again with her staggering 'mock-croc' platforms with 12 inch (30cm) heels, which she designed for her 1993 Anglomania collection (plate 61). The shoes achieved even greater notoriety when supermodel Naomi Campbell tumbled over in them, on the Paris catwalk.

The 'Fashion Forward' Shoe: a New Generation of Shoe Designers

Despite the emphasis on mass production and standardisation, many shoe designers have continued to produce original and exciting designs using traditional formulae. The name of Manolo Blahnik, for example, is synonymous with perfectly crafted women's shoes (plate 62). Having trained as an artist, he took up shoemaking in the early 1970s and soon became a leading London-based designer serving international markets. As well as relaunching the high heel, his innovative approach towards cut combines comfort with style and his beautifully sculpted designs can make the widest foot look sleek and narrow. He is also a master of colour, using vivid combinations of magenta, scarlet, bright orange, emerald green and saffron yellow to striking effect. Drawing inspiration from a variety of sources, he can capture the spirit of Georgian grace in a contemporary design or even the sensation of a smell:

Once, for example, I was driving through the South of France with George, my New York partner, and I said, 'George, stop the car immediately, right now!' We screeched to a stop, and there was this wonderful smell of mimosa mixed with jasmine, and from that I made a shoe ('Footnotes from Manolo Blahnik', *Vogue,* September 1990).

He continues to refine the seductive line of his shoe, and endowed the stiletto of the 1990s with a new sensuality and sensitivity.

Since the mid-1980s, a new wave of British shoe designers has linked the Cordwainers College in East London with innovation and style. Emma Hope was one of the first graduates to attract publicity, producing shoes under her own label in 1985. Her beautifully embroidered designs and 'elfin' pumps perfectly complemented the British love of dressing up (fig. 24). She designed footwear for Betty Jackson and English Eccentrics, matching their exuberant and exotic trends with her soft sculpted lines, elongated toes and romantic designs. Whilst historical influences remain vital to her unique sense of style, Hope is constantly original in her approach. Her sleek, velvet slippers, strappy evening shoes and slinky high-heeled mules have a modernistic appeal tinged with a sense of British nostalgia.

Another popular and enormously influential designer is Patrick Cox. Canadian-born, he launched his career while still enrolled at the Cordwainers College, creating radical designs for Vivienne Westwood in 1984 and Body Map in 1985. Cox's fleur-de-lis signature has become a symbol of avant-garde design as well as top quality workmanship. He has re-interpreted traditional men's footwear, such as the co-respondent shoe, and experimented with moulded plastic jelly sandals, embedding models of the Eiffel tower into the heels. He is also known as the hero of the 1990s loafer. He created his Wannabe range of chunky loafers for the Autumn/Winter 1993/94 collection (plate 63) and the style became so popular that a doorman had to be

Fig. 24 above 'Josephine Baker' shoes; British, 1988. By Emma Hope. Black velvet with red and beige appliqué work and yellow and black beads representing bananas and hair. Embroidery by Karen Spurgin Winter. These witty shoes personify Josephine Baker (1906–75), the celebrated international singer and dancer known as the 'Black Goddess' of cabaret, famed for her spectacular revues which included dancing on a mirror at the Folies Bergère wearing nothing but a string of rubber bananas around her waist. Given by Ms Emma Hope. T.157:1&2–1990

employed to manage the queues that formed outside his London shop. As Cox explained in a BBC radio 4 interview in 1997, the appeal of the Wannabe lies in its versatility:

I think the success of the Wannabe loafer is the comfort factor and the cult that built around it...the comfort is key because footwear trends come and go, strappy sandals, pointy toes...but they're trends and they're fads and they die, but with the Wannabe loafer, even if you don't want to wear them any more because one too many of your friends have them or too many pop stars wore them that week...you end up wearing them because they are so comfortable.

By 1996 he had designed a range of Wannabe clothes and accessories to go with the shoes, and 'the global image' remains a vital component of his style. In his Autumn/Winter 1998 collection, metallic snakeskin loafers (plate 63a) complement the futuristic look of the men's suits, while on other shoes velcro fastenings and zips (plate 63b) reflect the functional details of the sportswear tops.

For Jimmy Choo shoemaking is a mixture of sculpture and engineering (plate 64). He learnt the art and intricacies of the craft from his father, a Malaysian shoemaker, and came to London in the early 1980s to study footwear design. After graduating from Cordwainers College with a distinction he launched his own label in 1988. Since then he has produced exquisite shoes for major fashion designers, including Jean Muir, Katharine Hamnett and Bruce Oldfield, as well as a large international clientele. The actress Kate Winslet was apparently so taken with the lace-up boots that she wore in the film of *Sense and Sensibility* (1995), that she ordered some shocking pink satin shoes to match her Vivienne Westwood dress for the Hollywood Oscars ceremony. Although he introduced a ready-to-wear range in 1996, Choo's real passion is the made-to-measure shoe. Based in a small workshop, he designs footwear to match his clients' specifications, often advising on style; he will not, for example, create a heel that is over $4^1/_2$ inches (11cms) high. His sleek, elegant creations have been described as 'shoes for princesses with chauffeur-driven transport'. The late Diana, Princess of Wales, wore them for special occasions, and by publicising the work of designers such as Jimmy Choo she did much to promote the couturier shoe industry.

Plate 63 opposite Two men's Wannabe loafers by Patrick Cox. Right (a): Brown metallic-effect snakeskin; British, Autumn/ Winter Collection 1998. T.181–1998 Left (b): Black leather with zip over the instep; British, Autumn/Winter Collection 1998. Given by Mr Patrick Cox. T.182–1998

Plate 64 left Pink satin mules with silver insoles; British, Summer 1998. Designed and created by Jimmy Choo, especially for the V&A. T.284:1&2–1998

Plate 65 opposite Men's 'Soho' chukka boots; British, 1998. By Oliver Sweeney, from the 'Sweeney's' Collection. 'Pascagoule' brown leather with hand-stitched 'S' logo on the upper and blue leather lining. Given by Mr Oliver Sweeney. Photograph by Jeremy Hirsch; reproduced by kind permission of Oliver Sweeney Ltd. T.285:1&2–1998

Tradition and Innovation

Shoe trends come and go. Some styles are fairly constant, while others, too extreme to be fashionable for long, die or re-surface in a different form. Strappy sandals, high heels, boots, loafers and brogues have remained popular, but designers are constantly re-working the basic shapes to give a modern appeal. Oliver Sweeney, creator of a stylish range of hand-crafted footwear, has been described as 'the finest designer in the world of classic-with-a-twist men's shoes' (*The Independent,* 3 April 1993). Sweeney has revitalised the image of the Oxford, Derby and brogue through subtly combining traditional bespoke techniques with a flair for contemporary design (plate 65). Each shoe is modelled from a unique anatomical last, originally developed by Sweeney himself, and together with proper arch supports this ensures a sleek modern design: 'Most brogues have a countryish, slightly bulbous look to them…If the arches are held tightly, it makes the feet look long and narrow, instantly elegant' ('A walk on the classic side', Oliver Sweeney, *The Times,* 11 June 1991). His Storm Derby became something of a cult fashion shoe in the early 1990s, and he continues to re-interpret classic styles using squared-off toes, thick welts and a distinctive streamlined cut.

Technological advances, particularly in the sportswear industry, continue to exert a powerful influence on shoe design. Specialised

Plate 66 left Woman's 'Elast' ankle boots with square toes; Italian, Spring 1998. By Armando Pollini. Given by Mr Armando Pollini. T.84:1&2–1998

Plate 67 opposite Women's shoes, 'Clovis'; French, 1995. By Christian Louboutin for his Spring/ Summer Collection 1995. The hydrangea petals suspended in the Lucite resin sole were gathered from Louboutin's garden and then hand-dried. Given by Mr Christian Louboutin. T.729:1&2–1997

sports shoes made of high-performance techno-fibres and reflective materials have fed into mainstream fashion, and designer versions by Donna Karan's DKNY line have become the ultimate in trendy streetwear. The latest technology has also enabled many shoe designers to experiment with a vast range of synthetic materials as well as new methods of construction.

Others have explored existing sources to create innovative and exciting footwear. Armando Pollini's discovery of the stretch fabric, 'Elast', transformed the appearance of the ankle boot (plate 66). He stumbled across the stretch grosgrain in 1985, while sourcing new materials in a German firm which made corsets and bustiers. He patented the fabric under the name 'Elast', using it to create a range of close-fitting yet supple court shoes, loafers and boots. The vibrant colours and rich textures of the material complement the sculpted lines of his ankle boots, giving them a strong minimalist look. His work has been widely imitated but, as Pollini points out, 'the quality is absolutely not the same'.

French shoe designer Christian Louboutin is no stranger to innovation. After working as a freelance designer for Chanel and Charles Jourdan, he opened his first shop in 1991. Although his shoes are always extremely feminine he often combines chic elegance with theatrical fantasy to create novel and provocative designs. His most exuberant creations include gilded heels carved to resemble Assyrian columns, and a pair of mules with 'bra-strap' fastenings, inspired by the Serge Gainsbourg song, 'Sea, Sex and Sun'. He has even suspended hydrangea petals in clear resin to give the impression of walking on a carpet of flowers (plate 67): 'Gardens are a great inspiration for me...some designers might go to a Gauguin exhibition and say "Wow, what a beautiful blue", but when I close my eyes I see shades of colour from gardens instead' (Christian Louboutin, *Impression 'Sole Man'*, November 1995).

It is impossible to foresee what innovations shoe design of the future will hold. Perhaps the words of Patrick Cox best sum up the outlook of many young designers. When asked 'What comes next?' in a recent internet interview with *Vogue*, he responded, 'God, we've only just started!'

Glossary

Note: The use of the word 'shoe' also includes boots, slippers, chopines, trainers and overshoes, unless otherwise stated.

Albert side-laced boot with five buttons and usually a cloth top.

Artois buckle shoe buckle of enormous proportions, fashionable in the 1770s and 1780s. Named after the Comte d'Artois, later Charles X of France (1824-30).

Balmoral closed-front ankle boot with galosh. Worn by men and women, named after the country seat of Queen Victoria.

Blucher short, front-laced leather boot, named after the Prussian General von Blücher who played a decisive role in the Battle of Waterloo in 1815.

Brogue a laced shoe with punched decoration.

Brothel Creeper shoe, usually of suede, with thick crêpe sole.

Bulldog or Boston toe bulbous toe shape on men's shoes, popular in the United States during the late 19th century and in Britain in the early 20th century.

Buskins boots reaching to the calf or knee, usually made of supple or lightweight material.

Chape the pronged part of a buckle through which the strap is secured.

Chelsea boot ankle boot with pointed toe and elastic sides. Popular during the 1960s and associated with the fashionable King's Road in Chelsea, London. Also known as the Beatle boot.

Chopine see mule.

Chukka boot man's lace-tied ankle boot. Originally worn by polo players; adopted for general wear in the 1950s.

Clog leather-soled overshoe with straps across the instep, sometimes made to match the shoe with which they were worn.

Court shoe a low-heeled, slip-on shoe.

Cromwell medium or high-heeled shoe with decorative buckle.

Cuban heel heel of medium height with slightly curving back.

Derby lace-tied shoe with eyelet tabs stitched over the vamp.

Desert boot front-laced suede ankle boot with crêpe sole, a refined version of those made in Cairo during World War II for General Montgomery's Eighth Army.

Eyelet tabs front facings of the shoe through which the laces are tied.

Fastenette small buckle used to fasten the strap over the instep, often decorated with pastes. Served the dual purpose of a working buckle and an ornament.

Gaiters cloth or leather coverings for leg and ankle, buttoned or buckled at the side and often held on by straps under the foot.

Galoshes/goloshes/galoches overshoes worn outdoors to protect the boot or shoe.

Ghillie shoe of Scottish origin, with lacing through loops instead of eyelets.

Horned toe 16th-century shoe with two small horn shapes at the toe.

Hose a type of leg and foot covering, a precursor of the stocking.

Instep the raised area on the top of the foot above the toes.

Jackboots a) heavy, hard leather boots often with bucket tops to cover knees, worn for riding or outdoors; b) lightweight boots with back of knee scooped out to allow for bending.

Jelly sandal shoe made of soft plastic, with the bright, translucent look of jelly.

Jockey boot (later known as a top boot) leather boot with a turnover top and cloth straps. Originally worn for horse-racing, and adopted as fashionable wear during the eighteenth and early nineteenth centuries.

Langtry shoe of medium height, similar to the Cromwell but with a strap fastening or a large bow instead of a buckle. Named after the actress Lilly Langtry.

Lappets two bands of lace or linen hanging from the back or sides of a woman's cap. Popular from the late 17th century to the late 18th century, and again in the two middle quarters of the 19th century.

Last carved or moulded form on which the shoe is made.

Latchets straps which fasten across the instep by means of a shoe-tie or buckle.

Loafer casual slip-on leather or suede shoe, originating in the United States.

Louis heel heel of medium height, sharply curving inwards at the back, front and sides, and flared slightly at the base. Probably named after Louis XV.

Mule/pantoble/chopine types of shoe without heel quarters.

Oxford lace-tied shoe with eyelet tabs stitched under the vamp.

Pantoble see mule.

Patten overshoe with a wooden sole raised on an iron ring.

Pelisse an outer garment or coat.

Pinchbeck copper alloy which simulates gold. Invented by Christopher Pinchbeck in the 1720s.

Pinked decorative cut with saw-toothed edge.

Pump shoe with thin sole, soft or patent uppers and flat heel.

Quarter part of the shoe upper covering the sides and back of the foot.

Rand narrow strip of leather between the upper and sole, sometimes used as a decorative feature.

Slipper name for a mule which was in use from the later 17th century onwards.

Spats short cloth or leather gaiters.

Spool heel a heel composed of convex layers resembling the top and bottom outer edges of a cotton reel.

Stacked heel heel built up of horizontal layers of leather.

Straights shoes not shaped to distinguish between left and right, so could be worn on either foot.

Throat shaped part of the vamp resting on the instep of the foot.

Tongue part of the vamp which extends under the latchets or eyelet tabs.

Trainer sports shoe which has developed into a fashion accessory.

Two tone or co-respondent type of two-colour shoe originally worn for golf. It was adopted for more general wear in the 1930s and became known as the co-respondent probably because of its association with 'flashy' men of the type then cited in divorce cases.

Upper the part of the shoe which covers the top of the foot.

Vamp the front section of the shoe upper covering the toes and part of the instep.

Vandyked edge a serrated edging of lace or other material.

Wellington leather boot similar to the top boot but without the turnover top. Some styles have 'stockings' attached. Named after the 1st Duke of Wellington, famous for his part in the Battle of Waterloo in 1815.

Welt a narrow strip of leather sewn around the edge of the upper and insole to help attach the sole.

Winklepicker shoe with excessively pointed toes.

Major UK Dress Collections Featuring Shoes

Central Museum and Art Gallery, Northampton

Gallery of Costume, Platt Hall, Manchester

Museum of Costume, Bath

Museum of London, London

Shambellie House Museum of Costume, New Abbey, near Dumfries, Scotland (displays of costume from the National Museums of Scotland)

Shoe Museum, C&J Clark Ltd., Street, Somerset

Victoria and Albert Museum, London

Selected Bibliography

An Outline History of Footwear - The shoe as a mark of civilization and as an objet d'art. International Shoe Museum, Romans, France, 1996.

Arnold, Janet *Queen Elizabeth's Wardrobe Unlock'd.* W.S. Maney & Son Ltd., Leeds 1988.

Brooke, Iris *Footwear - A Short History of European and American Shoes.* Pitman, London 1972.

Buck, Anne *Dress in Eighteenth Century England.* B.T. Batsford Ltd., London 1979.

Byrde, Penelope *The Male Image – Men's Fashions in England 1300–1970.* B.T.Batsford Ltd., London 1979.

Byrde, Penelope *Nineteenth Century Fashion.* B.T. Batsford Ltd., London 1992.

Campbell, R. *The London Tradesman.* T. Gardner, London 1747 (reprinted 1969).

Catalogue of shoe and other buckles in Northampton Museum. Northampton Borough Council Museums and Art Gallery, 1981.

Chenoune, Farid *A History of Men's Fashions.* Flammarion, Paris 1993.

Costume The Journal of the Costume Society. Costume Society Publications, Leeds. Specific issues: Number 11 (1977), pp.28–33, Thornton, J.H. *A Glossary of Shoe Terms.* Number 18 (1984), pp.35–58, Buck, Anne and Matthews, Harry. *Pocket Guides to Fashion.* Number 22 (1988), pp.44–50, Swann, June. *Civil Uniform and Court Shoes in Northampton Museum.* Number 22 (1988), pp. 51–59, Du Mortier, Bianca M. *Men's Fashion in the Netherlands.* Number 26 (1992), pp. 32–39, Fawcett, Trevor. *Bath's Georgian Warehouses.* Number 31 (1997), pp. 49–67, Llewellyn, Sacha. *'Inventory of her Grace's Things, 1747' – The Dress Inventory of Mary Churchill, 2nd Duchess of Montague.*

Cunnington, C. Willett *English Women's Clothing in the Nineteenth Century.* Faber & Faber Ltd., London 1937.

Cunnington, C. Willett & Phillis *Handbook of English Mediaeval Costume.* Faber & Faber Ltd., London 1952.

Cunnington, C. Willett & Phillis *Handbook of English Costume in the Sixteenth Century.* Faber & Faber Ltd., London, first published 1954.

Cunnington, C. Willett & Phillis *Handbook of English Costume in the Seventeenth Century.* Faber & Faber Ltd., London, first published 1955.

Cunnington, C. Willett & Phillis *Handbook of English Costume in the Eighteenth Century.* Faber & Faber Ltd., London, first published 1957.

Cunnington, C. Willett & Phillis *Handbook of English Costume in the Nineteenth Century.* Faber & Faber Ltd., London, first published 1959.

Cunnington, Phillis & Mansfield, Allan *Handbook of English Costume in the 20th Century 1900–1950.* Faber & Faber Ltd., London, 1973.

De la Haye, Amy (ed) *The Cutting Edge: 50 Years of British Fashion 1947–1997.* V&A Publications, London 1996.

De Marly, Diana *Fashion for Men – An Illustrated History.* B.T. Batsford Ltd., London 1985.

Defoe, Daniel *The Complete English Tradesman.* Charles Rivington, London 1726.

Devlin, James *The Shoemaker - Guide to Trade.* Houlston & Stoneman, London 1840.

Dowie, James *The Foot and its Covering; comprising a full translation of Dr Camper's work on 'The Best Form of Shoe'.* Robert Hardwicke, London 1861.

Fashions for All - The Ladies' Journal of Practice Fashions. London 1912-17.

Grew, Francis and de Neergaard, Margrethe *Medieval Finds from Excavations in London: 2, Shoes and Pattens.* HMSO, London 1988.

Hughes, Bernard and Therle *Georgian Shoe Buckles.* Greater London Council 1972.

Laver, James (ed) *Costume of the Western World: Early Tudor 1485–1558.* Harrap & Co. Ltd., London, first published 1951.

Laver, James (intro.) *17th and 18th Century Costume.* HMSO, London 1951, 1959.

Ledger, Florence E *Put Your Foot Down.* The Uffington Press, Melksham, Wiltshire 1985.

Malcolm, James Peller *Anecdotes of the Manners and Customs of London during the Eighteenth Century.* Longman, Hurst, Rees and Orme, London 1810.

McDowell, Colin *Shoes - Fashion and Fantasy.* Thames & Hudson, London 1989.

Mazza, *Samuele Armando Pollini – Design e affinità elettive.* Leonardo Arte, 1997.

Pattison, Angela and Cawthorne, Nigel *A Century of Shoes - Icons of Style in the 20th Century.* Quarto Publishing plc, London 1997.

Probert, Christine *Shoes in Vogue Since 1910.* Thames & Hudson, London 1981.

Reynolds, Graham *Costume of the Western World: Elizabethan and Jacobean 1558-1625.* Harrap & Co. Ltd., London, first published 1951.

Ribeiro, Aileen *Dress and Morality.* B.T. Batsford Ltd., London 1986.

Ribeiro, Aileen *The Art of Dress - Fashion in England and France 1750-1820.* Yale University Press, New Haven and London 1995.

Rossi, William *The Sex Life of the Foot and Shoe.* Wordsworth, Ware 1989.

Swann, June *Shoes - The Costume Accessories Series.* General Editor: Dr Aileen Ribeiro. B.T. Batsford Ltd., London 1982.

The Footwear Organiser & Shoe and Leather Trades Export Journal. London: vol. 3, no. 1 (January 1920); vol. 6, no. 6 (December 1921).

The Whole Art of Dress or The Road to Elegance and Fashion. By a Cavalry Officer. Effingham Wilson, Royal Exchange 1830.

Victoria and Albert Museum: 17th and 18th Century Costume. Introduction by James Laver. HMSO, London 1951, reprinted 1959.

Vogue (British edition). Condé Nast Publications, Inc.

Weber, Paul *A Pictorial Commentary on the History of the Shoe.* Bally Shoe Museum, Basle 1982.

Wilson, Elizabeth and Taylor, Lou *Through the Looking Glass – A History of Dress from 1860 to the Present Day.* BBC Books, London 1989.

Wilson, Eunice *A History of Shoe Fashion.* Pitman, London 1969.

Wright, Thomas *The Romance of the Shoe.* C. J. Farncombe & Sons, London 1922.

Index